A NEW WAY OF SEEING

A NEW WAY OF SEEING

DISTANCE AND
TRAUMATIC MEMORY
IN THE POETRY
OF WORLD WAR II

MICHAEL
SARNOWSKI

LOUISIANA STATE
UNIVERSITY PRESS
BATON ROUGE

Published by Louisiana State University Press
lsupress.org

DESIGNER: Michelle A. Neustrom
TYPEFACE: Chaparral Pro

COVER IMAGE: A U.S. soldier walks through forest in the Bastogne area of Belgium as he returns from the front lines, 1944. Courtesy U.S. Department of Defense.

LIBRARY OF CONGRESS CATALOGING-IN-PUBLICATION DATA

Names: Sarnowski, Michael, author.
Title: A new way of seeing : distance and traumatic memory in the poetry of World War II / Michael Sarnowski.
Description: Baton Rouge : Louisiana State University Press, 2025. | Series: American wars and popular culture | Includes bibliographical references and index.
Identifiers: LCCN 2024048598 (print) | LCCN 2024048599 (ebook) | ISBN 978-0-8071-8399-1 (cloth) | ISBN 978-0-8071-8440-0 (epub) | ISBN 978-0-8071-8441-7 (pdf)
Subjects: LCSH: American poetry—20th century—History and criticism. | English poetry—20th century—History and criticism. | World War, 1939–1945—Literature and the war. | Simpson, Louis, 1923–2012—Criticism and interpretation. | Douglas, Keith, 1920–1944—Criticism and interpretation. | Hugo, Richard, 1923–1982—Criticism and interpretation. | Nemerov, Howard, 1920–1991—Criticism and interpretation. | Jarrell, Randall, 1914–1965,—Criticism and interpretation. | LCGFT: Literary criticism.
Classification: LCC PS310.W68 S27 2025 (print) | LCC PS310.W68 (ebook) | DDC 811.509—dc23/eng/20250121
LC record available at https://lccn.loc.gov/2024048598
LC ebook record available at https://lccn.loc.gov/2024048599

for Laura and Owen

CONTENTS

ACKNOWLEDGMENTS ix

INTRODUCTION 1

1 LOUIS SIMPSON
The Temporal Ambiguity of War 28

2 KEITH DOUGLAS
Closeness, Self-Elegy, and Remnants of War 75

3 RICHARD HUGO
Revisiting the Sites of Trauma 119

4 HOWARD NEMEROV
Reclaiming Narratives and Interrogating Memories
of "the Good War" 154

5 RANDALL JARRELL
The Vicarious Trauma of Processing War at a Distance 189

CONCLUSION 217

NOTES 227

WORKS CITED 235

INDEX 255

ACKNOWLEDGMENTS

The existence of this book is indebted to the support of individuals, mentors, and institutions that helped cultivate a passion for literature and a hunger to better understand the world. Like many people born in the latter half of the twentieth century, the roots of my curiosity about World War II grew from family connections to the war. Both of my grandfathers, Thomas E. O'Laughlin and Edward A. Sarnowski, served for the U.S. Army. Days spent with Grandpa O'Laughlin were among the most treasured of my childhood, and only learning of his war service after his death became a source of intrigue in trying to grasp his experience as an infantryman in North Africa and Normandy. Grandpa Sarnowski died months before I was born, and his absence was deepened when trying to learn about his life and World War II service in Italy. Studying the poems in this book helped me to feel more closely connected to others, both family and strangers.

Much of the research conducted for this book was supported by Liverpool Hope University. The supervision, mentorship, and support provided by Dr. Guy Cuthbertson and Dr. William Blazek was instrumental toward deepening discussion, expanding reading lists, and providing key feedback. I must also thank Viva examiners Tim Kendall and Peter Childs, whose expertise strengthened this book.

Material from the following archives and libraries has contributed to this study: the Louis Simpson Papers at the Library of Congress in Washington, DC; the Keith Douglas Papers at the British Library; the Keith Douglas Collection at the Brotherton Library at the University of Leeds; the Howard Nemerov Papers from the Washington University in St. Louis Digital Archive; the Randall Jarrell Papers from the University of North Carolina, Greensboro, Digital Archive; the Dennis and Joan Welland Papers at the John Rylands Library at the University of Manchester; the University of Oxford's First World War Poetry Digital Archive; and the National Poetry Library in London. Thank you to all of the librarians, archivists, and curators who have helped make this material accessible. Thank you, also, to the permissions managers and literary executors acting on behalf of these poets for permitting the reprinting of their poetry.

I appreciate the opportunity to have shared earlier explorations of this research and received feedback when speaking at conferences hosted by the University of Oxford, the University of Cambridge, and Liverpool Hope University. Thanks to the following journals and websites for publishing articles of earlier versions of this work:

"Revisiting the Sites of Trauma: The War Poetry of Siegfried Sassoon, Edmund Blunden, and Richard Hugo." *Journal of Literature and Trauma Studies,* vol. 7, no. 2, 2020.

"The War in the Air: Post-War Memory in the Poetry of Howard Nemerov and Richard Hugo." *War, Literature, and the Arts Journal,* vol. 31, 7 Nov. 2019, http://wlajournal.com.

"Revisiting Wilfred Owen's 'Exposure' in Louis Simpson's World War II Poem 'The Battle.'" World War I Centenary: Continuations and Beginnings. University of Oxford, 12 Oct. 2018, ww1centenary.oucs.ox.ac.uk/.

"Enemy Encounters in the War Poetry of Wilfred Owen, Keith Douglas, and Randall Jarrell." *War and Literature: Commiserating with the Enemy,* special issue of *Humanities,* edited by Rachel McCoppin, vol. 7, no. 3, 14 Sept. 2018, p. 89, doi:10.3390/h7030089.

I am also grateful that I received permission to publish portions of the following works and items:

Keith Douglas's "Book Diary." Undated. From the British Library Collection/copyright © Professor Desmond Graham. MS. 56360, Vol. X, Keith Douglas Papers, Western Manuscripts.

Robert Graves's "Letter: To Wilfred Owen." First World War Poetry Digital Archive, 25 July 2018, http://ww11it.nsms.ox.ac.uk/ww11it/items /show/8082. Reproduced with permission from United Agents Ltd on behalf of The Trustees of the Robert Graves Copyright Trust (Copyright © The Trustees of the Robert Graves Copyright Trust).

Randall Jarrell's "Item 001a Front." Series 1.1: Randall Jarrell Manuscripts—
Original Poems, Box 1, Folder 7: "Death of the Ball Turret Gunner,"
"The Wide Prospect," and "The Snow Leopard," December 1955. Randall Jarrell Papers, MSS 0009, Martha Blakeney Hodges Special Col-
lections and University Archives, University Libraries, The Univer-
sity of North Carolina at Greensboro. And Jarrell's "Page 043." Series
1.3: Randall Jarrell Manuscripts—Criticism, Box 4, Folder 5: Recent
Poetry—Rough Draft, 1955. Randall Jarrell Papers, MSS 0009, Mar-
tha Blakeney Hodges Special Collections and University Archives,
University Libraries, The University of North Carolina at Greensboro.
Keith Douglas's Marginalia. *A Book of Modern Verse.* Zodiac Books, Chatto &
Windus, 1939. Reproduced with the permission of Special Collections,
Leeds University Library, Brotherton Library Special Collections: Keith
Douglas Collection, BC MS 20c Douglas. https://explore.library.leeds
.ac.uk/special-collections-explore/8451/keith_douglas_collection.
Photograph of Douglas in uniform: carboard photo frame bears inscription
"Dulce et decorum est pro patria mori." 1940. Reproduced with the
permission of Special Collections, Leeds University Library, Brother-
ton Library Special Collections: Keith Douglas Collection, BC MS 20c
Douglas/1/Box C/A. https://explore.library.leeds.ac.uk/special-collec
tions-explore/416349/first_numbered_sequence_of_photographs.

I also thank the estates of Howard Nemerov and Louis Simpson for allowing me to use certain material throughout the book.

To James W. Long; LSU Press; the American Wars and Popular Culture
series editors, Matthew Christopher Hulbert and Matthew E. Stanley; and
all other editors and readers, I am so thankful for your consideration and
publication of this book.

I want to particularly thank the literature and creative writing profes-
sors who taught and encouraged me, gave their time, and shared their passion for poetry. Mark Jarman, Rick Hilles, and the rest of the Vanderbilt
University MFA Creative Writing staff and writers, as well as the Vanderbilt Department of English, your kindness, knowledge, and dedication to
helping others is appreciated without end. In addition, my time at the State
University of New York at Fredonia was defined by courses delivered by
Aimee Nezhukumatathil and Natalie Gerber, whose influence cannot be

overstated. They helped identify a love for writing and studying poetry, and gave extra time, support, and opportunity that surpassed what was expected of them.

A heartfelt thank you to Mom, Dad, Steve, Chris, and the extended branches of the Sarnowski family for the countless forms of support you have provided over the years. Thanks to the support networks of friends and colleagues in the places I've lived, with particular appreciation for my friends from Rochester, New York, and to the Hill family and those who have made the UK feel like home.

Most importantly, examining a period of great historical tumult and change while living through another has amplified the importance of love, support, stability, laughter, and happiness. This work is only possible because of the unwavering support of my wife, Laura, to whom this book is dedicated. Laura and Owen, you have my unending love.

As this book stems from examining the generational impacts of the decisions humans make, the thought of writing poetry in times of war, and in reflection of it, can appear so far removed from the physical intensity of armed conflict and its violent disruption. Yet, the importance of affirming one's humanity and the value of human expression, especially in times of war, is something to be thankful for and to continually seek out.

A NEW WAY OF SEEING

INTRODUCTION

These wars have been so great, they are forgotten
Like the Egyptian dynasts. My confrere
In whose thick boots I stood, were you amazed
To wander through my brain four decades later
As I have wandered in a dream through yours?
—LOUIS SIMPSON, "I Dreamed That in a City Dark as Paris"

The political, social, and psychological impact of World War II was unparalleled in the twentieth century. Visually evocative acts of combat, humanitarian crisis, destruction, and resilience from 1939 to 1945 have been seared into collective memory and have helped translate events that have been, at times, beyond belief. Memorable images from World War II include *Taxis to Hell—and Back—Into the Jaws of Death*,[1] Robert F. Sargent's D-Day landing craft photo of soldiers wading through water toward the beaches of Normandy while under fire (Sargent), and aerial footage of destroyed cities, such as Warsaw at the hands of the Luftwaffe, London smoldering during the Blitz, and Hamburg ablaze during the firebombings. Consider the ominous sight of Hitler posing in front of the Eiffel Tower in 1940, signifying Germany's occupation of France (H. Hoffmann), or the apocalyptic vision of a mushroom cloud rising from the atomic bomb dropped on Nagasaki as the war was brought toward a conclusion (Levy). Memorable, too, are photos capturing claims of victory like *Raising the Flag on Iwo Jima* (Rosenthal), *Raising a Flag over the Reichstag* to mark the end of the Battle of Berlin (Khaldei), and jubilant scenes like the sailor embracing a woman in *V-J Day in Times Square* (Eisenstaedt). Equally indelible are the visuals of utter depravity, such as photos and videos documenting the Holocaust and the

1

operation and liberation of concentration camps. While these static and moving images cast an unflinching eye upon a world submerged in conflict, so too do acts of sight, affirmation, witnessing, and reflection in World War II soldier poetry.

From Homer's *The Iliad* to the First World War trench lyrics and beyond, war narratives transmit sensory, emotional, and psychological perspectives of armed conflict. Eyewitness accounts of war inform the world and serve as historical record. Among World War II's many distinguishing factors, it is unmatched in its geographic spread, technological advancement of armed conflict, combatant and civilian casualties, and scale of human atrocity. The civilian experience of World War II has provided incalculable value to understanding the war, such as urban populations recalling bombing raids, Holocaust victims struggling for life and humanity, citizens grappling with the inhumanity of persecution and genocide, displaced communities desperate for security and a sense of belonging, and home front voices pensively waiting for news about loved ones. The perspectives of soldiers deepen our understanding of World War II by capturing varied aspects of combat, deployment, and duty. While scholars such as Santanu Das have deftly highlighted how "writings of the First World War are obsessed with tactile experience" (*Touch and Intimacy* 5), the poetry of World War II soldiers offers new forms of *seeing*. The literal sense of sight and figurative seeing, as in processing, in World War II soldier poetry serves to document, witness, and examine a vast range of experiences. Literal sight and figurative forms of vision are conduits for how soldiers processed distance and traumatic memory, themes that underpin the most evocative poetry by World War II soldiers. With these concepts as guides, a new way of seeing World War II soldier poetry is also possible for readers: as a definitive departure from the outdated reputation of World War II soldiers as a "Silent Generation."

Humans process the world through sensory perception, and, in the words of Mohan Matthen, "Perception is the ultimate source of knowledge about contingent facts" (1). Sight affirms that what we perceive is what is true. While one may consider a function of war poetry to be the sharing of battlefield visuals with the reader, the World War II poets examined in this study routinely use a visual landscape of war—both real and imagined— not just to inform the reader but to affirm to themselves their observations and feelings, that what they have witnessed is real, and that they have truly endured a traumatic psychological cost. The philosophy of perception is a well-trodden field, as are conversations surrounding the problem of perception, the idea that "reality and appearance can indeed diverge: its fundamental premise is that *illusions can occur*" (A. D. Smith 22). The objective of this study is to examine the real and illusory visions that soldier poets used to process distance and traumatic memory of World War II. The fact that traumatic visions of war disrupted the lives of soldiers for prolonged periods speaks to the importance of acknowledging the writings derived from traumatic experience.

The "Silent Generation" Debate

Critical attention has been slow to acknowledge the contributions of World War II poets, and the outdated reputation of generational silence has taken decades to evolve. The perception that World War II soldiers failed to produce impactful poetry began with newspapers and journals asking amalgamations of "Where are the poets of the war?" in the early 1940s (William and Brodribb 391). Literary critics such as Robert Langbaum reinforced the notion that soldiers insufficiently responded to World War II by writing, in a 1955 issue of *The American Scholar,* "the generation that fought the war and is now in its thirties and early forties, still seems, to everyone's dismay including its own, to have no character. . . . The Silent Generation is, I think, the name which will stick" (87). The "Silent Generation" typically denotes those with birth years from the mid-1920s to the mid-1940s (Troksa 7). Later, terms like the "Greatest Generation" (Brokaw viii) or "G.I. Generation" (Strauss and Howe 28) were popularized for the World War II generation. Critics have continually expressed disappointment stemming from the perception that World War II soldier poets responded to the war with relative silence.[2]

Even though more poetry was produced during World War II than during the First World War, "the [World War II] period is conventionally and misleadingly viewed as one of relative artistic silence" (Deer 12). As World War II soldier poetry began to be recognized, it faced both harsh criticism and the towering reputation of the First World War poets. Critics such as William Logan have simultaneously argued that the Holocaust and dropping of the atomic bombs pushed poets into silence (180), but also that, among the poems that were produced on World War II, there were "few worth writing and fewer worth reading" (173). Logan's view of World War II poetry is not alone, as many critics and scholars acknowledge, even when arguing to the contrary, that "It is received wisdom that the First World War—or Great War—was also the greatest of all wars in terms of the poetry it generated, and that the Second World War inspired very little poetry to rival it" (Waterman 1). Hugh Haughton's 2004 anthology *Second World War Poems* acknowledges the possibility of reinvestigating the canon when conceding that "whereas the canon of First World War poetry in English is relatively stable, that of the Second World War is still an open question" (xxvi). World War II soldier poets also encountered resistance from influential literary figures. T. S. Eliot was critical of war poetry for its immediacy and therefore absence of the perspective gained from time, and he was "glad that so little of what [young British war poets] write gives an answer to satisfy the sort of people who ask, 'where are our war poets?'" (C. Ricks 269). Eliot was, in contrast, far more receptive to First World War soldier poet David Jones, remarking that his book-length poem *In Parenthesis* was "a work of genius" ("A Note of Introduction" vii). The conclusion that poets of World War II are part of a "Silent Generation" has been a repeated, though gradually challenged, narrative, yet as Monique van Hout stresses, the very development of cultural memory involves "emphasizing, leaving out, or reinterpreting historic facts" (8). In other words, to define an era, one must decide when that era has ended and whose participation was noteworthy. This is a knowingly imperfect process because it fails to encompass the entirety of a history, yet its necessity demands that we revise our findings when new information arises.

For decades, the reputation of World War II soldier poetry has been made in relation to the output and reception of First World War poets. This generational comparison recurs for two reasons: the world wars are inextricably linked by proximity and historical context, and because, overwhelmingly, notions of influence, repetition or rejection, and uniqueness (or lack thereof) are fundamental for any effort to identify or compartmentalize. Writers of the world wars are routinely compared by how they shape public perception of war. Several literary critics and cultural commentators have suggested, as George Steiner claims, that World War II poetry is without "the control of remembrance achieved by Robert Graves or [Siegfried] Sassoon" (160). Historian John Keegan reinforces this line of thinking by arguing that, in contrast to the "eternal quality" of First World War writings, "Nothing which the Second World War evoked stands comparison with it" and that "the only important category of book which the Second World War established in England was the prisoner-of-war story" (283). Even while drawing attention to World War II poetry, Hugh Haughton recognizes that "The poetry of the Second World War . . . has nothing like the same currency as that of the First" (xvii). Kenneth Rose echoes how "it is one of the conventions of literary criticism that World War I produced great writers but World War II did not" (185). Focusing on British writers, Philippa Lyon's *Twentieth-Century War Poetry* asserts how "no Second World War figure equivalent to Brooke, Owen or Sassoon has taken hold in the popular imagination" (5). This critique echoes arguments made in the *Times Literary Supplement* (*TLS*) in 1957 that, unlike the First World War, World War II "does not seem to have produced in any of the writers who went through it any such prolonged aftermath of inner stress, nor on the other hand, has it produced any such memorable literature" (Fraser, "The Poet at War" 718). Despite abundant evidence to the contrary, this view has persisted in the *TLS*, as reflected in a 2019 article that excuses poets of World War II, opining, "It is hardly their fault that they were not Graves, Owen, Sassoon and Gurney" (James ["J.C."] Campbell). In *Modernism and World War II*, Marina MacKay affirms that World War II poets were expected to re-create the literary accomplishments of their predecessors: "The soldier poets of the Great War set the standard by which the literature of the second war was judged wanting" (5). Scholars such as Margot Norris believed World War II poets fell short of such expectations and produced little poetry of note, positing in *Writing War in the Twentieth Century* that "World War I . . . was a quintessentially literary war; World War II was not" (99) and that "the poetry of the Great War skipped a generation, leaving little trace of itself on the literature of World War II" (37).[3] This latter position is echoed in *Words to Measure a War* by David K. Vaughan, who believes "the tradition or mode of the English Great War Poets appears to have had little impact" on the poets of World War II (6). Even Ian Hamilton's 1972 anthology, *The Poetry of War: 1939–1945*, timidly suggests that "There is perhaps more honest effort than distinct achievement in most of the [anthologized World War II] poems" (9).

Despite such dismissive opinions of World War II soldier poetry, more recent texts have taken a more reformative approach, such as Desmond Graham's *Poetry of the Second World War: An International Anthology* and

Jon Stallworthy's *The Oxford Book of War Poetry* (and its updated edition), which offer a more inclusive study of war poetry, with poems by both civilians and soldiers. In addition to inclusion in anthologies, Stallworthy endorses World War II soldier poets by recognizing the contributions of Keith Douglas and Louis Simpson in contrast to the generally accepted belief that, "unlike the First World War, the Second produced no poetry of importance" (*Survivors' Songs* 181). Stallworthy's *The New Oxford Book of War Poetry* attempts to revise the perception that World War II poetry was insignificant by offering, "At no point in that history did man's inhumanity to man generate more eloquent testimony from more poets than in the two world wars of the last century, the Second no less than the First," adding, "the widespread ignorance of Second World War poetry is disturbing" (*New Oxford* xxxv). Loyd E. Lee echoes Stallworthy's sentiment by agreeing that "the critical neglect of American poetry of the Second World War is unfortunate" (298). Similarly, Simon Featherstone recognizes the shortcomings of many studies and anthologies of British war writing in *War Poetry: An Introductory Reader,* emphasizing that "The canon of Second World War writing is less well-established than that of the First World War" (271–72). In the words of Peter Childs, "The poetry of World War II has not had the same press as that of World War I, even though fine work was produced" (*The Twentieth Century in Poetry* 120). In *English Poetry of the Second World War: A Biobibliography,* edited by Catherine Reilly, Reilly writes, "The poetry of the Second World War has not yet attracted as much literary and critical attention as that of the First World War but it is a popular misconception that the poetry of the second war is inferior to that of the first" (xiv). Vernon Scannell acknowledged the belief that "from the First World War came a wealth of fine poetry and from the Second little of any merit is still extraordinarily widespread" (*Not Without Glory* 15). Peter Davison remarked on the dueling legacies that "The poets of World War I were much more interesting than the poets of World War II," because of a hatred for the futility of the First World War that was not shared toward World War II (Haygood). Mark Rawlinson's *British Writing of the Second World War* adeptly describes how "wartime literature is both critical" of the legitimating of military violence while also being "fully implicated in the reproduction and invention of alternative justifications of violence" (3). Adam Piette's *Imagination at War: British Fiction and Poetry, 1939–45* presents an elevated view of soldier and civilian war writing that tackled the disjointedness of World

War II in the British imagination. Dawn Bellamy's articles on the influ-ence and relationship between poets of the First and Second World Wars provide insightful analysis on issues of iconography, style, and sexuality.[4] Overwhelmingly, commentary on World War II soldier poetry is situated in relation to First World War poetry, and therefore any meaningful analysis of World War II soldier poetry must acknowledge the threads between the two generations, disentangling them when appropriate.

The propensity of critics for quick compartmentalization has also con-tributed to an underdeveloped examination of World War II soldier po-ets. Now, eighty years since the end of World War II, retrospective analysis and legacy-shaping is conducted with very few living veterans remaining. Among the poets central to this study, Louis Simpson (1923–2012), Rich-ard Hugo (1923–1982), Howard Nemerov (1920–1991), and Randall Jarrell (1914–1965) wrote for decades after the war ended, and their postwar writ-ing lives contain deep explorations of their war experience. Keith Douglas (1920–1944) died in service in Normandy, and therefore the posthumous publication of his writings, letters, and documents by those who knew him must suffice.

The impacts of a war extend far beyond the scope of the conflict itself, and it is particularly valuable to revisit the poets of World War II because it was not until after the war, or in some cases late in their lives, that these poets wrote some of their most thought-provoking poems reflecting on the war. As a result, literary critics more frequently categorize the soldier poets highlighted in this book by other characteristics. Louis Simpson is considered a "deep image" poet, Richard Hugo a "regionalist," Howard Ne-merov an existential nature poet who played with irony and duality, and Randall Jarrell a critic and poet who explored dreams and mythology with colloquial speech. Having died in combat, Keith Douglas is the one poet in this study whose literary legacy is chiefly aligned with the war, though one could argue that if he had survived and continued writing he might have been categorized as an "extrospective"[5] poet rather than as a "war poet." This is not to say that these categorizations are inaccurate, or that soldier poets should be limited to the scope of being exclusively seen as "war po-ets," but to point out that World War II soldier poets are rarely grouped together as a unified generation in the way the trench poets are. This has caused a dislocation in their poetic legacies, precluding them from being linked by their explorations of distance and traumatic memory.

Recognizing these links between World War II soldier poets would have also been difficult amid a rapidly evolving world and increasingly busy literary landscape in the mid-twentieth century. A range of other foreign engagements and cultural developments including wars in Korea and Vietnam, the growth of the film industry, and the rise of the Beat Generation and the Confessional poets pulled attention from soldier poets after 1945. In his updated introduction to the 1987 edition of Keith Douglas's *The Complete Poems,* Ted Hughes explained the delayed, gradual recognition of Douglas's poetry in relation to changing literary trends: "The critical odds against any immediate post-war recognition were quite weighty. The *Four Quartets,* published the year Douglas died, joined the continuing prime of Auden's generation, the emergence of Dylan Thomas's generation, and the rapid maturing of the survivors of the 1920 generation. On top of these . . . modern US poetry . . . the Beats . . . modern [world] poetry, [and] "that unprecedented boom of translation" [all demanded attention] (Douglas xvii). Hughes points out that it is not that Douglas's poems were suddenly discovered, but that a diverse range of poets and movements saturated the postwar years. In *British Poets of the Second World War,* Linda M. Shires reinforces Hughes's explanation that soldier poets such as Keith Douglas "remain ignored" because of being overshadowed by the influence of Auden, Larkin, and The Movement poets on 1940s and postwar literature (xv). While the poets examined here have, subsequently, earned substantial individual recognition and accolades, the objective of this book is to examine the historical and artistic value of their poetry as a generation of World War II poets, and how creative explorations of distance and traumatic memory are at the heart of that work.

Soldier Poet vs. War Poet? What Is a War Poem and Why Should We Read Them?

World War II and its diverse combat experience broadened the scope of armed service. *The Oxford English Dictionary* defines "Soldier" as "a member of an army," and the categorization of "soldier poetry" has historically referred to poetry by those in the military, whereas "war poetry" is inclusive of both soldiers and civilians. Different branches of the armed services have distinct titles for their members, such as army "soldiers," air force "airmen," navy "sailors," and the eponymous marines, with a range of more detailed roles within each branch. Such titles are complicated when discussing poets like Richard Hugo and Randall Jarrell, who were members of the U.S. Army Air Force, and Howard Nemerov, who served in the Royal Canadian Air Force before joining the U.S. Army Air Force. The U.S. Army Air Force began as a part of the U.S. Army in 1907 and did not become a separate branch of the U.S. military until 1947, after the conclusion of World War II ("Air Force History"). While Hugo, Jarrell, and Nemerov would technically be classed as "airmen" today, Jarrell referred to his own poems about armed service and the war as his "army style" poems (Pritchard, *Randall Jarrell* 100). Similarly, British First World War poet Rupert Brooke is known best for his poem titled "The Soldier" and is "Undoubtedly the most influential and renowned of the soldier poets during the [First World] War and for several decades afterwards" (Kendall, *Poetry of the First World War* 102), despite being a member of the Royal Naval Volunteer Reserve (National Archives, "DocumentsOnline"), a subset of the Royal Naval Division in which infantry conducted amphibious landings (Scutts). While nuance is required to recognize the interrelations and distinctions between each role and branch, this study will treat the poets of World War II inclusively, as a group of armed service members who share more unifying qualities than their military branch or role would suggest. Therefore, this study will employ terms such as "soldier" and "soldier poetry" in a traditional sense to refer to the armed service members of World War II, rather than dividing the generation by branch of service, or whether they participated in combat operations or served in a noncombat capacity.

The importance of examining the soldier's perspective within the broader field of war poetry is to examine the consequences and sustained repercussions of armed conflict. Soldier poetry offers testimony and the perspective of primary source witnesses to the irrevocable reshaping of history, politics, borders, sovereignty, and cultures. That does not mean that the experiential dimension of soldier poetry precludes it from critique. Addressing a feeling of exhaustion when reading war poetry, Alice Templeton asks, "what is the use of writing poetry in the consciousness of wartime" if "poetic language so seldom exceeds the us/them binaries and brutalities of uncritical rhetoric?" (44). While this is a completely justifiable question to ask, World War II soldier poets such as Louis Simpson, Keith Douglas, Richard Hugo, Howard Nemerov, and Randall Jarrell see enemies, civilians, and all people as part of their "us." The act of seeing, and therefore recognizing the humanity of another, is essential for understanding the tragic losses of World War II and to further understand war as an act of collective suffering.

In *Veteran Poetics: British Literature in the Age of Mass Warfare, 1790–2015*, Kate McLoughlin stresses that the importance of the veteran in literature is bringing to light questions such as, "What can be recovered from the past? . . . What is the value of experience? How can what has happened be communicated to others?" (1). These recovered histories are chances to share hard truths about the experience of war, and it is the same impulse of many creative works attempting to connect to others. Midcentury literary critics sought war poetry of firsthand experience for the same reason war poems conventionally command interest, its "subjective element" that carries "a mark of authenticity and truth that, paradoxically, more objective histories rarely attain" (Brosman 86). Readers turn to narratives of witness and testimony for its "experiential dimension," for vicarious knowledge of historical events that would otherwise be inconceivable (85). Furthermore, listening to "life stories" brings us closer to understanding the flow of history because they put "ordinary people back into the well-known narrative of major events" (Jarausch 1). Ordinarily, primary source historical insight is prized because it helps to locate "family stories in bigger, more universal, narratives," and memorable war poems locate a reader's understanding through the perspective of an individual (Winter and Sivan 3). With these purposes in mind—though the world moves forward with or without those who need time to heal and put their experiences into words—reexamining how soldier poets saw World War II is essential to understanding their experience.

The Field of World War II Poetry Criticism

While recent critical works such as Diederik Oostdijk's *Among the Nightmare Fighters* (2011) and Rory Waterman's *Poets of the Second World War* (2015) evaluate the poetry of World War II soldiers, this study is distinct from these books in argument, poet selection, and thematic continuity. Oostdijk's compelling *Among the Nightmare Fighters* concludes that American poets of the World War II generation were not "silent," but "quiet" (244), and were "self-consciously historical" because they had become "intellectuals filling the voids of their predecessors, recognizing the past and society's historical amnesia" (242). Oostdijk's book focuses exclusively on American poets, whereas this analysis seeks not to delineate the generation of World War II poets by nationality. As a result, Oostdijk only mentions Keith Douglas and, even while focusing on American poets, gives limited attention to Richard Hugo, while greater emphasis is placed on figures outside of the armed services, such as conscientious objector Robert Lowell. Meanwhile, Waterman's book takes umbrage with the title "'war poet,'" suggesting instead that many World War II poems are travel poems. In doing so, he responds to the repeated refrain of "Where are the war poets?": "They were all over the place" (4). As opposed to linking World War II poems by a shared sense of movement, this study offers a more nuanced explanation of location, time, space, and proximity, as components of the theme of distance. While Waterman's book selects both British and American soldier poets of World War II as its focus,[6] it ignores Hugo and only mentions Nemerov in passing.

This research also engages with a range of scholarly articles that have shared influential ideas about war literature. Catherine Savage Brosman's 1992 article "The Functions of War Literature" addresses the important overlap of the storytelling tradition with the "experiential dimension" of war (85), and the subsequent value afforded to authenticity (86), ideas that are echoed in James Scott Campbell's 1999 article "Combat Gnosticism." These research findings are not written in support of the theory of "combat gnosticism," which argues "the knowledge of combat is a prerequisite for the production of a literary text that adequately deals with war" (204). While these concepts are ubiquitous in war literature criticism, the war poems of Randall Jarrell challenge the notion that firsthand experience is a requirement for writing about a subject. Furthermore, a distinguishing characteristic of many of the World War II soldier poems examined in this study is that they are not depictions of combat at all, but more frequently reflections on how the war has reoriented the way they interpret concepts such as distance, memory, legacy, duty, guilt, and purpose. Steven Gould Axelrod's 1999 article "The Middle Generation and WWII" identifies five World War II–era poets who embody their generation's "refus[al] to glorify war" while describing it from "sharply divergent perspectives" (3). Axelrod's analysis includes soldiers, civilians, and conscientious objectors,[7] and the refusal to glorify war is pertinent to a deep field of soldier poets. To invoke Martin Jay, experience is "the intersection between public language and private subjectivity" because it "is both a collective linguistic concept . . . and a reminder that such concepts always leave a remainder that escapes their homogenizing grasp" (6). Narrative threads and through lines are interwoven in the poetry of soldiers, but for as much as these commonalities link them, their experience, reflections, and writings on war are not carbon copies. These writings are worthy of revisitation because each affirms the value of an individual human life amid an era that is often spoken of using expansive statistics of combatants, victims, and survivors.

Sight Manifested in Distance and Traumatic Memory

While many First World War soldier poems are linked by the "traumatic focus of the Great Wars' trenches" (Roderick Watson 318) and the response to "shell-shock" (Armstrong 63), the range and scale of traumatic events in World War II extend beyond battles—which provided new perspectives of air, sea, and ground combat—to events such as the Holocaust, Hiroshima and Nagasaki, D-Day, and the targeting of civilians. Since there is no singular World War II combat image equivalent to the communal experience of First World War trenches, such an assortment of experience poses a challenge to critics attempting to compartmentalize World War II poets. Despite these variables of experience, war influences the way humans process nearly incommunicable experiences. As Judith Herman explains, survivors are "subject to the dialectic of trauma" and must "find a language that conveys fully and persuasively what one has seen" (2). Herman's idea of response to trauma has been paraphrased as "the conflict between the need to publicly witness his encounter with violence and the compulsion to repress it" (Scranton 1). It is therefore understandable why World War II soldier poets would recurringly explore themes of distance and traumatic memory to cope, compartmentalize, and comprehend the violence they have seen or visualized. These themes allow for the creation of both a channel for their observations and a buffer to protect oneself from the psychological and physical stress of war. As numerous studies in recent decades have shown, cathartic or expressive writing can assist veterans and those with PTSD to reintegrate into civilian life, and help to reduce symptoms such as stress, anger, depression, and anxiety (Sayer). Among their most valuable contributions to the canon of war literature, poets of World War II creatively cast the war experience as a negotiation of literal and figurative distance and demonstrate war's repercussions by confronting traumatic memory through confessional and testimonial personas, often for decades after the war ended. It is precisely these diverse interpretations of distance and delayed processing of traumatic memory that resulted in an incomplete view of the contributions made by World War II soldier poets. The distance of time measured in short- and long-term retrospection on the war, and the inherent time required for traumatized individuals to process and confront their experience, meant that time, delay, and separation were required by soldiers to compartmentalize their war experience. The impatience of literary and cultural critics did not afford World War II soldiers the time needed to reflect, heal, and create, resulting in premature declarations of their silence and lack of creative output. While themes such as distance and trauma are not exclusive to World War II, they are consistently used lenses through which World War II soldier poets processed their experience.

Subsections within the chapters that follow will examine how poets of World War II used and manipulated sight for literal and figurative manifestations of distance. Literal distance—a measurable space or geographic spread—between self and enemy, target, home, civilians, or combat itself directly corresponds to how these poets engage with concepts such as landscape, imagery, and sight. Explorations of literal distances of space (between combatant and battle) and time (between the poet's present and past) are informed by Carolyn Forché and Duncan Wu's exploration of "poetry of witness" and the notion of proximity. Stemming from the experiential, the concept of "poetry of witness" is described as a "readerly encounter with the literature of that-which-happened, and its mode is evidentiary rather than representational" (Forché and Wu 21). The clearest linkage between Forché and Wu's scholarship and this study of distance and traumatic memory is the idea of the witness "*in relation*" to extreme events, about which Forché explains, "Relation is proximity, and this closeness subjects the witness to the possibility of being wounded" (25). As shown throughout this study, processing war through the distance or "proximity" to battle (in both literal and figurative ways) is a defining and unifying feature of World War II soldier poets. Furthermore, the act of creating such testimonial writings means "the writer must recognize the claims of difference, the otherness of others, and the specificities of their experience" (Forché, *Against Forgetting* 37). By acknowledging the limitless potential to interpret a historical event from each individual's perspective, Forché argues, "Witness, in this light, is problematic: even if one has witnessed atrocity, one cannot necessarily speak *about* it, let alone *for* it" (*Against Forgetting* 37).

Figurative perceptions of distance, a psychological separation or divide, also influences expressions of resentment, guilt, impersonality, and extrospection. Figurative distance can be understood by incorporating Heidegger's *Being and Time* theory of "distantiality" as a response to "Dasein" (German for "there-is," or being, one's presence) (Brady). Distantiality can be read as Dasein's loss of self, a separation from one's conception of self (Fynsk), which is demonstrated in Simpson's depersonalized and cross-generational war poems; Douglas's extrospective poetry, which brings isolated enemy soldiers into closer view;[8] and the poetry of Hugo, Nemerov, and Jarrell, who direct readers to empathize for the victims of war. The way Simpson, Douglas, and Jarrell shed their identities in favor of anonymous personas or speakers is itself an exercise of T. S. Eliot's declaration that "Poetry . . . is not the expression of personality, but an escape from personality" ("Tradition and the Individual Talent" 48–49). Contemporary theories on distance, such as Corinna Stan's 2018 idea from *The Art of Distances* that "interpersonal distance is crucial to the preservation of inner distances," aid in the analysis of using personas and the intent of distancing oneself in war poems (237). This balancing of external and internal distances is exemplified by Douglas's turn toward the extrospective mode and Hugo's use of external landscapes to translate internalized feelings.

Additional chapter subsections invoke the work of trauma theorists and writers to contextualize the presence of traumatic memory in the work of these five poets. Particularly insightful is the trauma theory of Sigmund Freud in *Beyond the Pleasure Principle*, which explains symptomatic latency and repression in trauma victims, relevant to the delayed response war poetry of Simpson, Hugo, and Nemerov.[9] Additionally, Cathy Caruth's view of trauma as a repeated suffering and a disruption in *Trauma: Explorations in Memory* and *Unclaimed Experience*, and E. Ann Kaplan's notion of "vicarious trauma," which she explains in *Trauma Culture: The Politics of Terror and Loss in Media and Literature*, are of notable importance. Manifestations of trauma from lived and vicarious experience influence each of the poets selected in this study, with Jarrell's poems of Holocaust victims typifying vicarious trauma.[10] Further sources of trauma theory that have added to this study include Dominick LaCapra's ideas from *Writing History, Writing Trauma* on the roles of temporality and distance to shape our understanding of historical trauma, particularly in the temporal ambiguity in Louis Simpson's poetry and Randall Jarrell's manifestations of distance. Psychological studies such as the Murray, Merritt, and Grey study on returning to sites of traumatic experience and their application of the Ehlers and Clark Cognitive Theory provide insight for analyzing Richard Hugo's postwar poems chronicling his return to Italy.[11]

Why Simpson, Douglas, Hugo, Nemerov, and Jarrell?

As with any attempt to encapsulate the literature of a generation, omissions will be inevitable. The estimation of this research is that these five poets— Simpson, Douglas, Hugo, Nemerov, and Jarrell—created the strongest body of World War II soldier poetry throughout their writing lives, and each offers a new way of seeing shared themes of distance and traumatic memory. Armed services poets from America such as Karl Shapiro, Richard Wilbur, John Ciardi, Lincoln Kirstein, Anthony Hecht, and James Dickey, and from Britain such as Alun Lewis, John Jarmain, Hamish Henderson, Sorley MacLean, Charles Causley, Henry Reed, and Sidney Keyes, among many others from all over the globe, also wrote valuable poetry on their World War II experience. In particular, Karl Shapiro's *V-Letter*, Richard Eberhart's "The Fury of Aerial Bombardment," James Dickey's "The Fire-bombing," Alun Lewis's "All Day It Has Rained," Henry Reed's "Naming of Parts," John Ciardi's *Other Skies*, Anthony Hecht's "Rites and Ceremonies," and John Jarmain's poems are notable war-inspired works.

To select a unified collection of the strongest World War II soldier poets, the following methodological variables were used: literary output (did the poet write a substantial body of war poetry?), critical acclaim,[12] war experience (were the poets enlisted and did they possess substantive insight on the war?), and, of particular importance to the cohesion of this generation and study, engaging themes of distance and traumatic memory. In addition to these variables, poets were omitted for various reasons, such as dying early in their war service (Lewis[13] and Keyes[14]), questions of authenticity (Dickey[15]), or for practical considerations of concision (to borrow Desmond Graham's words, this selection of poets is intended as "a gathering and not a monument" (*Poetry of the Second World War* xvi)). This study is rooted in the work of poets traversing a world at war, and such decisions will inevitably bear some degree of subjectivity.

As with any such methodological and subjective selection criteria, questions of representation of nationalities are expected. The selection of four American poets and one British poet is not a value judgment on the literary prowess of each country, but a result of the methodology described above and reflects representative numbers of World War II service members: "by the end of the war, 3.5 million had served in the British Army" while 16 million Americans served out of 50 million who were registered ("Soldiers in World War II"). While not a primary factor in poet selection, this approximate 4:1 ratio of American to British servicemembers is reflected in the selection of poets in this study. The inclusion of Keith Douglas in this cohort is essential because his output, experience, and thematic examinations of distance and traumatic memory situate him alongside his American contemporaries as a unified cohort of World War II soldier poets. Douglas's extrospective poems reflect upon combat, subvert pastoral landscapes, consider guilt, and demonstrate mechanized sights and weaponry. The abbreviated time between combat and the writing inspired by it speak to Douglas's intensity of reflection and production. These methodological determinants and shared thematic parallels align Douglas's war poetry with that of Simpson, Hugo, Nemerov, and Jarrell far more than nationality would distinguish them from one another.

Equally, simplifying Simpson, Hugo, Nemerov, and Jarrell as a homogeneous group of Americans would present its own issues. Simpson was born in Jamaica (then a British colony) to a half-Black Scottish father and Russian-Jewish mother and became an American citizen during his three years of service in the U.S. Army. Nemerov, who served in both the Canadian RAF and U.S. Army Air Force, was the son of Russian-Jewish immigrants. According to Edward S. Shapiro, it was not until the end of World War II that, for Jewish Americans, "the relationship between their Jewish and American identities was to be one of symbiosis and not conflict" (65). The diversity of heritage, region, and other identity constructs suggests that "American" is itself a nuanced and imprecise identifier.

Limiting the scope to these select poets may inadvertently reinforce a narrow view that war poetry is a field predominantly written by one demographic: white, male, English-speaking soldiers. The effects of war are never restricted to one gender, race, or other identifier, and therefore nei-

ther is the literature of war. The lack of racial diversity in World War II narratives is a direct consequence of systemic racism and inequality. Telling
the story of the contributions made by a more ethnically diverse range of
servicemen and servicewomen to Allied victory in World War II is a task
made increasingly difficult due to a disproportionately imbalanced amount
of source material curated from the war. For example, filmmakers looking
to turn Maria Höhn and Martin Klimke's book *A Breath of Freedom: The
Civil Rights Struggle, African American GIs, and Germany* into a documentary
"discovered less than 10 minutes of footage" of "black GIs in the final push
into Germany and during the occupation of post-war Germany . . . despite
the fact that among the 16 million U.S. soldiers who fought in World War II,
there were about one million African-American soldiers" (Höhn).[16]

Though there is a smaller body of published World War II poetry by
Black soldiers compared to that of white soldiers, one would be remiss not
to acknowledge the poems and literary contributions of Black veterans.
Among them is Dudley Randall, a member of the Air Force's Signal Corps
who served in the South Pacific (Randall, "Dudley Randall" 76). "Pacific
Epitaphs," Randall's series of short poems, elegizes dead servicemen using
place-names to frame his reflections (Randall, *More to Remember*). After
World War II, Randall became an influential figure in the Black Arts Movement as the editor of Broadside Press.[17] Owen Dodson is another notable
Black veteran writer. Dodson enlisted in the U.S. Navy, and while his creative output during the war was largely channeled through directing plays,
poems like "Black Mother Praying in the Summer 1943"[18] and "The Decision" were published in *Common Ground* in 1944. Other Black-run publica-
tions such as *The Crisis*[19] and *Phylon*[20] carved out space for social, political,
and creative expression and were critical resources highlighting the double
standards experienced by African Americans during World War II.[21]

A recurrent theme in a number of World War II poems by Black writers
is the idea of "double-consciousness," which can be traced from W. E. B. Du
Bois pointing out "this sense of always looking at one's self through the
eyes of others. . . . One ever feels his two-ness,—an American, a Negro;
two souls, two thoughts, two unreconciled strivings" (364). Grappling with
these identities, African American soldiers confronted a "two-front battle"
(Delmont) in which they fought the Axis powers abroad while fighting for
equality at home, hoping to achieve "a double victory" (Gates). These sentiments reverberate through the World War II poetry written by African

American civilians, the most widely recognized of which belong to major Black writers Langston Hughes and Gwendolyn Brooks. One can look to Hughes's "Will V-Day Be Me-Day Too?" in which each stanza frames the hypocrisy of America for fighting for equality and against prejudice abroad while exhibiting prejudicial and segregationist behavior against Black Americans at home. Hughes asks:

> When I take off my uniform,
> Will I be safe from harm—
> Or will you do me
> As the Germans did the Jews?

> ("Will V-Day Be Me-Day Too?" lines 52–55)

Similar to Hughes's "Will V-Day Be Me-Day Too?" is "Beaumont to Detroit: 1943," written in response to race riots in America during World War II, in which Hughes captures the sentiment of having to simultaneously fight for freedom at home and abroad: "How long I got to fight / BOTH HITLER— AND JIM CROW" ("Beaumont to Detroit: 1943" lines 31–32). Poet Gwendolyn Brooks also questioned the purity of American patriotism in a series of sonnets titled "Gay Chaps at the Bar" in her 1945 collection *A Street in Bronzeville*. Brooks writes of the blind, cyclical support for war in "the progress": "Still we remark on patriotism, sing / Salute the flag, thrill heavily, rejoice / For death of men, who, too, saluted, sang" (lines 6–8). While the fragility of this myth of American exceptionalism is on display in these poems, the speakers of these poems recognize the protection afforded to members of the armed services. For Hughes's speaker in "Will V-Day Be Me-Day Too?" the fear of being susceptible to discrimination comes "When I take off my uniform" (line 52), just as the speaker in Brooks's "the progress" admits—despite the blatant racial inequality in America—that "still we wear our uniforms, follow / The cracked cry of the bugles" (lines 1–2). The serviceman's uniform is seen as a partial shield from heightened discrimination, a thin veneer concealing the hard truth about racial inequality in America. In addition to writing about anonymous veterans, Brooks also used specific individuals to champion the contributions of Black servicemen. In "Negro Hero," Brooks channels the voice of Doris "Dorie" Miller, a U.S. Navy mess attendant who courageously carried his captain to safety and took up arms during the bombing of Pearl Harbor (Wamsley). In the poem, speaking as Miller, Brooks reminds readers in an aside that "(They are not concerned that it was hardly The Enemy my fight was against / But them)" (lines 11–12).[22] Other writers took up this critique of segregation and discrimination in the armed forces, such as poet and First World War conscientious objector Witter Bynner, who wrote in his 1944 poem "Defeat" that "On a train in Texas German prisoners eat / With white American soldiers, seat by seat, / While black American soldiers sit apart" (lines 1–3), concluding that "It is again ourselves whom we defeat" (line 10).

Asian Americans also faced heightened discrimination and questions of dual loyalty in response to the attack on Pearl Harbor, manifesting in the internment of more than 120,000 Japanese Americans (Frail), as well as segregated units for Japanese American soldiers ("Fighting for Democracy"). Cary Nelson's *Anthology of Contemporary American Poetry* thoughtfully includes a section titled "Japanese American Concentration Camp Haiku (1942–1944)." As a lasting repercussion of discriminatory policies, and the segregation of the U.S. military until 1948 ("Executive Order 9981"), we are now reckoning with an incomplete picture of history caused by a legacy of segregated and suppressed voices.

Of equal importance are the great literary accomplishments of women and civilian poets writing during World War II. Fortunately, twentieth-century war poetry by women such as Charlotte Mew, Vera Brittain, H.D., and others has been increasingly recognized in anthologies such as Catherine Reilly's *Scars upon My Heart: Women's Poetry and Verse of the First World War; Chaos of the Night: Women's Poetry and Verse of World War Two;* and *The Virago Book of Women's War Poetry and Verse,* Nosheen Khan's critical work *Women's Poetry of the First World War,* and articles such as Gill Plain's "Women's Writing in the Second World War." The indelible poetry of civilians affected by World War II such as Czesław Miłosz's "Dedication" and "A Song on the End of the World," Zbigniew Herbert's "September 17" and "Report from the Besieged City," Wisława Szymborska's "The End and the Beginning" and "Once we had the world backwards and forwards . . . ," Miklós Radnóti's "How Others See . . ." and his "Razglednicas," and Anna Akhmatova's poems of resistance such as "Requiem," to highlight just a few, also encompasses a broad body of scholarship that has been enriched by criticism, anthologizing, and commentary. No race, gender, nationality, role of witness or participant, or other identifier supersedes another in the value of war literature, and each offers important narratives and reflections on history. The aim of this book is to examine the traits and contributions of World War II soldier poets as one limb among the larger body of literature stemming from the 1939–45 conflict.

Structure and Overview

World War II soldier poetry provides innovative interpretations of distance and the persistent intrusiveness and psychological repercussions of traumatic memory. Therefore, each chapter will critically examine how Simpson, Douglas, Hugo, Nemerov, and Jarrell processed the war using these shared themes. The order of the following chapters reflects each selected poet's degrees of distance from battle, and how their processing of traumatic events mirrors the distance from which they experienced war.

The first two chapters focus on Louis Simpson and Keith Douglas, whose service was mostly conducted on the ground at relatively close proximity to the enemy. Arguably closest in experience to the battlefield experience of previous wars, Simpson experienced the ground war as an infantryman in France, Belgium, and Germany. Douglas also participated in the ground war, though as a tank commander in North Africa before dying three days into the Allied invasion of Normandy.[23] Both poets reflect on the proximity to enemy combatants in their writing, and it is through abbreviated distances that each processed traumatic experience. Coinciding with World War II's growing dependence on air offensives, the focus of this study will then shift to bombardier Richard Hugo and pilot Howard Nemerov. Hugo and Nemerov experienced the air war at a greater distance from the targets of their bombing runs than soldiers on the ground, and this added level of detachment is reflected in both their poetry and delayed processing of traumatic memory. Lastly, as a soldier stationed stateside, Randall Jarrell represents the greatest distance between soldier and combat of those examined in this research. Jarrell's distance from combat and heightened experience of vicarious trauma are indicative in the subjects of his poems, which commonly turn attention to the suffering of others. This book is structured on a gradient of growing distance between each soldier and his proximity to combat, and each chapter will analyze the emotional distance that modernized warfare cultivates in its participants.

American poet and member of the 101st Airborne Division, Louis

Simpson is the focus of chapter 1. After a brief introduction to Simpson's life and work, this chapter will contextualize his poetry and war experience and outline his contribution to World War II poetry. Simpson's recognition of the canonical weight of First World War poetry is demonstrated by reading his war poems alongside those predecessors, and through the repurposing of shared subject matter. A direct connection between Simpson and Wilfred Owen is documented in the preface to Simpson's *Collected Poems,* in which he specifically recalls encountering a First World War trench and how retreading this frozen ground in World War II made him feel as if he were reliving Owen's poem "Exposure" (xiv). Simpson's early war poems will be shown as invocations of Owen's war poems, the start of Simpson's efforts to write about different time periods simultaneously. The following section will turn to the tension in Simpson's war poems between feeling a connection to familiar landscapes and being distanced from civilians at the home front. Landscapes in Simpson's poems will be analyzed to show how Simpson advances a tradition of war poetry that subverts pastoral imagery. This subsection of generational comparison will work in tandem with an analysis of how the figurative distance between soldiers and civilians in Simpson's poems is exhibited through internalized feelings of resentment and neglect, a departure from the outward resentment voiced by First World War soldiers. Another hallmark of Simpson's war poetry is his shift toward impersonality and his use of temporal ambiguity. Subsequent sections focus on Simpson's engagement with traumatic memory, first with the relationship between touch and memory as demonstrated in the poem "A Bower of Roses." Then, using poems that employ dreams, nightmares, and visions, this chapter will conclude with an in-depth analysis of how Simpson uncovered traumatic memory through manifestations of the PTSD symptoms he experienced. The figures and settings of Simpson's reflective war poems pivot between self and other, now and then, World War II and all preceding wars, a sense of universality that will be shown as a commentary on war itself.

Keith Douglas is the subject of chapter 2. Neil Corcoran points to Douglas's line from the poem "Desert Flowers," "Rosenberg I only repeat what you were saying" (line 2), as proof that Douglas had "no illusions about the fact that the great war poems have all, long since, been written" (169). This refrain suggests World War II poets struggled to say something new about war in the wake of the literature of the First World War. Douglas was undeniably linked to the legacy of First World War poets because he was mentored by Edmund Blunden, was close friends with Hamo Sassoon (Siegfried Sassoon's nephew), and, as evidenced through archival research in the chapter, was a reader of Wilfred Owen and Isaac Rosenberg. Yet, Douglas's war writings and his connection to the previous generation demand greater interrogation than allowing the line "Rosenberg I only repeat what you were saying" to overshadow years of creative output. Complicating the relationship between war and distance is the desert landscape in which Douglas served, and the next section dissects the role of the desert in shaping Douglas's war experience. While Douglas is the only poet in this study who died during the war, one can read into his poems the presence and recognition of traumatic memory. Douglas's poetry exhibits moral distancing in the moments preceding, during, and following combat violence to comment on mortality and the absence of guilt for taking the lives of others. Douglas's most anthologized war poems are about the anticipation of death, specifically poems of self-elegy ("Simplify me when I'm dead"), the act of killing ("How to Kill"), and the consequences of death for loved ones of the deceased ("*Vergissmeinnicht*"). While these poems appear, on the surface, to be uniquely devoid of emotion, thoughtful explication reveals them to be among Douglas's most moving and insightful war poems, all of which manipulate literal and figurative distance through mediums of sight such as telescopic lenses and time. Sections herein will interrogate Douglas's invocation of traumatic memory through self-elegy, the presence and absence of guilt, and poems of remnants and ruins that quantify and recalibrate what war leaves behind. Keith Douglas's poetry offers a blunt yet nuanced voice and vision to the North Africa campaign of World War II, and his indelible poetry of distance and traumatic memory validates his presence among the most important World War II soldier poets.

Chapter 3 will turn to Richard Hugo, American poet and bombardier in the U.S. Army Air Force's Mediterranean campaigns. Hugo was a poet from Seattle who is primarily categorized as a regionalist for his poems of the Pacific Northwest, but his war poetry is split between spaces of perceived safety and danger: the land and the sky. Hugo's war poems are a by-product of the five miles of air that distanced him from his bomber's targets, and chronicle empathy for the civilians and bombing victims the bombers never have to see face to face. Hugo's empathic poems, such as "Letter to Simic from Boulder" and "The Yards of Sarajevo," reflect on the damage he caused and represent a postwar moral reckoning. Hugo's use of skyscapes and the relationship between the sky and land in his World War II poems are an extension of the landscape studies initiated in the Simpson and Douglas chapters. Twenty years after the war, Hugo returned to Italy, where he had been stationed, and the poems in his collection *Good Luck in Cracked Italian* (1969) resonate as a man attempting to find meaning in his life. Hugo's act of revisiting the sites of traumatic experience will be the focus of the next section, showing Hugo's attempts to bridge the gap between past and present through "then-now discrimination," a function in the Ehlers and Clark Cognitive Theory (Murray et al. 422). In Hugo's case, subconsciously engaging in "then-now discrimination" by comparing 1940s wartime Italy with 1960s postwar Italy gives him proof that local life and culture have survived and, though these locations have been forever changed by the war, allow him to accept that the war is over. Similarly, Hugo's poems of traumatic memory are linked to the act of war memorialization and those conflicted by acts of collective memory. This chapter will conclude by analyzing how Hugo explored guilt through writing ekphrastic poems while visiting sites of art and culture in his return trips to Italy. In this way, Hugo is both a creative voice of World War II air campaigns and one who navigated the complex field of remembrance and meaning for decades after the war.

Howard Nemerov was a pilot for the Canadian RAF and U.S. Army Air Force during World War II, and his war poems are the topic of chapter 4. While Nemerov wrote the occasional poem reflecting on or alluding to World War II in the 1950s and 1960s, it was not until later in his life and career that he felt an obligation to revisit the war more extensively. In large part due to disappointment over America's returns to armed conflict in the wake of two world wars, Nemerov felt it was a duty to share his war experience as he neared the end of his life. As posited by Diederik Oostdijk, among the World War II poets Nemerov was most "consistently and assertively" trying to "debunk 'The Good War' myth" ("Debunking" 222). Nemerov spoke as a moral authority against the appetite for war as someone with firsthand war experience. Nemerov's later work speaks against war and the narratives that governments employ to make war palatable. Nemerov's attempt to reclaim war narratives on behalf of the combatant will be the focus of the first section in this chapter. Particularly in his collection *War Stories*, Nemerov uses the distance of elapsed time from the war to compartmentalize world events while also using hindsight to point out their interrelations. For example, "Ultima Ratio Reagan" is a poem written in the height of the Cold War that expresses fear for younger generations that did not live through the atrocities of the past, and how willingly governments send them off to war, or, as Nemerov remarks, "The reason we do not learn from history is / Because we are not the people who learned last time" (lines 1–2). Sections in this chapter will show how Nemerov uses distance to chart his emotional investment in the war over time, reclaim the narratives of war, and demonstrate the influence of skyscapes on memory of the air war. This chapter will conclude by recounting how Nemerov actively navigates traumatic memory and guilt as topics of his war poetry. The poem "Redeployment" examines postwar life with symptoms of PTSD, while poems such as "The War in the Air" reflect on the nature of guilt as it relates to war and the discrepancy between personal and collective memory. For Nemerov, both PTSD and lingering guilt are examples of the psychological cost of war that he intends as warnings for younger generations.

Chapter 5 focuses on Randall Jarrell. Despite Jarrell being the only poet selected in this research not to have experienced combat, relegated to an instructional role stateside, he is arguably the most well-known soldier poet of World War II. As a poet and critic, Jarrell is best known for his five-line poem "The Death of the Ball Turret Gunner," one of the few consistently anthologized poems by a World War II soldier. Yet Jarrell's physical distance from the war in Europe and the Pacific situates him in a noncombatant soldier role, and this unique perspective of preparing others to carry out missions pushes Jarrell to focus on systematic aspects of war. The first two sections of this chapter will expose a cross-section of distance, mechanization, and the divide between the soldier and the state. Examples include one's search for individualism in the army ("Mail Call"), deadly training missions ("Losses"), and the perspective of the air war from someone who sends others into danger ("The Sick Nought"). Jarrell's use of a distanced perspective is not restricted to commentary on those in the armed forces but also extends to civilians. The presence of traumatic memory in Jarrell's war poems is rooted in the guilt of having a role in the death of others and as an example of "secondary" or "vicarious trauma," terminology used by E. Ann Kaplan to explain one's relationships or perceptions of distress experienced by others (91). Examination of these exercises of trauma and guilt will occur in separate sections of this chapter. First, Jarrell imagines the victimization of civilians during World War II as a way of generating empathy for others, and poems such as "A Camp in the Prussian Forest" and "Protocols" show Jarrell embodying the traumatic memory of others by attempting to give voice to voiceless Holocaust victims. Jarrell's recognition of the horrors endured during and after the war by individuals and nations is a symbolically important gesture of empathy for those affected. Then, Jarrell navigates a complex emotional landscape as a soldier who bears some degree of guilt for the death of others. Such psychological acceptance is demonstrated by Jarrell's sympathy for others, and in the overwhelming presence of dreams, nightmares, and visions in his poems of vicarious trauma. This self-awareness toward themes of distance and traumatic memory reinforces Jarrell's connection to generations of war poets and highlights his contribution to the body of World War II poetry.

Deductions from this research will address what it says about the nature of war to have thematic parallels between the poetry of the World Wars despite being dramatically different conflicts. Factors for why poetry of World War II is less recognized by critics and readers will be reexamined through the lens of distance and traumatic memory. Included in this discourse will be the difference in the generational reception and popularity of war poetry in relation to the timing of publication, the rise in film as an entertainment and news medium, the shifting focus of the public to new poetic movements and new wars, and the "latency period" after the war in which the world acquired knowledge of the Holocaust (E. Hoffman 84). The conclusion will also address Theodor Adorno's renowned declaration that "To write poetry after Auschwitz is barbaric," on the inadequacy of repeating cultural acts that were part of a culture that gave birth to an atrocity (34). Adorno's statement on how the Holocaust created a fissure in memory and meaning that cannot be bridged by traditional means demands a response. Such a response must recognize the output and testimonial of witnesses and participants in the war. In positioning this analysis in relation to existing literary criticism and cultural commentary, this study outlines the value in continuing to revise outmoded beliefs about the output, quality, and value of World War II soldier poetry. This palimpsest approach highlights how the reception of these war poets has been inadequate until recent decades, due, in part, to the prolonged period over which they wrote war poems after World War II had ended, a reflection of the delayed processing of traumatic experience. Literary criticism and cultural commentary rarely afford those with PTSD the necessary patience to process their complex experiences, often ignoring the indeterminate timeline of delayed or repressed memories. Dominick LaCapra paraphrased Sigmund Freud's idea that "Traumatic memory may involve belated temporality and a period of latency between a real or fantasized early event and a later one that somehow recalls it and triggers renewed repression or foreclosure and intrusive behavior" (89). Therefore, by revisiting World War II poetry and providing a new reading of the importance and contribution of these poets, this book provides a unifying vision of distance and traumatic memory as the dominant conduit themes of World War II soldier poetry. This argument furthers the reputational course correction of these poets and addresses a void in the field of war literature by offering a new way of seeing World War II soldier poetry, not as that of a "Silent Generation," but as that of a generation deserving of a significant place in the canon of war literature. The adequate remembrance of these soldier poets is not possible without proper representation.

■ ■ ■

The first half of the twentieth century contained two of the deadliest wars in human history, fomented by aggressive acts of nationalism and expansionism. These sanguinary conflicts were so immense in scope and consequence that they irrevocably demarcated the world. To glean a clearer understanding of the world wars, acts of reportage took many forms beyond conventional journalism, such as poetry, fiction, personal journals, memoirs, and the gradual technological development of film. The poetry written by soldiers of the First World War has been exalted and canonized as a warning to others of the horror and futility of war, while also revolutionizing the nature of war poetry, as war itself was evolving with modern technology and advanced weaponry. Roughly twenty years later, news of Germany's invasion of Poland was crystallized by W. H. Auden, who captured the feelings of many aware that there is no such thing as a "war to end all wars" but rather that war is a truly human act, destined to recur. As Auden wrote in "September 1, 1939," people were "Uncertain and afraid," and those feelings would not dissipate soon, or for some, ever (line 3).[24] Despite the cultural weight of Auden's poem at the outset of World War II, the war is not neatly bookended with a conclusive and widely read poem to mark its end. In that perceived absence one can, and should, look to poems by World War II soldiers that spanned the war and the decades that followed.

Though the soldier poets of World War II did not need to wrestle with the notion that their war was an act of futility, they nonetheless had to process a war that stayed with them as a tragic and unending psychological tremor. World War II resulted in a range of civilian atrocities that belie comprehension. In addition to coming to terms with the tens of millions of war dead from World War II, individuals struggled to grasp the scope of the systematic mass murder of Jews, Slavs, and other groups persecuted by Germany's Third Reich. To confront and comprehend the inconceivable horror of the Holocaust, historian Lawrence Rees proclaims, "history lives through eyewitness testimony" (*The Holocaust* 426). In every war, testimony serves an invaluable purpose in constructing an understanding of the conflict, and the soldier poets of World War II successfully forged empathic voices distinctly born out of their diverse experience. By examining the poetry of World War II soldiers Louis Simpson, Keith Douglas, Richard Hugo, Howard Nemerov, and Randall Jarrell, this study proposes that their poetry uses distance and traumatic memory to observe, reflect, and examine World War II and its lifelong repercussions. For a half century after the war, many critics reinforced the idea that World War II soldiers were a "Silent Generation," and despite a gradually changing tide of critical response, some still do. World War II soldier poems are linked through diverse interpretations of distance and delayed processing of traumatic memory, and it is time to acknowledge how these poets offer a new way of seeing the war, its connections to the past, and the lifetime of images it burdened them with.

1

LOUIS SIMPSON

THE TEMPORAL AMBIGUITY
OF WAR

> I did not wish to protest against war. Any true description of
> modern warfare is a protest. . . . My object was to witness and
> record. I wanted people to find in my poems the truth of what
> this war had been like.
>
> —LOUIS SIMPSON, *Air with Armed Men*

In the waning months of World War II as the Allied forces occupied Germany after V-E Day, Louis Simpson, a twenty-two-year-old member of the U.S. Army's 101st Airborne Division, wrote in a letter home: "P!S! We've just been given permission to tell where we are. We're in Berchtesgaden, Bavaria, the roost of the old bustard himself" (Letter to Lee). There is a sense that Simpson is marveling at his fortune, not just to be alive, but to have survived the D-Day invasion and the Battle of the Bulge, and to write home from Hitler's "Eagles' Nest" in Berchtesgaden, Germany. While there is levity in the play on words, referring to Hitler as "the old bustard" while writing from his nest, Simpson would struggle throughout his writing life to make whole the disparate experiences of a Europe fractured by World War II and an increasingly prosperous and suburban postwar America.

Louis Simpson is typically recognized for accolades such as a 1964 Pulitzer Prize for his collection *At the End of the Open Road,* and as a "deep image" poet, referring to poetry which allows "concrete images and experiences to generate poetic meaning" ("Deep Image"). Simpson's war poetry never garnered him critical recognition equal to that of the canonical war poets, and rarely has he been categorized as a "soldier poet." Yet, Simpson's war poems provide a unique vantage point of a World War II infantryman attempting to translate a seemingly untranslatable experience. Despite the inability of words to completely convey the physicality of battle, Simpson suggests in his memoir *Air with Armed Men* that "To a foot-soldier, war is almost entirely physical. That is why some men, when they think about war, fall silent" (143). Christina S. Jarvis believes that silence in the wake of World War II "stems from the pressures associated with hegemonic constructions of masculinity" and that "the absence of personal narratives may also be due in part to the general inexpressibility of pain and the nature of wounding" (92). While words may not come naturally to an experience that is largely absorbed as a barrage to the senses, Simpson acted in resistance to this anticipated silence, maintaining "poetry is written out of the need one has to write it" ("Love in the West" 48). Nevertheless, this concept of feeling physically and mentally overwhelmed by war evolved into a reputation that the soldiers of World War II were part of the "Silent Generation," failing to produce any significant war poetry like their First World War predecessors had, and early critics were let down because they "were expecting a new Lost Generation" (Langbaum 87). While soldiers such as Keith Douglas and Randall Jarrell published during the war, a remarkable body of soldier poetry was written and published after the war had concluded. Among that cohort of delayed-response poets was Louis Simpson, whose first book, *The Arrivistes,* was published in 1949. Though Simpson would go on to publish more than twenty books of poetry, memoir, and criticism, the impression that he was part of the "Silent Generation" was unsettling to him, as evidenced by his tongue-in-cheek reappropriation of the phrase. Simpson wrote the postwar poem "The Silent Generation," and an archival copy of a draft manuscript to his memoir *Air with Armed Men* (also *North of Jamaica*) was originally titled "Out of the Silent Generation" ("Life and Poetry" 1). "Out of the Silent Generation" is crossed out on the draft cover, with a second working title written above it, "Men Without Theories," which is also crossed out and replaced with the much more innocuous "Life and Poetry." Clearly, Simpson believed he and his generation had plenty to say and was facetiously responding to the notions that they were silent and without theories or ideas of their own. While a select number of Simpson's poems have appeared in war poetry anthologies—most commonly poems published between 1949 and 1955 such as "Carentan O

Carentan," "The Battle," and "Memories of a Lost War"—many of the poems of subsequent decades have not been acknowledged as poems of war.

Born in Kingston, Jamaica, in 1923 to a Scottish father who worked as a lawyer and Russian mother who came to Jamaica for an acting job, Louis Aston Marantz Simpson cultivated an interest in literature at preparatory schools. His parents separated, and, after the death of his father, Simpson moved to New York City, where his mother had relocated after the divorce. He attended Columbia University and studied under Mark Van Doren and Lionel Trilling. These studies were interrupted when Simpson decided to enlist in the army after the United States declared war against Japan and the Axis powers. In the preface to Simpson's first poetry collection, *The Arrivistes*, Theodore Hoffman summarized how "During his three years in the army, . . . [Simpson] won a bronze star and purple heart, U.S. citizenship, and had the luck to emerge with only frozen feet and delayed shock" (7). After the war, Simpson tried acclimating back to life in New York, where he experienced a mental breakdown from post-traumatic stress disorder. It was during this period that he turned to writing poetry more than fiction because he was only able to hold thoughts and focus for short periods of time. According to Bessel van der Kolk, "Trauma results in a fundamental reorganization of the way mind and brain manage perceptions" and our "capacity to think" (21). An archived letter from Simpson dated July 24, 1944, foreshadowed this struggle with memory and focus: "I of course didn't tell Mom anything about the fighting. But you know I had to tell somebody, and when I come home in '50, the memory may be too dim" (Letter to Dots and Ruth). Comparing this return to Robert Graves's life after the First World War, Simpson recalled: "I suffered from the condition described by Robert Graves and familiar to many an ex-infantryman: at every street corner, and when I passed an open place, I would look for a machine-gun position; at any whistling sound or bang my whole body would convulse" (*Air with Armed Men* 131). Simpson is describing these difficulties of struggling with the aftermath of traumatic experience before PTSD was introduced to the "American Psychiatric Association's Diagnostic and Statistical Manual of Mental Disorders III . . . in 1980" (R. Smith 39). While empathizing with Graves, Simpson describes conditions related to PTSD symptoms, previously classified as "shell shock" during the First World War, and named "traumatic neuroses" (Kardiner), "battle fatigue" or "combat stress reaction" in World War II (Friedman). After a period of rehabilitation, Simpson would return to Columbia for his B.A., M.A., and Ph.D. He would teach for the majority of his life at institutions such as Columbia University, University of California, Berkeley, and SUNY Stony Brook, receiving a Pulitzer Prize, Guggenheim Fellowship, and other awards, while earning a reputation as a poet of suburban American life and worldly curiosity.

Simpson initially framed his war experience by invoking the First World War poets and challenging how war was processed by civilians, as well as in his own subconscious. Channeling his war poet predecessors, Simpson's "The Battle" conveyed war as a cyclical and universal human experience, casting the Battle of Bastogne as an extension of Wilfred Owen's First World War combat experience in subzero temperatures. Simpson's war poems will be analyzed for their cross-generational traits, including their subversion of pastoral imagery of fields and forests, and expressions of resentment between soldiers and home front civilians. Next, this chapter will note the growth and individuality of Simpson as a poet through his manipulation of themes such as distance and time, an evolution that resulted in an impersonal voice as more time had passed from his war experience. Investigating the fluidity of time in Simpson's war poems, specifically his use of temporal ambiguity and the duality of experience, will prove crucial to understanding his subtextual commentary. The flexibility derived from impersonality and temporal shifts allows Simpson to incisively explore aspects of traumatic memory that had been a challenge due to PTSD-induced amnesia after the war. Simpson's poem "A Bower of Roses" will be used to examine the relationship between touch and memory, and this chapter will conclude with poems that more directly engage PTSD and the prevalence of dreams, nightmares, and visions in Simpson's war poems. By analyzing manifestations of distance and traumatic memory, invaluable aspects of Simpson's war poetry that are routinely overlooked or neglected will be highlighted. Ultimately, Simpson's range from traditional to innovative war poems further informs our comprehension of World War II and the lasting repercussions it had on its combatants.

Repurposing Wilfred Owen

World War II was a unique conflict in its modernity, scale, and civilian involvement, and while there are threads that suggest a narrative lineage from the First World War generation, the war poems of Louis Simpson have not received the attention or acclaim of his First World War predecessors. Just as Paul Fussell describes how "Every war is alike in the way its early stages replay elements of the preceding war," Louis Simpson's early war poetry invoked characteristics of First World War poetry (*The Great War and Modern Memory* 314). This section is presented in two parts, the first of which posits Louis Simpson's "The Battle" as a World War II recreation of Wilfred Owen's "Exposure," while the second highlights society's treatment of veterans by analyzing Simpson's "The Heroes" alongside Owen's "Disabled." The parallels Simpson draws between the wars reinforces feelings about war's recurrence and the failure of societies to learn from the conflicts of their past, thereby removing perceived distance between combatants, conflicts, and civilians.

One narrative thread that links Simpson to Owen is the retreading of ground, symbolic of man's return to war. In the preface to Simpson's *Collected Poems* he recalls his experience as a soldier in World War II, and how it resonated with him to encounter the same ground as his Allied predecessors from the First World War. "When I came upon an old trench of the First World War," Simpson writes, "I remembered the lines by Wilfred Owen: Our brains ache, in the merciless iced east winds that knive us . . . / Wearied we keep awake because the night is silent . . ." (xiv). Here, quoting from Owen's "Exposure," Simpson registers "the tragic simultaneity of experience" (Arrowsmith 292). Encountering a trench used by the Allied Powers to defend the Western Front, Simpson recognizes the cyclical nature of global conflict and the parallels between the experiences of infantrymen of the two world wars. Simpson continues: "Weeks later, in the snow around Bastogne, I could apply these words to myself and my companions. Poetry speaks from one generation to another, yet speaks to the individual as though it were meant for him or her alone" (*Collected Poems* xiv). For Simpson, this sense of personal relevance of a poem helps bridge the unreality of war across history and the individual's plight. Simpson had read the poetry of Wilfred Owen and was affected with a lasting impression; he was further surprised to find himself in Owen's position twenty-seven years after him. Owen's "Exposure" and Simpson's "The Battle" can be viewed as companion poems from separate conflicts, both speaking to the simultaneous struggles of man versus nature and man versus man. By recognizing the shared environmental stressors of war, Louis Simpson's poem "The Battle" uses presentation, language, imagery, and perspective shifts similar to that found in Wilfred Owen's "Exposure" to invoke Owen's descriptions of the mental and physical complexities of war.

Owen's "Exposure" and Simpson's "The Battle" begin in anticipation, as both speakers know the enemy is approaching. For the British regiment described by Owen, they can hear "Northward, incessantly, the flickering gunnery rumbles, / Far off" ("Exposure" lines 8–9). Awareness of an impending threat causes their brains to "ache," for the soldiers to feel "wearied," "worried," and "nervous" (lines 1–2, 4). This onset of fear causes Owen's speaker and his fellow soldiers to "cringe in holes" and drive "Deep into grassier ditches" (lines 22, 23). Similarly, Simpson, writes "Somewhere up ahead / Guns thudded," causing the speaker to reflect on his situation and mortality ("The Battle" lines 2–3). Surrounded by artillery fire, the speaker in "The Battle" says, "Like the circle of a throat / The night on every side was turning red" (lines 3–4). Echoing the response of the soldier in Owen's "Exposure," the soldiers in "The Battle" "halted and they dug. They sank like moles / Into the clammy earth" (lines 5–6). Both soldiers share these feelings of fear and nervousness before battle, and both poems continue their parallels with language, freezing temperatures, and the onset of fighting.

Both "Exposure" and "The Battle" use the term "sentries." Defined by *The Oxford English Dictionary*, a sentry is "An armed soldier or marine posted at a specified point to keep guard and to prevent the passing of an unauthorized person."[1] This serves as a dual alert, to emphasize to the reader that the respective soldiers are ready and awaiting notification of the approaching threat, and to allude to Owen and link the two poems. Owen writes, "Worried by silence, sentries whisper," and later proclaims that bullets are "Less deadly than the air that shudders black with snow" ("Exposure" lines 4, 17). Simpson is experiencing the same nervous anticipation as "the sentries, standing in their holes, / Felt the first snow. Their feet began to freeze" ("The Battle" lines 7–8). For both groups of soldiers, the natural elements are just as dangerous to their survival as the enemy, and express ironic examples of the fear of death coming from the natural world rather than in battle. When the fighting begins in the poems, parallels between the soldier's experiences are magnified.

The fighting in Owen's "Exposure" is marked by "Sudden successive flights of bullets" that "streak the silence," yet the focus for the remainder of the fourth stanza is on the snow in the air (line 16). Owen unexpectedly equates bullets and snowflakes as equally dangerous—ordinarily one is deadly while the other is delicate—because the soldiers are afraid not only of being shot to death but of freezing to death. Simpson repeats this framing by first detailing the onset of fighting—"At dawn the first shell landed with a crack" ("The Battle" line 9)—before drawing attention back to the threat of plunging temperatures: "Then shells and bullets swept the icy woods" (line 11). Both speakers fear the elements as much as, if not more than, the approaching enemy, and this contrast of fire and ice continues in each poem. Though it is unclear if Simpson is also using these opposite natural forces of fire and ice as a nod to Robert Frost's 1920 poem "Fire and Ice," in which each element "would suffice" as methods for the destruction of the world (line 9), Simpson's admiration of Frost is rooted in "a polarization of feelings between two characters" such as a husband and wife, and the complexities of such a literal or metaphorical "marriage" (Simpson, "The Poet's Theme" 105). Though it is hard to ignore the likely allusion to Frost that Simpson could be making with the life-and-death tension of fire and ice, his duplicitous use of fire as both a threat of death and reminder of life echoes Owen's usage in "Exposure."

In both poems, contrasting images of fire and ice are used to represent natural opposites and competing fears between death by enemy fire or freezing. For a war poem to invoke the word "fire" in a positive way is an ironic departure from what one would expect. Instead of using "fire" to mean shooting one's weapon, both "Exposure" and "The Battle" reference "fire" as a metaphor for life, comfort, and what is desired. "Fire" is a response to what each soldier fears; their lives are threatened by ice and cold, hypothermia and frostbite. For Owen, fire is evoked in a hallucinatory moment when his speaker imagines life at home: "Slowly our ghosts drag home: glimpsing the sunk fires" ("Exposure" line 26). Yet this comforting thought is cut short as the doors to home and safety are "all closed," and with the line, "We turn back to our dying," the speaker returns to the present battle (lines 29, 30). Equally, Simpson's speaker has his own moment of respite from the fighting in which he focuses on the "bright ember" of a cigarette in the hands of a fellow soldier ("The Battle" line 15). The threat to survival posed by ice and snow is contrasted with a small glimmer of light that the speaker finds solace in because the cigarette pulses "with all the life there was within" (line 16). Simpson's "The Battle" leaves us suspended in this moment of desperation where the speaker notes, "The tiredness in eyes, how hands looked thin," and this pulsing cigarette is seemingly the only sign of life (line 14). Owen's "Exposure" also shows soldiers clinging on to life as they are preparing for the brutal cold, fearing that "Tonight, this frost will fasten on this mud and us, / Shrivelling many hands, and puckering foreheads crisp" as those who are burying the dead in the frozen ground "Pause over half-known faces" ("Exposure" lines 36–37, 39). Neither "Exposure" nor "The Battle" is optimistic as a dispatch from the battlefield, but the deliberate choice by both to turn inward in a switch to first person speaks to a desire to relate their experience on a more personal level.

Owen's "Exposure" is written primarily in first-person plural, using "Our" and "we" for the subject throughout (lines 1, 2). The speaker is writing from the perspective of the collective, speaking for the regiment, and in turn speaking on behalf of all soldiers so that readers back home in Britain have a primary source for understanding what trench warfare is like, one that differed from many news dispatches that painted a cheerier vision of the war. Only in stanzas six and eight does the perspective temporarily shift to include a third-person plural. In stanza six, the home the speaker wishes he could be transported to, in reality and not just in memory, is now inhabited by mice who rejoice because "the house is theirs" (line 28). The recognized shift in perspective occurs only when the speaker is lost in thought, imagining what it would be like to return home. This hallucinatory shift between third and first person also occurs in Simpson's "The Battle," which is written in the third-person plural for the first three stanzas of the four-stanza poem. For these first three stanzas, Simpson could equally be drawing inspiration from his own experience in the frozen fields of Bastogne or could be telling the story of soldiers like Owen, whose experience he was keenly familiar with. This temporary ambiguity opens the reader up to the possibility that Simpson could be writing about World War II as an extension of the First World War, a parallel experience. In the final stanza of "The Battle," Simpson brings us to a position of clarity by shifting to a first-person perspective: "Most clearly of that battle I remember / The tiredness in eyes" (lines 13–14). Upon first reading, the inclination might be to assume this poem is autobiographical, a quite literal recollection of Simpson's participation in the Battle of the Bulge from which he had to recuperate from frostbite. By having the third-person plural dominate the poem and concluding with a first-person memory, Simpson blurs the line between autobiography and persona. Ultimately, by affording the possibility of this alternate reading of a persona, Simpson could be layering his experience with that of First World War soldiers like Owen. Though Simpson declares "The Battle" as a poem that captured his experience of "the defence of Bastogne—standing in a hole in the snow, or lying down in the snow, for hours and days," the richness of this poem is in its potential for subtle deception, the fact that his experience so closely mirrored Owen's (*Air with Armed Men* 114).

Louis Simpson is speaking to a cross-generational experience, and the oscillation between his experience as a soldier in World War II and the wars that preceded him is not a singular occurrence in his poetry. For example, "I Dreamed That in a City Dark as Paris" is a hallucination poem in which he imagines he is in the boots and fatigues of a French infantryman of the First World War, watching a dogfight above the city (*Collected Poems* 83). Additionally, "Carentan O Carentan" echoes Walt Whitman's "O Captain! My Captain!" as much of Simpson's poetry would for decades.[2] As a young soldier in World War II, Louis Simpson would understandably think of Owen's poems when encountering the very land and circumstances of those earlier poems, as evidenced in the borrowed presentation, language, imagery, and perspective from Owen's "Exposure" in "The Battle." Simpson's self-alignment with Wilfred Owen can be read in concert with earlier references to Heidegger's idea of distantiality. Corina Stan defines "distantiality" as the "nagging urge to compare oneself to others" (8), and Simpson's urge to compare his experience to Owen's is chiefly a response to the recurrence of human conflict as opposed to an attempt to self-validate.

Further links between Simpson and Owen were suggested in Mottram's 1963 *Times Literary Supplement* review of *Five American Poets*, which proclaims Simpson's poetry is "one of the nearest things to Wilfred Owen to come out of the last war" (886). The review goes on to assert that Simpson shares Owen's "persistence of life, the regaining of vision, against barbarian violence" (886). This optimistic interpretation of Owen's and Simpson's poems representing the "persistence of life" may be too simplistic a characterization, as both poets take a begrudging stance toward war by highlighting personal dissatisfactions and lamenting the human condition. As Owen wrote in a draft "Preface" to his own book of poems: "This book is not about heroes. . . . Nor is it about deeds, or lands, nor anything about glory, honour, might, majesty, dominion, or power, except war. . . . My subject is war and the pity of war. The poetry is in the pity. . . . All a poet can do is warn. That is why the true Poets must be truthful" (Owen 192).

Mottram is just in arguing Owen's stance against "barbarian violence," but the way Owen pivots in opposition to war is by describing it with precise detail. Owen does not glorify violence when describing wounds and the mangled bodies; rather these images are a critique of war before they ever serve as an exultation of life. Simpson aligns with Owen that to describe war exactly as it is experienced is itself a critique. Both were willing participants in their respective wars, and in an interview with Micheal O'Siadhail, Simpson explained, "The most effective anti-war writings, like the poems of Wilfred Owens [sic], though he does protest sometimes, mostly are just descriptions of the sheer horror of it. Just to see something is enough" (Simpson and O'Siadhail 16–17). Santanu Das proclaimed that, "Categories such as 'pro-war' and 'anti-war' often prove inadequate, when tested against the complexity of individual poems" (*Cambridge Companion* xx). Exemplifying Das's position, Simpson's nuanced poems challenge the conventional approach of categorizing pro- or antiwar poems, a further reason why Simpson has rarely been identified as a war poet.

Simpson's act of mimesis in "The Battle" of Owen's "Exposure" is more than an homage to a poet he admires; it is commentary on the nature of war as influenced through the prism of combat experience. Simpson has adopted a mode of letting his poems convey the impulse directly instead of instructing the reader in how the poems should be interpreted, and therefore the parallels of Owen's "Exposure" in Simpson's "The Battle" imply that the horrors of the past repeat themselves. One could point to George Santayana's statement, "Those who cannot remember the past are condemned to repeat it" (284), for what Simpson is suggesting, but if we trust in Simpson's methods, he is removing the psychological distance between generations by asking the same simple question posed in Owen's "Exposure": "What are we doing here?" (line 10).

■ ■ ■

Louis Simpson also looked to Wilfred Owen and the First World War poets when conveying the human cost of war, as shown in his 1955 poem "The Heroes," suggesting "the futility of heroism through war" (Gray 187). Characteristic of Simpson's war poetry, "The Heroes" begins with a dream: "I dreamed of war-heroes, of wounded war-heroes / With just enough of their charms shot away / To make them more handsome" (lines 1–3).[3] The poem extols the virtues of veterans, for even those maimed by war are perceived as attractive, masculine, and courageous. Rather than causing women to recoil at the sight of their wounded bodies, "The women moved nearer / To touch their brave wounds and their hair streaked with gray" (lines 3–4). The four-quatrain poem's musicality nears a ballad meter, with ABAB rhyming of lines comprised of ten, eleven, and twelve syllables, rhythmic patterns of stressed syllables that are lighter in tone. Upon return, they are given "doughnuts" (line 6), "bibles and marksmen's medallions" (line 11), and are committed to military hospitals and care centers. At this point the poem's tone darkens, for this homecoming is not a tickertape parade but a pat on the back followed by the implication that the veterans will stay out of the sight and mind of the public. This dismissive stance is reinforced in the final stanza, in which the intentionally ambiguous phrasing describes both the maimed veterans and the awards and accessories they were given: "A fine dust has settled on all that scrap metal" (line 13). As if the veterans are discarded parts no longer capable of helping their country, they are deliberately categorized in the same manner as the medals and ornaments one might collect. The poem concludes, "The heroes were packaged and sent home in parts / To pluck at a poppy and sew on a petal / And count the long night by the stroke of their hearts," lines that trigger a twofold response: First, they can be read as the downcast veteran counting the seconds of his life that remain, relegated to insignificance. Second, the overt reference to the First World War poets by invoking imagery of a poppy is a nod to the act of remembrance and the recurrence of the cycle of conflict to casualty ad infinitum.

The prevalence of poppies in First World War soldier poems by John McCrae ("In Flanders Fields"), Isaac Rosenberg ("Break of Day in the Trenches"), Edmund Blunden ("Vlamertinghe: Passing the Chateau, July 1917"), and Scottish World War II poet Hamish Henderson ("Dark Streets to Go Through") encouraged the poppy lapel movement to demonstrate remembrance of soldier service and sacrifice. Simpson's penchant for taking a universal approach to individual experiences and blending time periods, in addition to his use of traditional forms, has elicited critical response equating him to his predecessors. A *Times Literary Supplement* review of Simpson's work by M. L. Rosenthal reinforced this notion by asserting that Simpson "is closer to British poets of Wilfred Owen's and David Jones's generation than to his American contemporaries" (167). This argument is made because each of these poets addresses cultural indifference toward the war-wounded veteran, a theme at the heart of "The Heroes." Jon Stallworthy suggests the intersection of Simpson's "The Heroes" and Sassoon's "The Hero" is the contrast of "civilian illusion with military reality," both poems conveying the message that, dead or alive, soldiers are neglected either by those at home or the military apparatus in which they serve (*Survivors' Songs* 182). Such cross-generational comparisons of veteran neglect are made clear when reading Simpson's "The Heroes" alongside Owen's "Disabled."

The version of Owen's "Disabled" best known to his readers was a 1918 revision, late enough in Owen's life and war experience for him to have seen action at the Western Front, stay at Craiglockhart Military Hospital to recover from "shell shock," and return to service in France. It should come as no surprise that Owen had seen physically and mentally wounded soldiers, of whom he was one. In what could be a precursor to Simpson's portrayal of the wounded veteran, "Disabled" begins, "He sat in a wheeled chair, waiting for dark" (line 1). The unnamed veterans in both poems are waiting, one for dark, the other counting the seconds by the stroke of his heartbeat. Both are waiting for death to come as a respite from their diminished roles. Another parallel between "Disabled" and "The Heroes" is the thought of female touch and attention. In Simpson's poem, "The girls with the doughnuts were cheerful and gay" ("The Heroes" line 6), while in Owen's poem, the "Town used to swing so gay" ("Disabled" line 7) and "girls glanced lovelier as the air grew dim" (line 9) before the soldier lost his legs and half an arm. Now, the veteran in "Disabled" knows "he will never feel again how slim / Girls' waists are" (lines 11–12). In this battle-maimed state, the veteran relies on others to "put him to bed," wondering, as time passes and the night grows later and colder, "Why don't they come?" (line 46). At the conclusion of both "Disabled" and "The Heroes," the veterans are alone, waiting out their time and relying on others to help them. Both veterans are neglected by a society expected to care for them. While their service may be remembered with commemorative poppies and moral platitudes, to literally care for wounded veterans is a tactile experience. Human contact and genuine recognition are instrumental to the care of veterans physically and mentally wounded by combat, a greater task than symbolic shows of remembrance.

Herein is the tragic nature of Simpson's war poetry, its recognition of a need for a historical record paired with the understanding that eventually the memories of that event will fade and be supplanted by new wars and new societal intrigues. Simpson purposefully removes the distance between the world wars in "The Battle" and between combatants and civilians in "The Heroes," casting past and present wars as sedimentary layers.

Pastoral Landscapes and Home Front Resentment

The divide between soldier and civilian is also represented by a dichotomy in Louis Simpson's war poetry: the impulse to reach out to civilians in both inclusive and resentful ways. For Simpson, war wedged a gap between soldiers and civilians, and this space was experienced as a manipulation of literal distance and psychological distance. Simpson's "The Ash and the Oak" and "Carentan O Carentan" are extensions of the forest and field poems written by Edmund Blunden and Robert Graves, each using landscapes familiar to civilians in order to convey untranslatable sights. Simpson's "The Silent Generation" expresses resentment harbored by soldiers toward a fractured societal landscape. Each of these poems affirms the universality and repetitive nature of the war experience as antithetical to civilian life, and subsequently serves to literally and emotionally distance soldiers from civilians.

Understanding combat landscapes is crucial to understanding an individual's war experience. In response to Siegfried Sassoon's open letter of "wilful defiance of military authority" to his commanding officer in 1917 ("Finished with the War"), Winston Churchill, while serving as Minister of Munitions, reportedly responded to Sassoon the following year: "War is the natural occupation of man . . . war—and gardening" (Fussell, *The Great War and Modern Memory* 234). Though there is no audio or visual recording of this conversation, leaving us unable to determine the degree of seriousness or flippancy with which Churchill spoke, the humor (and warning) is in the equation of the two activities, war and gardening, as necessary activities of humankind. While Churchill's comparison is fruitful in bearing out the types of metaphorical parallels that exist between man's need for war and the land, Paul Fussell believed this connection between land and war to be essential.[4] In his seminal book *The Great War and Modern Memory*, Fussell argues that "writers about the war had to appeal to the sympathy of readers by invoking the familiar and suggesting its resemblance to what many of them suspected was an unprecedented and (in their terms) an all-but-incommunicable reality" (174). Civilians away from the cratered, sunken, flooded, and carved-out landscapes of trench warfare would be hard-pressed to visualize war without photographic evidence, so writers relied upon observations of the natural world.

The term "battlefield" could be used in a literal sense when discussing the First World War, considering most of the battles took place in rural areas and farmland. Even though there were small cities and towns dotted along the Western Front, including those that are now synonymous with major battles such as Arras, Ypres, and Verdun, major French, Belgian, and German cities were impacted by war but largely avoided the brand of wide-scale urban destruction common in World War II. Nonetheless, the First World War was a collision of eras, in which the notion of war as a chivalric experience was met with an unforgiving barrage of artillery. Millions of lives were lost as soldiers went "over the top" from the trenches and into no-man's land, or by horseback into battle, and were met by mechanized weaponry. The First World War created a fissure of memory and cognition between the conventional imagery of men and horses traversing fields and a once-peaceful landscape rendered unrecognizable by shellfire and dead bodies becoming one with the earth. For Siegfried Sassoon and Edmund Blunden, their love of cricket may have shaped their view of the open field landscapes of war, barbed wire posts like wickets demarcating the deadly pitch of no-man's land, an image later suggested by Keith Douglas in "Aristocrats": "These plains were their cricket pitch" (line 15). Remarking on World War II, Sassoon wrote to Blunden on 18 April 1943: "If only the Germans would cultivate Cricket instead of frontier expansion! We might then establish a workable human relationship" (Letter: to Edmund Blunden).

For First World War poets, the primary features of battlefield landscapes are contradictions. For example, instead of calling to mind the openness and flowers of fields, that imagery becomes emblematic of open-faced graveyards and danger through exposure to enemy fire. Forests and woods are no longer symbols of natural solitude but are dangers concealing potential threats. Mud created from the combination of upturned earth, the trench system, and rain debases soldiers by reducing their courageous actions to deeds conducted while living and dying in squalor. As described by Santanu Das, the muddied earth of First World War battlefields "enwombs and entombs" its combatants (Touch and Intimacy 46). Just as many of the prominent First World War poets saw some of the fiercest battles in the 1914–18 conflict, such as Wilfred Owen fighting in the Somme and Siegfried Sassoon in Passchendaele, Louis Simpson's war service in World War II brought him through the heart of the European theater. Each location he served in became rich fodder for poems that would be written in retrospect. Examples include "Carentan O Carentan," named after a small French town in Normandy where Simpson participated in the D-Day invasion; "The Battle," which recalls the Battle of the Bulge in Bastogne, Belgium; and "A Story about Chicken Soup," which describes life at the war's end at Hitler's mountain retreat in Berchtesgaden, Germany. These poets used such distinct locations to use relatable imagery of pastoral landscapes in order to convey the experience of battle to their civilian readers.

Simpson's poem "The Ash and the Oak" contrasts the simpler, languid pace of pre-1914 war with the technologically advanced clashes of shellfire and blitzkrieg in the world wars. Writing "At Malplaquet and Waterloo / They were polite and proud, / . . . And, as they fired, bowed," Simpson is respectively referencing earlier British battles, the 1709 Battle of Malplaquet during the Spanish Succession and the Battle of Waterloo in 1815, which ended the Napoleonic Wars (lines 9–10, 12). Simpson uses these conflicts to exemplify the poem's refrain, "O the ash and the oak and the willow tree / And green grows the grass on the infantry!" (lines 7–8, 15–16). This imagery of the earth growing over the war dead where they fell or were buried is intended to demonstrate a level of orderliness in nature and respect for the dead in the way battle was conducted. Yet, Simpson shifts focus in the final third of the poem to "Verdun and at Bastogne," referencing battles of both world wars to differentiate between the ways these modern battles were fought compared to earlier conflicts (line 17). Simpson describes these world war battles as "a great recoil" (line 18) where "blood was bitter to the bone" (line 19) and "death was nothing if not dull" (line 21). To cast war death as "dull" reflects the enormous quantities and repetitive nature in which soldiers were mowed down or obliterated in the world wars.[5] Simpson modifies the poem's refrain when referencing the First and Second World Wars, concluding, "O the ash and the oak and the willow tree / And that's an end of the infantry!" (lines 23–24). The focus is no longer on how soldiers are granted a brand of burial by becoming one with the earth but rather that there will be no more soldiers left if this style of mass war continues.

Simpson's "bows boomed" ("The Ash and the Oak" line 5), Blunden's "brute guns lowing at the skies" like cows ("Vlamertinghe" line 8), and Owen's search for "passing bells" recognizing "those who die as cattle" ("Anthem for Doomed Youth" line 1) typify the twentieth-century war poem tendency to pair sound with landscape.[6] Such aural observations contribute to the surreal nature of war landscapes and one's perception of distance. For instance, a 1916 newspaper published the remarks of a soldier's wife who had traveled to Kent along the south coast of England for a holiday, hoping to leave behind the reminders of war in London:

We were not to forget. . . .

From the first day of our arrival we lived to an orchestral accompaniment—the distant boom, boom, and shuddering sound of the guns in France. At first some of us did not realise what it meant, and only when one of our company who had just returned from the front said, "It is the battle of the Somme" did we understand. Then we thought. If we could hear the terrific bombardment here, fifty miles away, what could the reality be? What the feelings of those enduring incessantly the noise and anguish of that hell? (National Library of New Zealand)

This reminder that war was just across the English Channel would erase any sense of security civilians had, shattering the illusion that one could detach from a war that could be reached in a few hours. Similar auditory observations were present for First World War combatants, as seen in Blunden's 1928 poem "Concert Party: Busseboom." In the foreground of the poem soldiers are enjoying live entertainment, but they are quickly humbled by the theater of war they hear in the background, "We heard the maniac blast // Of barrage south by Saint Eloi, / And the red lights flaming there" (lines 16–18). While they are resting behind the lines in Busseboom, a rural area outside of Ypres, Belgium, they can see and hear the battle "by Saint Eloi" less than ten miles away. This stark contrast of the jovial with the terrifying undercuts the sense of escapism for the soldiers and reminds them of the looming weight of war. The sarcastic suggestion that these soldiers are called to "dance to the latest air" extends the theatricality of the moment (line 20). The soldiers are reminded of the close proximity of the war they will be returning to soon: "To this new concert, white we stood," writes Blunden, frozen in that moment when "Cold certainty held our breath" (lines 21–22). The disparate theaters, musical and combat, amplify the bleak reality that these soldiers cannot escape the war, "While men in tunnels below Larch Wood / Were kicking men to death" (lines 23–24). Blunden uses sensory observations to show the proximity of the war, and how the seemingly serene landscape of a wooded area conceals that which takes place within it, or in this case, in the tunnels beneath enemy lines where hand-to-hand combat took place. Like the aforementioned soldier's wife who cannot escape the literal sounds of war even from across the English Channel, Blunden's soldiers resting behind the lines are not afforded an escape from battle and may never mentally absolve themselves of the stresses and trauma of war. Blunden's view of fields and forests transmogrifies, as the proximity of war transforms serene landscapes into sinister tableaux.

Like Blunden's warnings, Louis Simpson's "Carentan O Carentan" shows the repetitiveness of war by showing the devolution of peaceful landscapes into landscapes of death. In a 1997 essay by Simpson titled "Soldier's Heart," he explains the origin of "Carentan O Carentan": "One night while I was in Paris I dreamed that I was walking with G Company along a strip of land with trees. There was water on each side. Suddenly shells began falling and I was lying prone. Bullets were sweeping the trees—a trunk a few inches above my head was slashed white. Someone close by was calling for his mother in Italian. The next morning I wrote out the dream in ballad stanzas" (547). Imagining similar landscapes helps Simpson recover previously inaccessible memories from his war experience, realizing "it wasn't a dream but a memory . . . our first contact with the enemy" (547). For both Simpson and Blunden, the aural memory of shells, gunfire, and fearful screams decorate the landscapes in equal measure as the flora. Echoing Blunden's "Concert Party: Busseboom," Simpson's "Carentan O Carentan" establishes the setting of a "shady lane" (line 2) beside a "shining green canal" (line 5), where "the ground / Was soft and bright with dew" (lines 9–10). This peaceful pastoral landscape is marred only by the recognition that "Far away the guns did sound" (line 11). Simpson personifies war in childlike description, explaining the danger felt from afar:

The sky was blue, but there a smoke
Hung still above the sea

Where the ships together spoke
To towns we could not see.

(lines 13–16)

Both Simpson and Blunden are confronting the inability to appreciate what would otherwise be picturesque landscapes when war rages nearby. The loss of innocence in "Carentan O Carentan" is tracked by the transition from a false sense of security to a violent reality (Oostdijk, *Among the Nightmare Fighters* 27). These aural cues are recurrent in world war poetry, as is the fear that comes from the gradual crescendo of gunfire and falling shells, the anticipation of war. Simpson's soldiers hear a "whistling in the leaves / And it is not the wind" ("Carentan O Carentan" lines 37–38), and in a further allusion to Owen's "winds that knive us" ("Exposure" line 1), Simpson's stanza concludes, "The twigs are falling from the knives / That cut men to the ground" (lines 39–40). While Owen is describing the threat of death that comes from freezing temperatures and icy winds, Simpson is borrowing and transposing that terminology to represent the threat of bullets and shells that whistle like the wind in their approach. Yet, to complete this re-creation of the uneasy feeling in Blunden's "Concert Party: Busseboom" of soldiers being killed in the woods while a party carries on nearby, the final four stanzas in Simpson's "Carentan O Carentan" transform peaceful landscapes to deadly ones. Simpson's speaker calls out to high-ranking service members one by one for direction, only to realize they have all been killed. First, Simpson's speaker requests, "Tell me, Master-Sergeant, / The way to turn and shoot" before recognizing that "the Sergeant's silent" (lines 41–42, 43). Echoing Walt Whitman, the speaker then turns, "O Captain, show us quickly / Our place upon the map" but is without luck because "the Captain's sickly / And taking a long nap" (lines 45–48).[7] In the second-to-last stanza, the infantile soldier looks to his "Lieutenant" to ask, "what's my duty?" but comes up empty-handed again because "He too's a sleeping beauty" (lines 49, 51). The final stanza is the awakening from innocence to experience for the young soldier narrating the poem, as a picturesque town with a canal snaking through it is transformed:

Carentan O Carentan
Before we met with you

We never yet had lost a man

Or known what death could do.

(lines 53–56)

Like "Concert Party: Busseboom," "Carentan O Carentan" shows the stark acceptance that war has the power to corrupt and transform beautiful landscapes into a stage for death. "Carentan O Carentan" is often critiqued for its simplicity of language, but from Simpson's perspective this is a poem about "simple men. They were not literary critics. Most of the hard and dangerous work of the world is done by such men. During the war I learned to respect them and have done so ever since" ("In Transit" 630). The generational echoes of violence are endured by Simpson in World War II, just as they were by Blunden in the First World War, and Walt Whitman during the American Civil War (M. Murray). Each generation of soldiers, awoken by the trauma of war, comes into awareness of the brutal realities that inexorably change an individual. For poets like Blunden and Simpson, translating that shift through the familiarity of landscape is a method of conveyance that allows those distanced from war to examine it up close.

Louis Simpson also felt a connection with First World War soldier poet Robert Graves through similar experience. Graves uses nostalgia to elegize the environmental and psychological casualties of war. Throughout time, uncivilized land has been used as a metaphor for purity, freedom, wildness, and possibility, and Graves laments in the poem "1915" that land has been stripped of its "Red poppy floods" and replaced with bloody substitutes (line 4). One of Graves's most anthologized poems, "A Dead Boche," also shows the natural world transformed to the grotesque. Presented as an antidote to the exuberance for killing that war stirs in the unaffected, "A Dead Boche" chronicles how Graves's speaker "found in Mametz Wood / A certain cure for lust of blood" (lines 5–6). In the second stanza of "A Dead Boche," Graves describes a dead German soldier "propped against a shattered trunk" (line 7) who has been there for days, as evidenced by his smell, his "face a sodden green," and his body bloating in death (line 10).[8] Graves must confront the invasive and lasting image of the dead soldier each time he is in the woods or sees a tree stump. Such traumatizing visions stayed with Graves, as he reinforced in his memoir *Goodbye to All That:* "I was still mentally and nervously organized for war; shells used to come bursting on my bed at midnight . . . strangers in daytime would assume the faces of friends who had been killed. When strong enough to climb the hill behind Harlech and revisit my favourite country, I could not help seeing it as a prospective battlefield" (235). Persistent traumatic hallucinations give Graves's dead German soldier a haunting presence both for Graves and (he hopes) for the reader, so that one may temper the bloodlust prompted by war. By perverting pastoral imagery, Graves hopes he may relate to those who have not seen firsthand the horrific sights of war, whether they are in Harlech in North Wales or Mametz Wood in northern France.

Similarly, Louis Simpson recognized in his postwar life that he "had still not recovered from the war," and he would "see bodies lying about" in his room, such as a dead "German officer who kept reappearing on the furniture" ("In Transit" 629). The sustained traumas of battle for poets such as Simpson, Blunden, and Graves resurface when processing postwar landscapes. Graves's nightmares of being under fire in his civilian life were shared by Simpson, who scoured New York City streets for machine gun perches, both equating the fields and forests of combat to the spaces they inhabit in more peaceful times. In the words of Carolyn Forché, "The poetry of witness frequently resorts to . . . the invocation of what is *not* there as if it *were,* in order to bring forth the real" (*Against Forgetting* 40). Their poems are channels for civilians to comprehend war because they hinge on rebranding familiar landscapes to describe abnormal circumstances. Fields and forests were the primary landscape of Simpson's war service, and in his war poems they become the staging ground for contrasts between the Edenic pastoral and the war-afflicted psyche of the individual.

■ ■ ■

Just as landscapes like fields and forests can be transformed into disturbing settings in war, social landscapes can also transform the home front. Once demobilized, Simpson showed a frustration and disconnection over the ways war service has the potential to push some soldiers against the establishment, elevate fellow soldiers in contrast to noncombatants, create resentment toward civilians, and illuminate the neglect of veterans. Arthur Hadley refers to the divide between the military and civilians throughout the twentieth and twenty-first centuries as "The Great Divorce," a consequence of changes in society, the military, and causes of war (T. Ricks).

Emerging from a trend in First World War poetry by Siegfried Sassoon and Alan Seeger of exposing the resentment soldiers had for civilians and the neglect of veterans returning home, Louis Simpson's poem "The Silent Generation" exemplifies the perceived distance between soldiers and civilians, and the neglect and powerlessness felt by veterans.

World War II soldiers were pressured to produce literature that would serve as a narrative voice for the war and carry the same weight as First World War poets and writers such as Owen, Sassoon, Hemingway, Remarque, and Fitzgerald. Though the World War II generation is heralded in America and Britain as the "Greatest Generation," the poets of World War II—whose war poems were largely written after the war in contrast to during it—were chastised as the "Silent Generation." Louis Simpson bristled at this reputation, and Simpson's poem titled "The Silent Generation" speaks to the divide between soldiers and civilians by reminding readers of the mission of World War II soldiers to defeat the spread of fascism, illustrating the struggle to adjust back to civilian life and how the feeling of accomplishment and triumph has dissipated.

Simpson begins his 1959 three-sestet poem "The Silent Generation" by reminding his readers of Hitler's determination: "When Hitler was the Devil / He did as he had sworn" (lines 1–2). The simple gesture of the first line is the implication that civilians may have lost sight of how the Allied forces faced unquestionable evil, as if to bitterly say *in case you forgot* . . . now that many American civilians were living in relative comfort, having rebounded from the Great Depression, and were economically thriving in the postwar boom. The second stanza is a response to this reminder: "It was my generation / Who put the Devil down" (lines 7–8). Having helped to defeat the Axis powers, Simpson now struggles with feeling directionless, writing of soldiers, "our occupation / Is gone. Our education / Is wasted on the town" (lines 10–12). Transitioning from life-or-death situations in the army to the comparatively mundane happenings of domesticity has left soldiers with no chance to tap into the thrill of soldiering, and little opportunity to apply the experience of their service. From noting the "enthusiasm" (line 3) of Hitler to seek control to the "enthusiasm" (line 9) Allied soldiers showed in resistance, Simpson now admits the soldiers who returned home "lack enthusiasm" (line 13). The thrill and heightened emotions of war have subsided, and soldiers now try to find where and how they belong in a new stage of society. Simpson resorts to categorizing how

"Life is a mystery" by comparing it to "the play a lady / Told me about: 'It's not . . . It doesn't have a plot,' / She said, 'It's history'" (lines 15–18). Simpson compares feeling directionless to a play without a plot and implies that people are playing their role within something that has no distinguishable direction. For as much as he struggles to find a sense of purpose after the war, he is reminding critics that war is not a play. War does not have a set plot. Soldiers and leaders are not actors required to fulfil prescribed roles for public entertainment. In other words, to criticize soldiers for their lack of immediate poetic production is to have a misdirected set of priorities. In contrast to the resentment felt by First World War poets toward civilians who promoted the war effort from a safe distance, Simpson resents the media and literary critics who long for a resurgence of war narratives resembling those from the First World War.

Simpson's "The Silent Generation" is an addendum to First World War poems that express resentment toward noncombatants, albeit with a different underlying conceit. Simpson's speaker directs resentment at a society that no longer has a place for those who defended it. Feeling estranged and resentful, "The Silent Generation" is a departure from how those themes were expressed by poets of the First World War, who felt civilians did not understand the sacrifices soldiers made and the physical and emotional wounds they endured. For example, after leaving Craiglockhart Military Hospital in 1917, Siegfried Sassoon wrote, "Suicide in the Trenches," a poem depicting a naïve "soldier boy" not yet tainted by war (line 1) who grew "cowed and glum" in the "winter trenches" (line 5) before putting "a bullet through his brain" (line 7). What bothers Sassoon most about this devolution is the grim fact that "No one spoke of him again" (line 8). For Sassoon, the true tragedy is the absence of public response to the struggles of soldiers and the ignorance civilians demonstrate alongside their outpourings of patriotism. The final stanza, biting in its accusations of the public turning a blind eye to the loss of innocence for soldiers, reads:

You smug-faced crowds with kindling eye
Who cheer when soldier lads march by,
Sneak home and pray you'll never know
The hell where youth and laughter go.

(lines 9–12)

Sassoon is critiquing the willful ignorance of civilians and the hypocrisy of cheering on those returned from war while being unwilling to truly understand the experience they endured. According to Andrew J. Kunka, Sassoon believes these onlookers "are guilty of false mourning because they lack or suppress essential information gained through first-hand experience with death, and their attempts to appease sorrow through faith and patriotism succeed only in diminishing the value of the soldiers' sacrifices" (76). By glossing over the details of the war experience and giving parades and hollow gestures of support, one is neglecting what makes a happy and innocent soldier in one stanza suicidal in the next.

Alan Seeger's 1916 poem "Sonnet 9: On Returning to the Front after Leave" is another example of a soldier's resentment toward civilians.[9] Seeger's poetic reputation is as one who uses traditional war lyric traits such as invoking honor, duty, and patriotic sacrifice, though "Sonnet 9" is a departure from a mere rallying cry. For Seeger, those who serve are "Brave hearts" (line 7), and noncombatants are the "shams and imbeciles" (line 8) who belong to "that poor world we scorn yet die to shield" (line 13). Even though Seeger affirms throughout this poem (and many of his poems) the honor of serving in the military, it is hard to ignore the boiling resentment he holds for the home front, referring to it as "That world of cowards, hypocrites, and fools" (line 14). The volta in this poem is the revelation of the irony of fighting to defend a world that one resents. As the title suggests, the act of returning to the front after leave initiates these feelings, a fresh reminder of the difference between the disarray felt between soldiers and noncombatants and the camaraderie felt among soldiers.

Louis Simpson's early war poetry showed a kinship with the First World War poets who preceded him by invoking similar imagery, diction, themes, landscapes, and expressions of neglect and resentment felt between soldiers and civilians. Simpson dredges up comparable experiences and feelings about the recurrence of war and the shortcomings of society's inability to learn from history and conflict. Simpson's use of landscape imagery is a way to process war using images more familiar to civilians than conventional war images of large-scale violence and destruction. By repurposing pastoral landscapes in ominous war narratives, Simpson allows parallels to surface between war from one generation to the next, and the implied questions of purpose, duty, guilt, and sacrifice that inevitably follow suit. Simpson also uses social landscapes to convey postwar feelings of resentment between soldiers and civilians. Simpson differs from his predecessors by repurposing the imagery of fields and forests to comment on war's recurrence, while his feelings of resentment toward the home front were an internalized frustration, in contrast to the outright condemnations made by First World War poets. Simpson's poetry is rooted in his firsthand experience of World War II, but the temporal fluidity of his poems complicates the role and recognition of veterans, and casts traumatic memory as an active state. Like trauma, writing war poetry is not just a reflection from a state of recovery but a persistent struggle to balance one's life with the rupture it has endured.

The Shift toward Impersonality and Temporal Ambiguity

In response to the hallucinatory quality of Simpson's war poetry, C. B. Cox explains that, "Like Wilfred Owen, [Simpson] presents the people and events of war not fixed by their particular backgrounds, but like shadows in some cosmic drama that involves all humanity" (72). Initially, this self-awareness of relating the trauma experienced by the individual to the experience of humanity was not a natural impulse for Simpson. As he explained in the 1997 essay "Soldier's Heart" about his feelings toward his own PTSD, "I used to think that having such dreams was a thing to be ashamed of. For what had I suffered in comparison with others?" (549). A strength of Simpson's poetry is presenting the repercussions of war as suffering endured by all people, before, during, and after World War II. By writing about World War II as if retelling the experiences of the First World War, Simpson is arguing that the universality of war and the persistence of traumatic memory are reinforced generation after generation. As opposed to Siegfried Sassoon's turn toward impersonality to warn future generations of the threat of war,[10] Louis Simpson pairs his World War II experience with that of First World War soldiers to create a palimpsest to reflect on the past. Though the conditions, time, and conflicts of the world wars are different, Simpson layers the two engagements as parallel experiences to comment on the linkages of historical moments. Simpson's retrospective war poetry takes the long view of history, an introspection that compensates for the passion and pressure forged in the immediacy of the poems written during armed service.

Exemplifying Simpson's temporal ambiguity and shift toward impersonality, the poem "I Dreamed That in a City Dark as Paris" from his 1959 collection *A Dream of Governors*, is a tempered reflection on order and chaos that blurs generations of war. Additionally, Simpson's poem "On the Lawn at the Villa" from his 1963 collection *At the End of the Open Road* uses disorientation to complicate a perspective of war, simultaneously discomforting readers through the proximity of war while speaking to the longevity of wartime memory. Scattered throughout Simpson's body of war poetry are temporally ambiguous poems that layer eras and armed conflicts to recast war as an event of cross-generational consequence. These poems exemplify Simpson's use of distance through both close-range perspective and the separation of time, ultimately arguing that the space between the individual and the history of combat is veil thin.[11] Simpson's use of impersonality and temporal shifts to look to the past generate an inevitable self-reflection and question the effectiveness of war as an act of conflict resolution.

At the outset of Louis Simpson's poem "I Dreamed That in a City Dark as Paris," the speaker stands alone in a Parisian square, having been left behind, and observes a "flickering horizon" (line 5) where "The guns were pumping color in the sky" (line 6). Dressed in the garb of a French *poilu*, the speaker watches the fighting at "the Front" from afar while a dogfight brings a burning fighter plane to the ground nearby (line 7). This displacement of self, or perhaps more accurately the embodiment of a soldier from a bygone war, is a response to the generational call to military conflict. Simpson is speaking of war from an observational viewpoint, but rather than telling the experiences of fellow soldiers, he is recalling the visions of a French First World War soldier as if they belong to him. As Duane Locke notes, Simpson is prone to invoking an "I" that "is usually a stranger, or someone apart, so much apart from the ordinary amusements of humanity that he can make the perspicacious observation" (64). This hallucinatory moment, though "awkward," is a literal transposition; "I was the man," the speaker says, convinced he is seeing the world through the eyes of his French predecessor ("I Dreamed" line 15). The fourth stanza marks the poem's volta, where the poem's speaker returns from the hallucinatory moment to acknowledge that "These wars have been so great, they are forgotten" (line 22). This turn is a critique of the rhetoric of memorialization after war and catastrophic loss. Simpson illuminates the irony of nations urging the public to remember the sacrifices made and the unhealed wounds of loss, while driving themselves back into perpetual states of conflict.

Simpson looks to the past by acknowledging the fears and disbelief of previous generations, confounded that after the horrors experienced at war humankind would return again to armed conflict:

> My confrere
> In whose thick boots I stood, were you amazed
> To wander through my brain four decades later
> As I have wandered in a dream through yours?

> (lines 23–26)

This stanza addresses a French First World War soldier who doubtless too has imagined himself as a soldier in another time period, asking if the amazement at this transposition is shared. The sentiment of this poem can be rooted in the word "amazed," an understatement that references the dreamlike bewilderment with which, one generation after the next, these soldiers find themselves returning to combat, begrudgingly armed with the knowledge that their work and sacrifice will soon be overshadowed by the inevitable next conflict that will boil to the surface. Simpson cultivates empathy by transcending time and identity to equate cross-generational experiences. While paraphrasing Julia Whitehead, the CEO of the Kurt Vonnegut Memorial Library, Alex Horton writes, "Post-traumatic stress can bend time . . . and the sense of how recent or distant something is can be distorted when a memory is triggered," a reaction recurrently seen among war veterans. Simpson acknowledges that ending a war does not end conflict or prevent war from returning, and that no matter how inevitable war is, it still represents "The violence of waking life" that "disrupts / The order of our death" ("I Dreamed" lines 27–28). Like a horror film in a moment of quiet suspense, war is an interjection that derails the trajectory of one's life. The poem concludes, "For dreams are licensed as they never were," a mournful expression that one's dreams (both the literal unconscious imagination and one's figurative aspirations) are appropriated by greater forces (line 29). Soldiers are at the mercy of governments, nations, and the will of decision-makers whose reach extends to all facets of society. The subconscious exploration of "I Dreamed That in a City Dark as Paris" equates combatants across time, and Simpson's blend of dislocated identity and temporal ambiguity offers an incisive reflection on willing sacrifice—that of both soldiers and leaders—and the unreality of war.

Louis Simpson's 1963 *At the End of the Open Road* is a collection that further disorients with a critical eye fixated on American culture and Whitman's vision of American opportunity and potential. In this collection, the poem "On the Lawn at the Villa" lulls its reader into a false sense of security with a title that doubles as the first line. Even Simpson is amused with the pleasantness of the opening, remarking, "That's the way to start, eh, reader?" (line 2). A similar blurring of identities observed in "I Dreamed That in a City Dark as Paris" can be found in "On the Lawn at the Villa," and although the speaker does not transcend time or existence, he interrogates what it means to be American in a world divided by culture, ideology, and history. Sitting with the speaker at the villa is "a manufacturer of explosives, / His wife from Paris, / And a young man named Bruno" who are referred to as "malefactors" (lines 7–9, 11). Initially, the speaker positions himself as "somehow superior. By that I mean democratic," though this opinion gets hazy as the poem progresses (line 13). Directly, the speaker lays out the conundrum that has prompted the poem: "It's complicated, being an American, / Having the money and the bad conscience, both at the same time" (lines 14–15). Having believed himself to be the guardian of a moral superiority when placed beside an arms maker, the speaker implies that this manufacturer profited from war and is unconcerned with the ramifications of those financial rewards, and that guilt should be shared by all parties. As a survivor and benefactor of the war, the American speaker must negotiate how to feel about being from a country that benefited from World War II, in economic growth and global prominence. The underbelly of "On the Lawn at the Villa" points out the hypocrisy of the American's sense of superiority because the speaker's guilt is inward (one's "bad conscience"), whereas the European arms maker is unapologetic in his motivations, soaking up the sun in this "expensive" (line 3) villa after "the diversions of wealth" (line 5) at the conclusion of the war (Stitt, *The World's Hieroglyphic Beauty*). All parties have gained from their participation in the war, but the willingness to admit that is what separates the Americans and Europeans in the poem. In its final stanza, this hypocrisy and moral bankruptcy are on full display as the participants sit "paralyzed / In the hot Tuscan afternoon" (lines 17–18), seemingly devoid of emotion, though "the bodies of the machine-gun crew were draped over the balcony" (line 19). Peter Stitt remarks that in this moment "Everyone in the scene . . . ignores this very basic reality, and are all equally guilty," suggesting that all are equally participatory in war and therefore equally responsible for the casualties and other ramifications ("Louis Simpson" 358). Whether you are the one making the weaponry or the one firing it, it is naïve to act obliviously to the human cost of one's actions. The final line, "So we sat there all afternoon," serves the dual purpose of showing the willful emotional ignorance of the participants and the contemplative mode of the speaker (line 20). Since the guilty parties are tanning in the Tuscan sun, they are soaking up their surroundings. What they absorb beyond the warmth and picturesque surroundings is unclear, but it is obvious to the reader that the guilt that lingers like the mowed-down machine-gun crew is what they are trying to ignore. Archived early drafts of this poem reveal that arguably the most shocking moment in this poem—the surreal revelation of the dead soldiers draped over the balcony amid an otherwise placid scene—was added in later drafts. The absence of this penultimate line meant the original draft's final stanza read: "We were all sitting there drinking / In the hot Tuscan afternoon. / So we sat there all afternoon" (Simpson, "On the Lawn at the Villa" draft). Omitting the deadly scenery suggests an initial desire for the realistic depiction of war death to be subtext, an implied guilt. Yet, the jarring addition of the line "And the bodies of the machine-gun crew were draped over the balcony" magnifies the unwillingness of the figures to fully acknowledge the obvious sacrifices made in exchange for their financial gain.

Ultimately, Simpson shows the way distance can manifest in the mind. By tangling memory, dream, the subconscious, and one's conscience, Simpson highlights the inseparable nature of memory, imagination, and the mind. Despite fourteen years passing between the end of the war and the publishing of "I Dreamed That in a City Dark as Paris," and another four years until "On the Lawn at the Villa" was published, the persistence of memory and the pervasive quality of trauma are evidenced by these poems. Both poems utilize the type of impersonal distancing and temporal ambiguity representative of a traumatic event. In these poems Simpson demonstrates the trouble Sigmund Freud had in analyzing First World War traumas. Explaining Freud's question of the relationship between trauma and consciousness, Cathy Caruth writes, "The traumatic reliving, like the nightmares of the accident victim, seemed like a waking memory, yet returned, repeatedly, only in the form of a dream" (*Trauma* 151–52). If we are to imagine the traumatized figures of Simpson's poems experiencing dreamlike visions as if they are a First World War soldier observing the fighting from a Parisian square, or an American having a pleasant afternoon with arms manufacturers and other war beneficiaries while there are irrepressible images of dead soldiers strewn about a balcony, the poems themselves act as recurring pulses of traumatic memory. Simpson layers his poems with commentary on the lasting effects of war and the struggle the mind must cope with to process these memories. Inherently, while the delay between the trauma of World War II and Simpson's attempts to confront it affords more time to distance oneself from the event, the power and persistence of traumatic memory is confirmed. As a victim of traumatic experience would seek to look to the past to close fissures of memory caused by the brain's defense mechanism of shutting down during a traumatic event, Simpson is looking to the past not only to make whole the gaps of his memory but to use cross-generational reference points to contextualize feelings of disbelief, fear, and guilt.

Temporal ambiguity is also present in Simpson's poem "The Heroes" through use of the poppy as a sign of war memory and commemoration. While the poppy lapel signals that the soldier in "The Heroes" is a veteran living in a post–First World War world, it is unclear whether they fought in either the First or Second World War.[12] Simpson's catalogue of war poetry often layers time with intentionally confounding effects, most notably showing World War II soldiers embodying the roles and locations of First World War soldiers. By casting armed conflict as an inevitable recurrence, Simpson's traumatic memory is understood as a generational reverberation. In addition to "I Dreamed That in a City Dark as Paris," examples of this include speakers who wait along an embankment ready to charge "like infantry in World War One" in "On the Ledge" (line 15), and who encounter the decayed remnants of First World War battlefields in "The Runner." For Simpson, World War II is merely the surface layer in a view of wars throughout time.

In the 1959 poem "The Runner,"[13] Simpson fictionalizes his experience as a runner passing messages between battalions. Giving himself the alias Dodd, he encounters a relic from a past war:

The earth gave
Under his boots. He picked up a small scrap
Of wire, and it crumbled. He surmised
This was a trench dug in the first Great War.
Who knew? Perhaps an older war than that.

(stanza 9, lines 102–6)

The symbolic significance of retreading the ground of an earlier war, and for a wire from the First World War to be crumbling in one's hands, is a fertile embodiment of the cyclical and generational memory of war and, ultimately, the disintegration of war memory. While "The Runner" is referenced somewhat frequently in discussion of Simpson's poetry, it garnered criticism from fellow soldier poet John Ciardi. In an archived 1955 letter from Ciardi to Simpson, Ciardi criticizes "The Runner" as "a mistake" for its narrative form in poetic structure, fully committing to neither. Simpson took this feedback to heart, as he agreed with Ciardi in a 1981 interview:

DRURY: How do you feel about your early poems, when you were writing in traditional forms?

SIMPSON: I don't read them anymore. I don't deny them. There are one or two I still read. The poem "Carentan O Carentan"—the war poems I still read. For one reason, I think that the traditional form was very well suited to some of that material.

DRURY: What about "The Runner?"

SIMPSON: No, I don't read that.

DRURY: Well, it's much longer.

SIMPSON: And it's blank verse. I think that it was the wrong form. (Drury and Irwin 104)[14]

Simpson would reflect on this stylistic shift, explaining, "There was no precedent for the kind of poetry I wanted to write. Some years ago I had broken with rhyme and meter and learned to write in free form. Now I discarded the traditional ornaments of language, especially metaphors. I wanted to render the thing itself exactly as it happened" (*The King My Father's Wreck* 80). Simpson, his peers, and his critics may validate the argument that "The Runner" was an ambitious albeit uncharacteristic poem, but it nonetheless affirms the self-awareness Simpson had for his historical position and the importance of writing about war as a shared struggle of humanity.

If one were to position this shift toward impersonal and temporally ambiguous poetry by Simpson, one could weigh these decisions beside noted works of literary theory on the relationship between self, subject, and influence, such as T. S. Eliot's 1919 essay "Tradition and the Individual Talent" and Harold Bloom's 1973 book *The Anxiety of Influence*. Eliot's "Tradition and the Individual Talent" claims that the poet undergoes "a continual surrender of himself as he is at the moment to something which is more valuable. The progress of an artist is a continual self-sacrifice, a continual extinction of personality" (43). This act of self-sacrifice and the extinction of personality can be seen throughout generations of soldier poetry. Figuratively speaking, poets like Simpson shift focus from the self to others, absolving themselves as the focal points of their poems in favor of telling the stories of others to explain the predicament of war. Literally speaking, all soldiers perform acts of self-sacrifice in their service, knowingly subjecting themselves to the threat of death on behalf of a greater cause. As soldiers, they have accepted an "extinction of personality" by conforming to the structure of the army, being given a number and taught obedience to orders, a departure from which could mean death. While Eliot champions the scope of literature as a universe in which all of history contributes to the present moment and poets engage the ideas of those that came before them, Bloom argues that poets are continually trying to assert themselves against influence in "a ritualized quest for identity" (65). Yet, more so than "an escape from personality" and a "quest for identity," these increasingly impersonal and temporally ambiguous poems by Simpson exhibit an overarching desire for an understanding of cultural memory. What is universal in these poems from separate conflicts, whether Sassoon is looking forward in caution or Simpson is looking back for explanation, is the pleading for society to remember and learn from history and to eschew the passivity and cultural amnesia that would allow one to license dreams away.

Touch and Memory in Louis Simpson's "A Bower of Roses"

Returning to the subject of war later in life is like hearing an echo reverberate across a canyon, getting fainter with each aural pulse. While memories may fade with each passionate retelling of the intensity of physical engagement, there are powerful reasons to return to a subject decade after decade. Such is the case with Louis Simpson's poem "A Bower of Roses," published in his 1980 collection *Caviare at the Funeral.* "A Bower of Roses" is a sensory experience that weaves in and out of reflection and revisits the narratives that surround the individual and collective experience of World War II. Santanu Das, in his book *Touch and Intimacy in First World War Literature,* defines First World War literature as work that utilizes touch more than sight to convey the experience because it is a "more apt register for recording the horrors" of trench warfare (7). In contrast, the World War II poem "A Bower of Roses" is a poem of implied touch, the anticipation of touch, and retaliation to the contact of others.

"A Bower of Roses" is a poem about a sexual relationship with a prostitute, and it begins with the sensory experience of smell: "Algerian tobacco, / wine barrels, and urine" (lines 2–3) that the speaker will "never forget" (line 4) even if he lives "to be a hundred" (line 5). The sense of smell is closely tied to emotion and memory (Gaines-Lewis), and Simpson's speaker reinforces the persistence of war memory as he recalls the ambience of a Parisian brothel. Whether Simpson is writing autobiographically about his recovery period in Paris after the Battle of the Bulge, when his feet were frozen, during the Parisian day trips he would make from Sens to retrieve supplies for the "regimental newspaper" he was put in charge of (*Air with Armed Men* 125), or intentionally creating separation between himself and his speaker by using the third person, this episode mimics Simpson's out-of-body approach to writing about the war, as if it happened to someone else. Through this adoption of a persona or a distancing of oneself from reality, there are echoes between "A Bower of Roses" and Simpson's earlier poem "I Dreamed That in a City Dark as Paris," in which memory returns to the speaker in dreams. Even though "A Bower of Roses" is written in the third person, in which the central "he" is unidentified, and "I Dreamed That in a City Dark as Paris" is written from the first-person perspective, both speakers are cast as if they could be soldiers from various wars. The speaker of "I Dreamed That in a City Dark as Paris" dreams he is wearing the uniform of a First World War French *poilu* (line 13), as if he is reliving the Great War and seeing the firefights, planes, and explosions illuminating the night sky. Though "A Bower of Roses" is more specific to World War II, the "he" is gradually acknowledging that his experience—the joy of experiencing human touch, enduring battle wounds, the desire for an unregimented life, and learning the tragedy of war—is not unique, but nearly universal for war combatants.

The speaker in "A Bower of Roses" recalls life during wartime when he is on medical leave and recuperating in Paris. The casual attitude away from the front is reflected in small talk with prostitutes who cast aspersions on other prostitutes about how much more active they must be to afford to feed their dog, a Great Dane. In his memoir, Simpson comments on civilian desperation for money toward the end of the war: "They were prostitutes, but then so many of the women of France at this time were prostitutes that the word had lost its meaning" (*Air with Armed Men* 125), and how "women who had been friendly with the Germans" had their heads "shaved by patriotic Frenchmen" (126). When the speaker receives permission to step out of the hospital, "he would make for the bar in Rue Sainte Apolline / Margot frequented" in search of sexual release (lines 24–25). The details return to the speaker in frankness and simplicity, such as the "ten thousand francs" (line 30) it would cost to stay the night with a prostitute, though he would also need to account for "a thousand for the concierge, / The maid, too, must have something" (line 32–33). Here, the anticipation of touch is met with practicality, and the poem refrains from documenting the sexual transaction, like a memory in which touch is just out of reach.

The third section of the poem sees the speaker's return to the front after medical leave, catching up to "the division in Germany" (line 40). Here, there is another transaction of contact, an exchange of German and American shells, during which Simpson reminds his readers of the economic realities of war. Like the arms manufacturers who meet in Simpson's "On the Lawn at the Villa," "A Bower of Roses" shows how profiteering corporations are represented in combat: "For every shell Krupp fired / General Motors sent back four" (lines 44–45). While corporate interests are secured by a sustained war effort, the speaker notes that "The areas on the map of Germany / marked with the swastika kept diminishing, / and then, one day, there were none" (lines 55–57). This imagery of shelling and the growing swathes of land gained by the Allies repeats the anticipation of contact and touch, and the calming de-escalation of enemy control. The successful war effort results in the speaker being sent back to France, and in this final section of the poem Simpson's speaker confronts the dissonance between his worldview and reality.

Close enough to return to his old Parisian haunts, "Once more he found himself climbing the stairs" of the brothel (line 60). Here the anticipation of touch is finally satisfied as the soldier and prostitute hold each other in a surprise reunion. "My God," she responds, "cheri, / I never thought to see you again," and this dialogue seems so ordinary it nearly eludes interrogation (lines 65–66). The reader does not know if the woman's response is a by-product of being a non-native English speaker or if she literally means what she said. There is an enormous semantic separation between what one would expect to hear in this moment, *I thought I would never see you again* (alluding to the obvious threat of death faced by a soldier, and an undercurrent of hope of being reunited), and what she actually says, "I never thought to see you again," which conveys the clear absence of sentimentality between a prostitute and her John. While the mind wants to hear the warmer sentiment of longing and surprise, *I thought I would never see you again,* the true feelings of the prostitute are unclear, and the speaker is equally unconcerned with knowing what she meant. By returning and consummating their agreement, the man is afforded a moment of reflection with a clear mind. "That night, lying next to her" (line 67), the soldier puts the prostitute on a pedestal for her sexual promiscuity in contrast to the "young women / he had known back in the States / who would not let you do anything" (lines 68–70). The tragic underpinning here is a soldier caught in a moment of anticipatory nostalgia when contrasting the sexual proclivities of sex workers in a recently occupied country during wartime and the perceived puritanical ethics of young women in 1940s America. He knows he will soon long for this sexual liberation, even if it is a luxury he must pay for. He now sees the ironic truth in a song from the First World War era, "How Are You Going to Keep Them Down on the Farm? / (After They've Seen Paree)," about the fear of losing men and boys from rural upbringings to the excitement and liberalism of cities, foreign lands, foreign women, and exoticized cultures (lines 72–73). This moment has a remarkable impact on the speaker, who recognizes the scenario posited by the ragtime song. He sees himself reflected in the song; *he* is one of those men you would have to drag out of Paris. In this moment of clarity, he is just like the countless other soldiers whose path he will retread by going off to fight a war in foreign lands and, by surviving, become a statistic, a stereotype, a carbon copy of those who came before him. This crystallized moment of self-awareness is conveyed in one of the most incisive stanzas from any poem of World War II:

> He supposed this is what life taught you,
> that words you thought were a joke,
> and applied to someone else,
> were real, and applied to you.
>
> (lines 74–77)

Everyone shoulders the tragedy of war. World War II soldiers learn the same harrowing lessons as their predecessors who fought in bygone wars. Like the 400,000 British soldiers of the First World War who were treated for venereal disease from patronizing French brothels (Makepeace 67), the same quests for sexual release, closeness amid war, or simple recognition as an individual, if only momentary, are repeated by soldiers in subsequent generations. To attribute Robert Warshow's ideas about Richard Wright's novels to Simpson, recognizing the universality of human experience depends on being able to see "the experience of particular human beings in a specific situation" (Hutchinson 79). The unflinching sadness in the final lines of "A Bower of Roses" points to the universality of some historical experiences, as well as the unfortunately predictable nature with which they recur. After all, Simpson's generation grew up in the wake of "the war to end all wars," only to fight in one of their own.

Thirty-five years had passed since the end of World War II when "A Bower of Roses" was published, and many of Simpson's poems written in the interim seemed to be inching toward this sentiment of realization in its final four lines. One can see Simpson trying to find the words to convey the lesson that no individual is immune from the trials endured by others, and that for one human to endure hardship is equal to the suffering of all humans. This theme is consistent throughout Simpson's poetry, beginning with the 1949 poem "The Men with Flame-Throwers" from his first collection, *The Arrivistes*. In this poem, "The men with flame-throwers . . . Are looking for us" (lines 1, 3), and reflecting on dropping an atomic bomb on Nagasaki, the speaker wonders what has been broken, concluding, "No city but ours" (line 28). George Hutchinson is the only critic who has commented on "The Men with Flame-Throwers," and he does so by briefly explaining that Simpson is conveying the knowledge that "what happened to 'them' could happen to 'us'" (362). Simpson revisits this dark knowledge in the poem "The Silent Generation" from his 1959 collection *A Dream of Governors,* in which the speaker realizes that even defeating Hitler is seen by some civilians as if it were a play, a part of "history," and irrelevant to the current moment (line 18). One's own experience always means more to oneself than to anyone else, and even great historical events are eventually relegated from the minds of those who were bystanders. A few pages later in *A Dream of Governors* is "To the Western World," in which the speaker recalls "our fathers in their wreck" (line 7), who met new frontiers and homelands with "silence" (line 10). Simpson would go on to modify "fathers in their wreck" as the title of a 1995 memoir, *The King My Father's Wreck,* which is an allusion to Shakespeare's *The Tempest:* "weeping again the king my father's wreck" (1.2.394).[15] When the speaker comes of age, he realizes that each successive generation sacrifices as "grave by grave we civilize the ground" ("To the Western World" line 15). From one generation to the next, conflict recurs as forms of routine sacrifice and costly conquest. Simpson's commentary on one's predetermined and inevitable path in life is also present in his 1963 poem "In the Suburbs," here in its entirety:

There's no way out.
You were born to waste your life.
You were born to this middleclass life
As others before you
Were born to walk in procession
To the temple, singing.

Simpson implies that the lives of others that are envisioned with the beauty and grace of song are just other forms of order and duty. Like the revelation in "A Bower of Roses," the speaker is self-identifying as a cog who had mistaken individual experience for uniqueness. Each of these admissions is tinged with a feeling of resentment, anger over not knowing or being told that this is what life would be like. While the opening stanza of "A Bower of Roses" suggests the man will never forget the smells of the brothel, by extension this sensory recall could be applied to the memory of shedding innocence for experience, both sexually and in terms of one's worldview. The man will never forget how it felt to realize what he perceives as the truth of modern life.

As a guest poetry editor for the May 1957 issue of *New World Writing*, Simpson explained a guiding principle for his selection process for the journal's feature titled "Poets of the 'Silent Generation'" by posing the question "*Does it move?*" (112). He goes on to clarify, "By movement I do not mean emotion—though where there is real emotion, there is likely to be movement. Rather, I have demanded that the poem evolve a definite action of narrative, idea or metaphor" (112). "A Bower of Roses" is undoubtedly a poem of movement from military leave to brothels to redeployment and back, but it is chiefly a poem of developmental movement. In other words, though this poem's subject matter is the anticipation of touch between a man and prostitute, the poem's underlying exploration is in the acknowledgment of how it feels, figuratively, to change.

Dreams, Nightmares, and Visions: Louis Simpson's Poetry of PTSD

Louis Simpson's poems "On the Ledge," "Memories of a Lost War," and "A Story about Chicken Soup" further the concept that war irrevocably changes the individual. Simpson's focus on writing poetry was not until after the war, when he could focus only for short periods while trying to recall the memories he had lost of his war experience. The presence of dreams, nightmares, and visions in these poems is characteristic of a mind grappling with the balance between reality and imagination, memory and the present moment, and a traumatic past and an uncertain future.

A reflective mode is perceptible in Simpson's poetry through acts of reliving and recovering traumatic memory. In a 1997 essay Simpson detailed some of his symptoms, such as "hearing voices" ("Soldier's Heart" 544) and, "For some years after leaving the hospital I was subject to the sudden onsets I have mentioned: a heart that beat faster, and shaking, and sweating. I would imagine shells falling and hear the sound of guns. I could not stand being confined" (545). In addition to these daytime afflictions, while he was sleeping Simpson's symptoms continued, as he explains, "I relived the war almost every night in my dreams. This continued for years. When Miriam and I married she woke one night to sounds that were coming from different parts of the room: sounds of battle, shelling and gunfire. They were coming from me! I was projecting them like a ventriloquist" (549). While these startling dreams and nightmares affected Simpson's day-to-day life, they also played a role in his recovery and writing because it was through dreams that "memories of the war began to return" (547). Abandoning the cold and clinical terminology of PTSD, Simpson opts for the Civil War–era diagnosis, a more delicate name for his condition: "Soldier's Heart." While this notion is devoid of the decades of clinical research that has come with evaluating those who have survived traumatic experiences, Simpson finds the archaic classification strikes him "as the best, for it describes an illness that involved my heart as much as my head" (543). Simpson's body of writing must be framed within the actuality of his traumatic experience. One's writing and worldview will inevitably evolve after an experience that irreparably changes an individual, like war, a notion supported by T. R. Hummer, who claims "Simpson is, in a real sense, always writing about shell shock" (119).

The speaker of the 1980 poem "On the Ledge" is a soldier whose unit is pinned down on an embankment by German bullets and shells. Fear heightens when comparisons are made between the soldiers' positions "side by side in a straight line, / like infantry in World War One / waiting for the whistle to blow" (lines 14–16). The fragility of the position and anticipation of a movement that may resemble First World War soldiers going over the top of trenches into the battlefield is compounded by the awareness that "The Germans knew" their location and were firing relentlessly (line 17). Simpson registered generational parallels between the First and Second World Wars in his memoir, writing: "We were like infantry in the Great War waiting to go over the top. I had read about trench warfare and looked at photographs . . . a line of men with helmets and rifles looking up at the camera. In a few minutes many of them would be dead" (*The King My Father's Wreck* 54). Ordinarily, given the immediacy of life-threatening danger, this would not be an intuitive moment to get lost in one's thoughts, but the speaker is reminded of Fyodor Dostoevsky's *Crime and Punishment* and envisions facing a choice that the character Raskolnikov had once heard. Simpson recalls "a man being given the choice / to die, or to stand on a ledge / through all eternity" (lines 22–24). Dostoevsky's protagonist, Raskolnikov, wracks his brain trying to remember where he had heard of a hypothetical choice one considers while awaiting death:

Where is it I've read that someone condemned to death says or thinks, an hour before "his death, that if he had to live on some high rock, on such a narrow ledge that he'd only room to stand, and the ocean, everlasting darkness, everlasting solitude, everlasting tempest around him, if he had to remain standing on a square yard of space all his life, a thousand years, eternity, it were better to live so than to die at once! Only to live, to live and live! Life, whatever it may be! . . . How true it is! Good God, how true!" (191)

Simpson describes his experience as an infantryman under fire by using Raskolnikov's contemplation between death or a life in which one is forever confined to an isolated space.[16] Simpson is describing another form of facing execution by firing squad in "On the Ledge"; in his case, it is Nazi soldiers firing at his position among hedgerows, and he too weighs the choice to stand and face death or persist without any sign of a pending reprieve. Ultimately, Simpson is reflecting on what has become of his postwar life, as if thirty-five years after the war's end he is confined to the "everlasting darkness, everlasting solitude, everlasting tempest" of post-traumatic stress disorder. The speaker then considers this choice, recalling others who have "stepped off the ledge" where facing death is a form of *knowing,* as if death brings a knowledge that is off-limits to the living (line 29).

Common to Simpson's war poems, "On the Ledge" equates World War II to bygone wars through visions of battle and thinking of those "who survived the Bloody Angle, / Verdun, the first day on the Somme" (lines 31–32). Bloody Angle is a reference to a battlefield location during the Civil War's Battle of Gettysburg, while Verdun and the Somme are major First World War battles. As the decades rage on, each battle and war aligns as a historical demarcation of a world calved into a before and after. As Diederik Oostdijk reasons, instead of using intertextuality to distance himself from his predecessors, Simpson is comforted by the Dostoyevsky passage, for it helps him "articulate a traumatic experience" (*Among the Nightmare Fighters* 28). By first experiencing traumatic events through the writings of others, whether it be Dostoevsky's persecution in Russia or the war trauma conveyed by the First World War's trench poets, Simpson first underwent the "vicarious trauma" of others before those terrors were reignited by his own combat experience. One of E. Ann Kaplan's descriptions of how an individual can experience vicarious trauma is by "reading a trauma narrative and constructing visual images of semantic data" (91–92). Simpson's deep familiarity with the lives and writings of soldier poets such as Wilfred Owen and Robert Graves would satisfy this example of vicariousness, from which "pain evoked by empathy arousing mechanisms [interacts] with their own previous traumatic experiences" (M. Hoffman 17).

Luckily for the soldier in "On the Ledge," his reprieve comes in the form of Allied air support, which "flew over our heads, firing rockets / on the German positions" (lines 35–36). The conclusion to the poem is a stark relief after its initial stress and anticipated casualties one comes to expect from war stories, and while the speaker makes it clear the momentary conflict is over, the internal conflict is permanent. Even though "it was easy" (line 37) for these soldiers who "just strolled / over the embankment" (lines 37–38) after the enemy positions were bombed, the speaker corrects readers from thinking the episode is over. The speaker describes how "like the man on the ledge, / I still haven't moved" (lines 41–42). Since he did not have to make the choice to face death, he is frozen on the ledge, "watching an ant / climb a blade of grass and climb back down" (lines 43–44). In other words, like the individual Raskolnikov is remembering, having survived this brush with death, the soldier is forever condemned to a limbo, watching life pass him by as an ineffectual observer. Simpson alludes to Dostoevsky to convey how his traumatic experiences have kept him feeling like he remains motionless on that embankment, well into his postwar life.

Decades after his service, Simpson would explain how war memory and a war mentality extended into civilian life:

When I went walking I would keep an eye peeled for an enemy position. If there were an open field I would think, "How are we going to get across that?" I imagined lying again on a railroad embankment in Normandy, waiting to be told to go over it in spite of the bullets that were sweeping to and fro directly above me. That day I was sure I would be killed. Or I was in a graveyard in Holland with shells falling and the living getting mixed in with the dead. I was in the Ardennes, standing in a foxhole among trees covered with snow, and stamping my feet. They were freezing. ("Soldier's Heart" 545)

The confusion between Simpson's postwar life and recurrent visions of battle is manifested here in military strategy, as ordinary life was interrupted by possible movements and decisions that would have kept him alive during combat operations. Simpson's 1955 poem "Memories of a Lost War" from his collection *Good News of Death and Other Poems* further demonstrates the detachment he experienced between real and imagined life.

Simpson begins "Memories of a Lost War" proclaiming "The guns know what is what" (line 1). In personifying weaponry, Simpson suggests it is indisputable that the machines of death know what war is about, while in contrast soldiers cower "underneath / In fearful file" (lines 1–2). Yet, the reliability of one's memory is called into question as "The scene jags like a strip of celluloid" (line 5). This imagery of a film reel skipping on projection alters the sense of perception in the poem. The individual does not rely upon steady memory or sight to convey the scene but compares it to a flawed or imperfectly projected film. Initially, one may presume this response is an extension of Simpson's struggle to reclaim traumatic memories from his war experience from the period of mental breakdown after the war, but instead, this is confirmation of successful reclamation of memories. The lines that follow are definitive statements, seemingly cementing his memory: "A mortar fires, / Cinzano falls, Michelin is destroyed" (lines 6–7). These short, undecorated, declarative statements continue in the fourth stanza: "The thunder's blunt. / We sleep" (lines 14–15). Since these lines do not afford any room for alternate interpretation, the reader does not instinctively question the reliability of the narrator. Trauma theorists have proposed conflicting arguments about the relationship between traumatic experience and the accuracy of one's memory. The "traumatic superiority argument" suggests traumatic memories are more clearly remembered than positive memories (Porter and Peace), while the "traumatic memory argument" suggests traumatic experience impairs one's memory of the event (Kihlstrom and Shobe). While there is not a consensus for how a traumatized individual will respond or remember an event because every individual and traumatic experience is unique, the speaker in "Memories of a Lost War" would likely fall somewhere in the middle. On one hand, he tells his reclaimed memories with confidence, while on the other hand, the focus on basic observations suggests a tunnel vision of standout moments, impairing the memory of broader context. These direct observations are occasionally offset with an emotional counterbalance, such as when night falls and the soldiers fatalistically prepare for sleep because "this may be / The last of days" ("Memories of a Lost War" lines 11–12). Even the soldiers' dreams are cast as "a faint platoon" (line 15) passing "Toward the front" (line 16). Simpson oscillates between the traumatic superiority argument and the traumatic memory argument in which memories are either restricted to basic recall of war destruction, thunder, sleep, and dreams, or can be contextualized with emotions, fully cognizant of the danger narrowly avoided and surviving against the odds.

Consistent with many of Simpson's early poems, "Memories of a Lost War" is guided by form. The six-quatrain poem has a set meter of alternating ten-syllable and four-syllable lines in an ABAB rhyme scheme. For a poem that explores the confirmation of memory and understanding an event, this form may reflect such a theme. The structure of repeating lines with syllable counts of ten and four may be a subtle allusion to the ten-code communication call "10–4," meaning acknowledgment, or that one's message has been received and understood (Sawicki). "Memories of a Lost War" is an acknowledgment that despite the dreams endured by traumatized soldiers in their postwar lives, they have temporarily outlasted death. When soldiers wake from those dreams, "Though they may bleed / They will be proud a while of something death / Still seems to need" (lines 22–24). Simpson directs this poem at Death as someone who has evaded its touch through the war, a fate more fortunate than that of his predecessor Wilfred Owen, who died on 4 November 1918, one week before the First World War's armistice (Cuthbertson 292). The simplicity of "Memories of a Lost War" validates the responsibility many soldier poets felt to report the war as it happened. Speaking about the power of directness and truth, Simpson stated in an interview:

> SIMPSON: There's a way of saying things directly, you know. There is a way of saying the right thing. And also being poetic about it.
>
> IRWIN: Truthful.
>
> SIMPSON: Yeah. The poetry resides, as Wilfred Owen said, in the truth. The poetry's in the pity, he said. That's a great statement. It doesn't mean that you're not going to have problems with language or structure. God knows, from what I've said you must understand how hard I think about this whole thing. But it does mean that you can't bamboozle the reader with just sheer erudition. (Drury and Irwin 103)

In contrast to figures like Sassoon who publicly spoke out against the war, and Owen who wrote "My subject is War, and the pity of War. The Poetry is in the pity" ("Preface"), which Simpson paraphrases above, Simpson outlined his own position on the role of war poets in his memoir, writing, "I did not wish to protest against war. Any true description of modern warfare is a protest" (*Air with Armed Men* 144). Whether wanting to retain a more objective stance or perhaps armed with the confidence imbued by the previous generation who rebelled against patriotic impulse and government-sponsored nationalism, Simpson felt that to tell of war as he experienced it would be sufficient.[17]

Simpson's 101st Airborne Division participated in many of World War II's fiercest battles, and his 1963 poem "A Story about Chicken Soup" reflects on the experience of taking control of Hitler's mountain retreat in Berchtesgaden. Simpson's mother was a Russian Jew, and he only learned of his Jewish heritage in his late teens during a visit from his maternal grandmother. After experiencing World War II and learning of the Holocaust and immense numbers of Jewish casualties, Simpson ruminates on individual and collective guilt through the prism of traumatic experiences in "A Story about Chicken Soup." Perspectives of guilt are explored in three sections, the first on the murder of Simpson's Russian ancestors, the second on a young German girl amid a platoon of American troops, and the third on the expectations of how one is expected to behave in the wake of such incomprehensible events.

"A Story about Chicken Soup" begins by looking to the past, to Simpson's Russian ancestors who despite life in "the old country—mud and boards, / Poverty," always had chicken soup in the house (lines 2–3). He then paints an image of a simpler time, in which "out of her savings" (line 5) his grandmother would send "a dowry" for a pending marriage (line 6). The tonal shift in the third stanza is immediate, when the speaker ceases to reminisce, concluding "But the Germans killed them. / I know it's in bad taste to say it, / But it's true. The Germans killed them all" (lines 9–11). This frank interruption to otherwise homely scenes of rural Russian life justifiably apportions guilt for World War II and the loss of innocent civilian life on the actions of Germany.[18]

The second section is self-reflexive as the speaker, an Allied soldier, is swimming in a stream in the small Bavarian town of Berchtesgaden when a young and emaciated German girl sees the soldiers. The "German girl-child— / . . . all skin and bones" sat nearby, smiling at the soldiers (lines 15–16). The Allied soldiers "splashed in the sun" and initially felt disrespected when the girl laughed at them (line 19). Just like the third stanza in the first section, the third stanza of the second section also makes a drastic dark turn. From the perspective of the soldier, "We had killed her mechanical brothers, / So we forgave her" (lines 21–22). The speaker reabsorbs guilt, aware that the Allied war effort has killed her fellow Germans. He is willing to let a minor slight slide because all combatants bear some burden of guilt for the deaths of others. For this girl to smile and laugh in the face of death and hunger reintroduces light and life into a world dominated by death. An archived draft of this poem contains a stanza removed before publication: "It's as painful as a wound, / And cold, and hunger, / Accepting love." "Accepting" is crossed out and Simpson replaces it in the margins with the word "Relearning" (Simpson, "Chicken Soup" draft). This edit reflects how the transition between offense and forgiveness cannot be a passive endeavor, but one that an individual must actively undertake. The encounter between Simpson's Allied soldiers and the young German girl has a peculiar resonance with Wilfred Owen's "Strange Meeting," as both poems exhibit a palpable confluence of oppositional figures. In Owen's poem, the two dominant voices that carry the text are deceased soldiers from opposite sides in the First World War who meet in Hell and recognize each other's humanity. This curiosity between foes is echoed in Simpson's memoir, in which he writes, "Wanting to get as close as possible to the one you hate, the one who's done his level best to kill you—it's a strange attraction" (*Air with Armed Men* 122). Owen's "Strange Meeting" is an encounter between equals; Simpson's "A Story about Chicken Soup" depicts a power disparity between soldier and child. Simpson attempts to find a balance between wartime foes and humans who, aside from Nazi ideology, would presumably share similar aspirations in times of peace. Further elaborating the tragedy of such a divide, Simpson wrote, "the final harm that the Germans did was to damage mankind's confidence in its own essential goodness" (*Air with Armed Men* 139). Since World War II was a conflict in which civilian population centers were incorporated into military strategy as targets, Simpson's encounter with an innocent civilian of the enemy side accentuates the moral and human implications of wartime offensives.

This tug-of-war between good and evil, happiness and sadness, plays out further in the present-tense third section, in which "The sun is shining" but the speaker feels the eyes of the deceased watching him ("A Story about Chicken Soup" line 23). The speaker feels the sacrificial weight of what others have given so that he could live, as "they have some demand on me— / They want me to be more serious than I want to be," and recognizes a tonal insensitivity for those in the wake of war who exude levity rather than solemn reflection (lines 25–26). The speaker is pressured by the weight of history to return to the ways of his Russian ancestors, acknowledging, "They want me to wear old clothes, / They want me to be poor, to sleep in a room with many others," as if progress is an offense to the past (lines 29–30). The speaker displays survivor's guilt and the pressure he feels to be living with a quiet respect for the dead, an alternate way of demonstrating how war is sustained in the minds of its participants. Despite Simpson's description of the mindset of soldiers at war, saying, "What most of them wanted was to get the fighting over with and go home . . . to the good life," the implication in "A Story about Chicken Soup" is that the past can never truly be left behind ("Soldier's Heart" 551). The final stanza of the poem appears to layer the three eras through intentional temporal and spatial ambiguity, in which the speaker knows he is relegated "Not to walk in the painted sunshine / To a summer house, / But to live in the tragic world forever" ("A Story about Chicken Soup" lines 31–33). Is the house referred to the house of his Russian ancestors, the German girl in Berchtesgaden, or his own in postwar America? While the answer to that is intentionally unclear, believing that they are all part of the same human experience, Simpson is arguing that each generation carries its own tragedy, and the speaker has no option but to carry the burden of his experience.

"On the Ledge," "Memories of a Lost War," and "A Story about Chicken Soup" are three among many of Louis Simpson's war poems that use visions, dreams, and nightmares to address the themes of traumatic memory, guilt, and their permanence in the mind of those who experience and survive war. Having been a soldier who endured war trauma that caused a mental breakdown, Louis Simpson is always negotiating past and present in his poetry, aware of the ways in which they interrelate. The persistence of traumatic memory as it overlaps with one's sense of time, place, and identity is what divides Simpson's poems between the traumatic superiority argument and the traumatic memory argument. Simpson's poems of traumatic experience can be positioned at some intersection between clarity and directness, and ambiguity and misdirection, and his subconscious was a breeding ground for exploring these possibilities:

I dreamed of encounters with the Germans that I never had. But I had anticipated such meetings as this was my job. I walked alone among trees or over fields, carrying a message from G Company to Battalion. Or I dreamed about horrors . . . the field in Holland I had to walk through night after night. It was strewn with the dead bodies of German infantry and American paratroopers who had shot each other at close range. The bodies changed, putrefying and swelling. I had to walk around arms and legs and faces shining with corruption. ("Soldier's Heart" 549)

The mind imagines the terrible sights Simpson may encounter as a way of preempting shock and using dreams to recapture memories temporarily lost to PTSD.

■ ■ ■

Louis Simpson's war poetry consistently addresses themes of distance and traumatic memory. As an infantryman whose deployment saw some of the most intense ground battles of World War II, Simpson suffered a mental breakdown as a result of his combat experience and PTSD. Simpson's body of war poetry shows the reclaimed memories of war, symptoms of trauma, and search for meaning, clarity, and closure in a life that has been bifurcated by war. Louis Simpson wrote poetry about World War II over the course of roughly four decades, yet he receives limited recognition as a war poet. When occasional poems of his are included in anthologies or critical analysis, they overwhelmingly tend to be from his first few collections. Poems such as "Carentan O Carentan" (1949) and "Memories of a Lost War" (1955) are Simpson's most likely works to appear in anthologies of war literature (for example, both appear in Lorrie Goldensohn's *American War Poetry* anthology and Harvey Shapiro's *Poets of World War II* anthology), while "The Battle" (1955), "The Runner" (1959), and "I Dreamed That in a City Dark as Paris" (1959) are occasionally selected or discussed. Even fellow American World War II poet and critic Randall Jarrell questioned Simpson's first poetry collection, writing, "There isn't a good poem in *The Arrivistes*, but Louis Simpson is as promising a new poet as I've read in some time" ("Poetry, Unlimited" 189). Jarrell's backhanded compliment, like much of the attention given to World War II poetry within a decade of the war's conclusion, has contributed to a broader shaping of Simpson's reputation, respected but inadequately recognized as a war poet. As focus on World War II poetry waned under the misconception that World War II soldier poets were part of a "Silent Generation," Simpson's later war poems have largely been omitted from anthologies and are infrequently remarked upon, with some exceptions such as Harvey Shapiro's *Poets of World War II* anthology and Leon Stokesbury's *Articles of War* anthology, which both include "A Bower of Roses." Overwhelmingly though, literature anthologies that are not assembled around the singular theme of war or the World War II era have neglected soldier poets of World War II. Notably still, major war poetry and general literature anthologies such as *The Faber Book of War Poetry* and the *Norton Anthology of American Literature* do not include Simpson. Such exclusions are consistent with points in Simpson's career in which "his poetry suffered from a degree of critical neglect" (Lazer 10).

Simpson used the preceding generation to make a prescient prediction on the relationship between the purpose of war writing and the act of remembrance: "Why write about such things? Are they not better forgotten? After a war the millions who have been through it want to forget . . . time passes and the number of those who remember is suddenly diminished. Who remembers the Great War?" ("Soldier's Heart" 550). Yet, remembrance, celebration, and honor are bestowed upon British First World War poets, as resoundingly demonstrated in 2014–18 centenary events reflecting on the Great War. Despite being a quieter voice of war amid a generation believed to be silent, the war poems of infantryman Louis Simpson offer invaluable perspective, vision, and reflection on many of World War II's key engagements, and the mental and physical landscapes he traversed.

2

KEITH DOUGLAS

CLOSENESS, SELF-ELEGY, AND
REMNANTS OF WAR

> Well, I am thinking this may be my last
> summer, but cannot lose even a part
> of pleasure in the old-fashioned art
> of idleness. I cannot stand aghast
> at whatever doom hovers in the background;
> while grass and buildings and the somnolent river,
> who know they are allowed to last forever,
> exchange between them the whole subdued sound
> of this hot time.
>
> —KEITH DOUGLAS, "Canoe"

Keith Douglas's premonitions of death in the poems "Canoe" and "Simplify me when I'm dead" were tragically confirmed on 9 June 1944 when he was killed in action in Normandy, France, just three days into the Allied invasion. While his "last / summer" (lines 1–2) was not the 1940 season in Oxford when "Canoe" was written, speaking in a moment of serenity against a European backdrop of chaos and terror, his four years of armed service proved Douglas was not one to "stand aghast" as danger approached (line 4). The threat of death would have been unlikely to dissuade Douglas from his final reconnaissance mission to determine the location of German soldiers in a French town. Douglas's military service mirrored the observational eye and his goal of writing extrospective poetry, both seasoned by a series of events in which he ran toward heated engagements in search of the euphoria derived from the physicality of war. The pursuit of an extrospective poetry, verse that is "practical, journalistic, economical, objective, and realistic," is a hallmark of Douglas's work and distinguishes him as an important, innovative, and underrecognized war poet (Lowery 87). Douglas's poetry is unflinching in its perceptions of distance in mechanized warfare and desert landscapes, and how traumatic memory prompts self-elegies, guilt, and reflections on the remnants of war.

In the opinion of Michael Hamburger, Douglas was "the one British poet of the Second World War who can bear comparison with those of the First" (Scammell 207). Douglas recognized the long shadow of his soldier poet predecessors and that his poetry must offer a perspective unique to World War II if it were to have any lasting value. Douglas understood that poetry of World War II ran the risk of echoing the poets of the Great War, and he "had no desire to repeat the work of his predecessors" (Kendall, *Modern English War Poetry* 165), though he did draw upon First World War poetry, whether in direct influence or the osmosis of both cultural and personal connection. Douglas was a pupil of Edmund Blunden's at Oxford, and a 11 September 1939 letter from Douglas to Blunden reads, "Thank heavens I can't see what is going to happen to us all as clearly as you must be able to" (*The Letters* 74–75). Eight days later, Blunden would respond, "My dear Douglas, I deplore this vast disturbance which has broken in on your university career. . . . My view of the future is a bit wonky, but I rather imagine that as events have been so surprising in recent years the present matter too will not proceed 'as planned,' and more extraordinary turns of history lie ahead of us" (Letter to Keith Douglas). Though Blunden was a champion of Douglas's poetry, the most obvious reference made by Douglas to his First World War predecessors was not to Blunden but Isaac Rosenberg. In the poem "Desert Flowers," Douglas admits, "Rosenberg I only repeat what you were saying" (line 2). In a further nod to his predecessors, a military portrait taken of Douglas in 1940 shows him standing in uniform, bordered by illustrated hearts, laurels, Greek columns, and a banner emblazoned with a quote from Horace (ironically repurposed by Wilfred Owen), "dulce et decorum est pro patria mori" (Photograph of Douglas, 1940). Undoubtedly affirming a sense of lineage with the poets of the First World War, Douglas was aware of the risks of war and the ways in which it could sour the notions of duty and honor.

Douglas's proponents were also skeptical of literary accomplishments generated from World War II. For example, two years after Douglas was killed in Normandy, his mentor Edmund Blunden wrote in a May 1946 issue of the *Times Literary Supplement*, "The second war with all its novelty of aspect and its shifting of emphasis has not weakened the commanding position of Wilfred Owen in the poetry of the age" (Swift 24). Just as many of the now-exalted writings of the First World War did not see publication until the mid- to-late 1920s, there was a delayed recognition of Douglas's writings. Douglas's memoir *Alamein to Zem Zem* was posthumously published in 1946 (a publication date pushed back because, as editor and publisher M. J. T. Tambimuttu wrote to Douglas's mother, "war books don't sell very well at the moment and it would have more of a success if it came out later"). This memoir appeared before his poetry was reinvigorated by the publication of Douglas's *Collected Poems* in 1951 and the subsequent public support of Ted Hughes. The prevailing notion in these post–World War II years was that Owen and the trench poets were still the authority and definitive voice of modern war poetry, and even Douglas feared that all war poetry written after them would be "tautological," as he proclaimed in his 1943 essay "Poets in This War" (*The Letters* 352). Despite these self-doubts, the innovative reimagining of modern combat in Douglas's war poetry cannot be overlooked. Vernon Scannell's 1976 analysis of World War II poetry, *Not Without Glory*, made a case that Douglas's war poems would ultimately "prove to possess at least the lasting qualities of the best of Wilfred Owen" (51). More than forty years later we are still awaiting that degree of recognition.

Douglas viewed the extrospective mode both as the appropriate response to war experience, and as a necessity to distinguish himself as a war poet. Douglas's drive to write "extrospective poetry . . . even if it is not attractive" is what ultimately directed his poetry away from the initial influence of the poets of the Great War (*The Letters* 352). Even though both Douglas and his war poet predecessors like Wilfred Owen championed truth and using personal experience in poetry, the poems made of that firsthand exposure to war were distinctly different (Kendall, *Modern English War Poetry* 147–48). Owen's poetry is defined by the way he evolved an aural tradition toward pararhyme, creating slight dissonance and discomfort to reflect the unsettling nature of up-close warfare and the suffering of the individual soldier "in the trench or the war hospital" (Cuthbertson 219). In contrast, Douglas embodied T. S. Eliot's argument that "Poetry is not a turning loose of emotion, but an escape from emotion; it is not the expression of personality, but an escape from personality" ("Tradition and the Individual Talent" 48–49). Douglas's escape from emotion, a photographer's eye for detail that preempts any narrative nudging that would tell his reader how to feel about the scene, is punctuated by unnatural syntax and strategic line breaks that force the reader to slow down and reread lines for basic comprehension. One could extract motivation for the extrospective in notes Douglas wrote on T. S. Eliot's essay "On Metaphysical Poets": "Must become more and more comprehensive, allusive, indirect in order to free language (dislocate if necessary) into his meaning" ("Book Diary"). Douglas used disjointed thoughts and multiclause sentence structures such as "Death, like a familiar, hears // and look, has made a man of dust / of a man of flesh," an example of atypical phrasing that prioritizes incremental comprehension over fluidity ("How to Kill" lines 12–14). To be writing poetry with this, at times, atomized and near-Cubist approach bolstered the desire for making meaning in a time of chaos by breaking complicated scenarios and emotions into more easily digestible pieces.[1]

Douglas's journalistic approach to the war is in part a by-product of the increased distance and mechanization of warfare. The added barriers of combat distance and technologically advanced weaponry compared to the experience of the trench poets affirms, in addition to the greater geopolitical motives, that World War II was a distinctly different conflict. Furthermore, equipment used in combat, such as the telescopic sights Douglas used as a tank commander, provided a new form of seeing, a characteristic of World War II that would alter how soldiers would emotionally process their actions. Douglas's time in North Africa further accentuated the differences in the way combat was experienced by the average soldier between the two world wars. Arid plains of sand dunes and unrelenting sun were as far a cry as imaginable from the rain-filled "slimescapes" of the First World War battlefields in France and Belgium (Das, *Touch and Intimacy* 35). Each of these issues shows the direct and subtle ways in which Douglas processed the theme of distance in his war poetry, both cognizant of his war poet predecessors and departing from the fear of writing carbon copies of the trench lyrics for the World War II generation.

In addition to distance being a consistent theme in the poetry of Keith Douglas, so too is the presence of traumatic memory. A student of Edmund Blunden, who was himself aware of terrible sights born out of war, Keith

Douglas wrote poems exhibiting vicarious trauma. Exemplified by "direct observation of another's trauma" or "reading a trauma narrative and constructing visual images," and then experiencing trauma directly, "vicarious [or secondary] trauma" can be found in the poems of Keith Douglas in which one has internalized the traumatic experience of others before having those feelings reawakened by their own traumatic experience (Kaplan 91). Douglas faced the mortal danger of combat, bracing himself for the possibility he would not return alive. In spite of the obvious risks of entering military service, Douglas viewed the war as a test of his vitality and masculinity. By acknowledging the risk involved, writing self-elegiac poems was one method Douglas would employ to ballast his emotions for what he perceived to be a tempestuous future at war, to brace against the horrors of combat by engaging with traumatic memory. Douglas evolved as a poet while at war, transmitting battlefield scenes with unflinching details and subdued emotions. The startling absence of guilt and the brand of extroverted pity and critique popularized by poets of the First World War make Douglas's poems about killing, enemy corpses, and physical denigration of the body an unforgettable contrast. For Douglas to refrain from casting judgment on these scenes so that the reader can devise their own opinions of war is a creative complement to the field of war poetry. To recall Louis Simpson's approach to writing war poetry that "Just to see something is enough," Douglas was confident that his poems would be making a statement on their own, without needing to overtly comment on the nature or state of war (Simpson and O'Siadhail 17). Not only did Douglas suppress emotions and feelings of guilt to complete his duties, his preoccupation with what war leaves in its wake is telling of how Douglas likely would have felt had he survived the war. His poems about leaving lovers, relinquishing one's youth and innocence, and profiling the dead bodies of civilians and enemy soldiers suggest an attempt to normalize a fractured experience. Acts of self-elegy, an absence of guilt for the enemy while recognizing the humanity in their loved ones, and taking stock of all that war leaves behind are examples of how traumatic memory shaped the war poems of Keith Douglas.

Vernon Scannell suggested that Britain sought either a Rupert Brooke or Wilfred Owen type to write about World War II, "someone young and handsome and brimming with patriotic fervor, or a rebellious protestant against the suffering and futility of war, someone 'inspired'" (*Not Without*

Glory 16). Douglas does not file easily into either one of these categories, for though he expressed eagerness to serve and make a difference, he was not driven by cause of country; rather, it was "simply a case of fighting against the Nazi regime," as he wrote in a letter shortly before his death in 1944 to Edmund Blunden (*The Letters* 328). Desmond Graham explains that Douglas was never bound to be the outspoken antiwar poet that had been expected: "In hospital Douglas had made no attempt to take up the protests of the Great War poets: his impulse had been consistently to explore and comprehend, not to attack" (*Keith Douglas* 191). Even though the "antiwar" poets of the First World War have a more complicated dedication to their war service than their reputation of being objectors suggests, the fact that Douglas is more difficult to categorize as pro- or antiwar is one factor contributing to the underrecognition of his poetry.

Born in Tunbridge Wells, England in 1920, Keith Castellain Douglas was adventurous and unapologetic, qualities that would surface in his poems of World War II. He was the son of a First World War soldier who struggled to find steady employment in the years that followed, and a mother whose ill health and financial instability made raising Keith, primarily as a single mother, difficult. Douglas's parents divorced after years of hardship and separation, and Douglas declined opportunities to reconnect with his father in the late 1930s since his father had been an inconsistent presence, largely an absence, in Keith's childhood. Early childhood anecdotes provide glimpses into the man Keith Douglas would become, such as playing war with soldier and cavalry figures (Graham, *Keith Douglas* 1) and writing a war poem at age ten titled "Waterloo" about Napoleon charging the English army (15). Whether re-creating war as an effort to fill the void of his father's absence, or out of a common boyhood interest in soldiers, Douglas's adolescent years marked the development of an enthusiastic and rebellious spirit.

Douglas's reputation as a poet grew exponentially from the initial publication of his early work during World War II to the revisiting and promotion of his poems by Ted Hughes in the 1960s. In the eyes of many, including Douglas's biographer Desmond Graham, "Douglas was the only British poet to continue in that different war what he saw as the tradition established by Owen, Sassoon, and Rosenberg" (*Keith Douglas* v). Judged in relation to the monolithic legacy of the trench poets, Douglas's war poetry both absorbs and departs from his war poet predecessors. As evidenced by Douglas's personal library, which is stored at the University of Leeds Brotherton Library, Douglas had read the work of the First World War soldier poets. Included in the archive is a copy of the 1939 *A Book of Modern Verse* in which Douglas has placed marks in the table of contents to draw attention to poems such as Wilfred Owen's "Exposure," "Insensibility," and "A Terre," as well as Isaac Rosenberg's "Dead Man's Dump," among others ("Keith Douglas Marginalia"). What message Douglas is sending to himself by jotting an *X* beside these poems is unknown, but it is revealing to see his marginalia, each notation a hint that these poems registered some resonance to him and were worth revisiting. Perhaps while crafting extrospective poems such as "How to Kill" on the necessity of callousness when taking someone's life, Douglas took inspiration from these lines from Owen's "Insensibility":

> And some cease feeling
> Even themselves or for themselves.
> Dullness best solves
> The tease of doubt and shelling.

> (lines 12–15)

Or was the imagery of Owen's "A Terre," in which "Dead men may envy living mites" (line 40) and the dead find comfort "when turned to fronds" (line 60), a precursor to Douglas's "Dead Men," in which the deceased "rest in the sanitary earth" (line 13)? Or the verbiage itself, as Douglas describes the aftermath of a war scene in which steel is "torn into fronds" in the poem "Landscape with Figures" (line 13).

Douglas's connection to the poets of the First World War was not merely as a casual reader, but through personal connections and relationships. Most notably, Douglas's mentor as a university student at Oxford was Edmund Blunden. Blunden was a reader for his work who helped to forge connections in the publishing world, even getting Douglas's poems in the hands of T. S. Eliot. In a 1941 letter, Eliot wrote to Douglas that his poems were "extremely promising" and that he had finished a phase of "juvenilia" and had started in a phase he had "not yet mastered" (Douglas, *The Letters* 164). Douglas, even down to his handwriting, believed that his tutor Blunden was "beginning to have some kind of influence over me, as I am beginning to write like him. See that incredibly neat signature—I shall be putting E. Blunden without thinking soon" (*The Letters* 82). In a further connection to the poets of the Great War, Douglas befriended Siegfried Sassoon's nephew Hamo while studying at Oxford (Graham, *Keith Douglas* 67). With these connections it is no surprise that Douglas is seen as carrying the torch of war poetry for the World War II generation whose responsibility it was "to hold it high" ("In Flanders Fields" line 12). Yet, during his life, Douglas downplayed the connective tissue between the two world war generations and the potential for originality, particularly in a 1943 essay "Poets in This War." In this essay, Douglas proclaims that "In the fourth year of this war we have not a single poet who seems likely to be an impressive commentator on it" (*The Letters* 351). Although at this point in the war there was indeed very little poetry by soldiers that would garner critical acclaim, Douglas believed "The reasons are psychological, literary, military and strategic, diverse" as to why World War II poets were failing to create a distinct voice from the poets of the First World War (352). Stifled by the experience of war on such a scale, prevailing opinions argued that there was nothing new to say about war. What Douglas argues is ultimately more a condemnation of the repetitiveness of war's horrors than the inability to write inventively about World War II. As his essay continues, there are two reasons why he believes the poetic achievement would be difficult to re-create for World War II poets:

> Hell cannot be let loose twice: it was let loose in the Great War and it is the same old hell now. The hardships, pain, and boredom; the behaviour of the living and the appearance of the dead, were so accurately described by the poets of the Great War that every day on the battlefields of the western desert—and no doubt on the Russian battlefields as well—their poems are illustrated. Almost all that a modern poet on active service would be inspired to write, would be tautological. (352)

Often, this quotation is used as ammunition to defend the opinion that there were few poets of importance in World War II and that their writings would only rehash the subjects and style of the trench lyrics. Yet, the underlying message here is that war is hell and it would not be a sufficient contribution to the field of war poetry for the poets of World War II merely to reach that established conclusion. Douglas reinforces this stance in personal communications as well, writing in a 1943 letter to poet and Oxford friend J. C. Hall, "To be sentimental or emotional now is dangerous to oneself and to others" (*The Letters* 295). For Douglas, emotionally espousing the horrors of war and the drudgery of soldierdom was not an original or useful aim. Instead, Douglas's objective was "to write true things, significant things" (295). Whether intentional or not, Douglas's extrospective leanings reinforce a New Critical approach to reading literature that requires "distance or detachment on the part of the reader" to maintain "literature as a self-enclosed, self-contained verbal entity" (Kasprisin 57). This journalistic approach to poetry, largely devoid of emotion, became characteristic of Douglas's extrospective war poems, which served to create a heightened dissonance when he wrote unemotionally about otherwise life-changing events such as killing another human. Fatalism and an eye for brutal detail remained qualities in Douglas's war poetry, earning him publication for some of his poems while he was still alive, as well the planned publication of his memoir on the North Africa campaign, *Alamein to Zem Zem.*

Douglas's poetry explores themes of distance and traumatic memory in several ways. First, Douglas utilizes closeness and mechanization in battle, and revisits and revises the soldier-as-witness perspective popularized by Wilfred Owen. Second, Douglas's best war poems manipulate notions of combat distance and emotional distance through sights and telescopic lenses. Third, as undoubtedly the most acclaimed British poet of World War II and the North Africa campaign,[2] Douglas conveyed his war experience through descriptions of tactile desert landscapes. Furthermore, though Douglas did not survive the war and therefore his readers are not afforded poems of reflection and retrospection of his postwar life, the presence of traumatic memory in his poetry is found in three concepts that will be analyzed: the occurrence of self-elegy, the presence and absence of guilt in his poems, and reading his poems as a study of the people and memories left behind. Each of these sections will contribute to a fuller picture of the contribution Keith Douglas made to the body of World War II poetry, demonstrating he is more than just a name that critics feel obligated to mention when acknowledging that there were World War II soldiers who wrote poetry, too.

The Distance of Battle: Closeness and Mechanization

War is invasive, both by definition and through the mental and emotional impact on its participants and affected civilians. As the technology, proximity, and spaces of war evolve, so too have notions of distance and landscape. The brutal close combat strategy of trench warfare in the First World War was largely abandoned in World War II. Not only were the Battles of the Somme and Verdun reminders of catastrophic casualties from failed strategies, but the technological advancements that were made in the interwar period drastically changed the way war was conducted. This shift toward air attacks, while still fighting on land and sea, produced a change in mindset for combatants. As explained by Diederik Oostdijk, "The mechanized, industrialized nature of modern warfare had eroded the possibility of heroic dueling, and according to the World War II poets, heroic agency thus belonged to the past" (*Among the Nightmare Fighters* 30–31). For this reason, there are few World War II poems that capture the same close-range observations between combatants. Nonetheless, poets like Douglas chronicle the transition of warfare between close range and far distances. In his poems, Keith Douglas references the use of telescopic tools to show the distance between combatants, and this conceptual act of removing space between people or things is an exploration of closeness, distance, enemy encounters, mechanization, and absence. Some of Keith Douglas's most recognizable poems, specifically "*Vergissmeinnicht*," "How to Kill," and "Simplify me when I'm dead," as well as a scarcely anthologized early poem, ".303," use the sense of sight and manipulations of distance in both literal and metaphorical ways to cater to the evolution of global conflict.

To contextualize war poetry that influenced Keith Douglas's poems of distance and enemy encounters, one must first be cognizant of First World War soldier poets Robert Graves and Wilfred Owen. Presenting the enemy as anonymous, monstrous figures, as Robert Graves does in his elegiac "Goliath and David," is a mode that faded over the course of the First World War (Fussell, *The Great War and Modern Memory* 78).[3] Casting the enemy as monstrous validates the belief that, in the words of Hans Queiser, "In order to be a useful soldier, a man must overcome his natural aversion against the killing of a member of his own species" (Jarausch 102). While some major poets of the First World War such as Graves amplified the anonymity or sub- or superhuman nature of enemy soldiers, projecting an *us versus them* mentality, other defining voices of First World War poetry countered this militaristic impulse to dehumanize the enemy. This pivot toward describing the First World War more like a humanitarian crisis than an epic of good and evil is most notable in poems that chronicle close-range encounters between combatants. One such example, Wilfred Owen's 1918 poem "Strange Meeting," begins with a movement mimicking Dante's journey into the depths of hell in *Inferno*.[4] Owen uses the enemy soldier as a conduit to express the same message that threads through many of his most recognized poems, such as the loss of youth and "the pity of war" (line 25). The irony of this moment is that the similarities recognized between Owen's speaker and this enemy combatant are only learned when they meet face to face in death. Confronting one another in close combat reminds soldiers that the opposition is human and that one witnesses the violence committed with a degree of intimacy. Keith Douglas invoked a similar degree of knowing one's enemy in *"Vergissmeinnicht,"* by identifying a corpse through their relation to loved ones.

Most of "Strange Meeting" is spoken by a deceased German soldier, and giving voice to an often anonymously depicted enemy soldier is a rarely displayed act of compassion and humanity. While Owen gives voice to the enemy, Douglas's *"Vergissmeinnicht"* also shows closeness by recognizing the individualism of the deceased enemy soldier. One reason this individualism is rare is that it is easier to train soldiers to carry out orders when they view themselves as part of a collective, or in other words, "the Army's high command to imposing an institutionally-sanctioned collective identity upon the mass of soldiers" (Lukasik 197). The same anonymization happens when soldiers view the enemy as a collective evil rather than an army of individuals with their own thoughts, backgrounds, and aspirations. Regardless of the inspiration for Owen to write about this encounter— whether a literal meeting between soldiers in the figurative hell of war, drawn from the experience of encountering a dead enemy soldier, or an imagined encounter of two deceased soldiers meeting in hell—he is cultivating a sense of empathy for the enemy and contextualizing the nature of the conflict within geopolitical aims and not personal motivations.[5]

Yet, Owen's "Strange Meeting" and Douglas's *"Vergissmeinnicht"* differ in important ways. While Owen is not suggesting that opposing soldiers share political aims or personal goals, they are both cogs in the bloodied wheels of warfare throughout history. He presents this image with the archaic description of "when much blood had clogged their chariot-wheels / I would go up and wash them from sweet wells," implying that his role as a soldier is to keep the wheels of war moving (lines 34–35). By intentionally referencing the use of a chariot, Owen is speaking about war in the twentieth century as if it is no different from the battles fought by the Roman Empire. Despite technological advancements from the chariot wheel to the continuous track of tank wheels, Owen is making the case that war is still war, and the killing of others that it entails is all the more harrowing when conducted at a range close enough to console someone. Furthermore, the enemy soldier in "Strange Meeting" refers to the initial speaker in the second person—"I knew you in this dark" (line 41)—a markedly more intimate address than the third-person framing of "the soldier" in *"Vergissmeinnicht"* (line 4). Though Douglas's speaker encounters a corpse at close range, *"Vergissmeinnicht"* relies on emotional distance between speaker and corpse, and the physical distance between corpse and lover, as barriers to achieving the compassion Owen exhibits.

Inspired by his experience as a British tank commander in the North African campaign, Keith Douglas reforms the tradition of Owen's "Strange Meeting" of personalizing and humanizing the enemy in the poem *"Vergissmeinnicht."* Coming close enough to the dead enemy soldier to rummage through his personal belongings, Douglas's speaker finds "the dishonoured picture of his girl / who has put: *Steffi. Vergissmeinnicht,"* which translates as *forget me not* (*"Vergissmeinnicht"* lines 10–11). Though Douglas jeers the dead soldier for the rigor mortis that has set into his "equipment," the poem conversely exhibits sympathy for the loved ones who will experience the loss of this soldier (line 15). This recognition of the service and emotional weight of noncombatants is relatable for many soldiers, but World War II's heightened focus on civilian targets prompted an added attention to civilian loss. In *"Vergissmeinnicht,"* Douglas draws our attention to the dead enemy soldier's lover, Steffi, contrasting her loss with the soldier's undignified death, remarking "she would weep to see today / how on his skin the swart flies move" (lines 17–18). Though the enemy soldier has been killed, it is his lover, Steffi, who will undergo "mortal hurt" (line 24). Douglas struggles to humanize the enemy, but he recognizes the humanity of the loss as experienced by the loved ones of combatants. In contrast to the bond Owen establishes between enemy combatants through enduring the battle together, Douglas extends the locus of suffering to those who will bear the suffering and grief of the soldier's death. This compassion only comes to fruition because of the intimate interaction of sifting through enemy's valuables, as the speaker is forced to recognize the enemy as human by learning of their life outside of the war. The speaker of "*Vergissmeinnicht*" responds akin to Zoë H. Wool's description in *After War* of the postwar lives of injured American veterans who served in Iraq and Afghanistan: "suspended in that tension—the sometimes uncanny ordinariness of such seemingly extraordinary circumstances—when the most intimate contours and forms of life are rendered into matters of grave consequence" (19). The speaker shares a bond with the deceased enemy; war has distanced both from their loved ones. Heidegger's *Being and Time* encapsulates this notion when describing *Dasein,* or being, in relation to experiencing the death of others: "Death does indeed reveal itself as a loss, but a loss such as is experienced by those who remain" (282). Knowing that the German soldier's death will bring grief to his lover, Steffi, means the speaker must acknowledge the enemy as human despite inclinations to dehumanize them, particularly those complicit in atrocity.

The uneven syllable counts in the lines of "*Vergissmeinnicht,*" ranging from seven to eleven, and inconsistent rhyme scheme mirror a disjointedness of binaries in the poem: life and death, love and war, known and unknown. The dissonance is best encapsulated in the final stanza, in which rhymes like "mingled" and "singled" are offset by pararhymes "heart" and "hurt." Similar sensations of orderliness versus feeling unsettled are echoed in the syllable count of the final stanza, where line 21 is eleven syllables and line 23 is nine syllables, while lines 22 and 24 are iambic tetrameter, a shift between imbalance and control. The vacillation of the poem's mechanics—lines of orderly meter versus free verse, rhyme versus slant and pararhyme—mirror the binaries of closeness and mechanization. The binary choices of rhyme and meter Douglas makes magnify the sense of imbalance in the poem between the speaker and the corpse, the living and the dead, the lover at home and their defiled sweetheart abroad, and the seer and the seen. Each of these divides represents the navigation of a physical or psychological distance, and while the speaker distinguishes between "us" and "them" through these seemingly emotionally detached observations—even permitting the poem's title, "*Vergissmeinnicht,*" to be the German-language sign-off of the dead soldier's lover—each binary is an acknowledgment of the other, a cohabitation.

Douglas's "How to Kill" is a poem that uses the technological sight of a scope as a frame for the distanced perspective of scouting an enemy soldier. Originally titled "The Sniper" in a draft sent to J. C. Hall, "How to Kill" was written while Douglas was stationed in North Africa in 1943 (Graham, *Keith Douglas* 220). Douglas's "How to Kill" surprises readers with an atypical focal point, a speaker guiding us through the methodical and gratifying act of killing. Most notably, the speaker in "How to Kill" is "amused / to see the centre of love diffused" (lines 15–16), and in disbelief over "How easy it is to make a ghost" (line 18). What makes this poem unique to the process of a war fought by technological means is the target drawn into focus "Under the parabola of a ball," the opening line calculating the necessary trajectory to strike from distance (line 1). Through the sight the speaker zeroes in on his soon-to-be victim, walking the reader through procedural motions: "Now in my dial of glass appears / the soldier who is going to die" (lines 7–8). The telescopic sight used to identify the target is a visual and emotional barrier that separates the soldier from the life he is about to take. If the act is committed without the use of one's natural sight, much like how modern-day drone operators can conduct attacks from significant distances using video surveillance to watch the outcomes, the guilt is less immediate as if the perpetrator has not directly committed the act (Press). Similar to *"Vergissmeinnicht,"* "How to Kill" is a voyeuristic invasion of privacy where the enemy soldier is unaware he is being watched as "he smiles, and moves about in ways / his mother knows, habits of his" (lines 9–10). Again, the focus momentarily shifts from the battlefield to the home front, as the enemy soldier is described by the absence he has left in the home life of his family. When the speaker orders the shot to be taken, the enemy soldier's absence from the ranks of the living is described in simplistic terms: "Death . . . has made a man of dust / of a man of flesh" (lines 12–14). Sympathy for the family of the soldier evaporates just as quickly, as the extinguishing of life is self-congratulatory, referred to as "sorcery" and an act that causes the speaker to feel "amused / to see the centre of love diffused / and the wave of love travel into vacancy" (lines 14, 15–17). In amazement, the speaker acknowledges "How easy it is to make a ghost" (line 18) and describes the act of killing as where "man and shadow meet" (line 22). The final stanza speaks to the delicacy with which a life can be taken, comparing pulling a trigger or firing a bomb to how a "weightless mosquito touches / her tiny shadow on the stone" (lines 19–20). The cumulative effect of this commentary on extinguishing an enemy soldier is one aspect of how distance influences one's response to culpability and guilt.

In contrast to the sustained recognition in *"Vergissmeinnicht"* of loved ones left behind, the undercurrent of "How to Kill" is a fascination with the ease of killing, framed by the distance between an emotionally detached speaker and their victim. Douglas's emotional void is conveyed without any mention of the weaponry itself. The only technological tool mentioned in "How to Kill" is the scope through which the speaker views his target, which shortens the distance between the speaker and the enemy soldier without feeling the closeness of human connection found in *"Vergissmeinnicht."* Douglas commanded a British Crusader MKII during the Battle of El Alamein, a lighter-weight and more maneuverable tank outfitted with a "No. 30" sight scope that magnified objects by 1.9 times, with a twenty-one-degree field of view (D. Boyd). The telescopic sight through which the speaker of "How to Kill" views their target is a medium, a technological barrier that makes the act of killing feel impersonal. The use of mechanical sight in Douglas's poems mirrors the transformative "impression of having walked through the looking-glass that touches a man entering a battle" (Douglas, *Alamein to Zem Zem* 6). "How to Kill" exemplifies Heidegger's ideas of spatiality as "characters of de-severance and directionality," which his translators take to mean *"abolishing* a distance. . . . It is as if by the very act of recognizing the 'remoteness' of something, we have in a sense brought it closer and made it less 'remote'" (Heidegger 138). Douglas's speaker uses the telescopic sight to identify a remote enemy soldier, and in doing so, abolishes the distance between them, bringing the enemy soldier closer to the speaker, both in vision and a perceived sense of understanding. While mechanized vision had a psychological effect on soldiers, it also presented military advantages for tank crews who Douglas believed were "the best informed of all" because "Before the mind's eye the panorama of the battle is kept" (*Alamein to Zem Zem* 114). Soldiers in World War II were learning to deal with advancements in weaponry that made killing from great distances possible, while maintaining minimal risk for the perpetrator. For this reason, as Peter Lowe suggests in his analysis of Douglas's work, "modern war poetry often seeks out the dissonance between Homer's text and the near-mechanized slaughter of the Western Front," a contrast used to show how twentieth-century war poets possess a "distrust of anything that seeks to make war sound more elevated than it is" (301).

Douglas chronicled his World War II experience with simplicity and directness, devoid of a sense of glory. As its title could imply, Douglas's "How to Kill" is seen by Lorrie Goldensohn as the successor to Sassoon's "How to Die" (*Dismantling Glory* 128). While Sassoon ironically critiques the sacrificial nature of soldierdom as devotional and learned behavior, declaring "they've been taught the way to do it / Like Christian soldiers" ("How to Die" lines 13–14), Douglas knows that in this isolated moment there is no disguising the fact that the weaponry he possesses is "*a gift designed to kill*" ("How to Kill" line 6). By describing the mindset and action taken, ignorance and neutrality are removed, and the reader is made complicit in the act. Effectively, war poems that chronicle death in detail force readers to accept a broader view of the war. In other words, to support the war is to support the acts of brutality it fosters, and one cannot reap victory without consenting to the death of others. Though Goldensohn describes "How to Kill" as being written with a "sober decency" for its plain speech, it is proof of an emotionally callous speaker (*Dismantling Glory* 128). Acknowledging how little effort is necessary to kill, the speaker in "How to Kill" is detached from the act, a degree removed since he commands a sniper to take the shot: "I cry / NOW" (lines 11–12). Far from any feeling of guilt, the speaker in "How to Kill" feels more like they are conducting a supernatural feat, making "a man of dust / of a man of flesh. This sorcery / I do" (lines 13–15). "Sorcery" draws attention to itself, as if the speaker is simultaneously acknowledging the awesome power they possess—to have someone killed by saying a single word—while also suggesting the power is beyond belief, beyond human capability. In the poem's closing lines, "A shadow is a man / when the mosquito death approaches," Douglas intentionally uses a blood-sucking insect to convey his idea that such a seemingly insignificant thing—an insect bite, like a trigger pull—can cause the transition from life to death (lines 23–24). It is worth noting that the de Havilland DH.98 Mosquito was an Allied aircraft used for reconnaissance and bombing, known for its speed and largely wooden construction (*De Havilland Mosquito*). This affords the image of the mosquito's shadow and landing interpretive flexibility of alluding to both the insect and airplane.

Rather than depicting a typical heroic act of defense, "How to Kill" is a matter-of-fact, proactive, procedural retelling of the ease of killing from the point of view of the aggressor. As described by Desmond Graham, in Douglas's poems "there is a focusing of detachment upon that experienced by the soldier himself: his distance from what he does and the damnation which that distance reveals" (Douglas, *A Prose Miscellany* 9). Despite using technological sights and mechanized weaponry to abbreviate the distance between speaker and enemy, these conduits simultaneously serve as barriers between the speaker and feelings of guilt, remorse, or shame. Yet, as Tim Kendall describes, the "ethics of sight proposes that to look is a moral act" (*Modern English War Poetry* 161). The speaker capitalizes on the absence of these feelings that result from being complicit in the murder of an enemy soldier from afar. In contrast to the First World War poems that captured the pressure and relentlessness of trench warfare, Douglas's speaker in "How to Kill" seems caught off guard by how little engagement is necessary to kill the enemy and is grappling with the unexpected speed and relative technological ease with which war is now fought. "How to Kill" is a stunned response to the literal distance between combatants and the figurative distancing that occurs when the enhanced mechanization of war challenges the conventional relationship and emotional engagement of soldiers during combat.

Written in May 1941, "Simplify me when I'm dead" is another poem that manipulates distance through sight, this time reducing the body by its elements in the hope of finding what makes man's life worthwhile. Douglas knows it is not "the brown hair and blue eye" that will be of lasting value but something intrinsic and more elusive (line 5). The bulk of the poem enacts this stripping down of the extraneous and nonbiological facets of one's life, the "particular memories" (line 13), "pain I bore" (line 14), "the opinions I held" (line 15), and "even my appearance" (line 16), but Douglas knows these things "will be no guide" (line 17). Rather, it is "Time's wrong-way telescope" that will show the truth (line 18). Though a telescope is a technological device that aids human sight by increasing the size of objects from distance, Douglas is imagining one can use a telescope to look into the future. Through this telescope, Douglas sees "a minute man ten years hence / and by distance simplified" (lines 19–20). This image could have multiple meanings depending on how one reads the word "minute": either as the simplification of a man in the future, as if there is less complexity and detail when viewing someone or something from afar, such as a man through a telescope, or alternatively, "a minute man" could be referencing members of a militia prepared to join into conflict on short notice, an implication that Douglas sees a future of chaos and conflict. Through this telescopic sight, the figure is "by distance simplified," which in its own way is an admission that nothing is learned from the image beyond proof of existence. Yet, this recognition is what Douglas desires, as the poem is bookended with the requests "Remember me when I am dead / and simplify me when I'm dead" (lines 1–2, 27–28). In practical application, if Douglas is on active duty and looking through a telescope at enemy soldiers, he likely will know nothing about them as individuals beyond which country they serve based on their uniform. Douglas acknowledges the shortcomings of this type of distanced identification and recognizes that he, too, may be the subject of such analysis. Douglas continues with arguably the most crucial tercet of the poem, writing, "Through that lens see if I seem / substance or nothing: of the world / deserving mention or charitable oblivion" (lines 21–23). The act of simplifying and reducing a human, identifying one from a distance and over time, hinges on the word "substance." Douglas's speaker is asking if he is worth anything to the world, if he is noteworthy or irrelevant, and welcomes this judgment. Like many people, the desire to have a legacy and be remembered is a motivator, so whether it is through his service as a soldier, or his writings, the speaker wants to be remembered and understood with "Edge and exactitude," to quote his Oxford mentor and First World War soldier poet predecessor Edmund Blunden from his poem "Can You Remember?" (line 3). "Simplify me when I'm dead" does not prescribe what constitutes "substance" as opposed to "nothing." Perhaps of subconscious importance is that telescopic sight—whether purely visual or imagined over time—can only provide a bigger and more detailed image of what is far away, but it cannot inform the observer with any greater clarity as to the substance of one's subject. In other words, the tools of war are indiscriminate.

The emotional distancing espoused by Douglas from replacing one's feelings with one's actions was a conscious decision, reinforced by a letter to J. C. Hall in which Douglas wrote "Reportage and extrospective poetry . . . has to be written just now even if it is not attractive" (The Letters 352). For Douglas, writing extrospectively meant "honesty, economy of expression, writing from first-hand experience, writing in a way that resembles 'reportage,' and writing poetry that was outward-looking, as opposed to introspective, lyrical, or inward-looking" (Lowery 85). Douglas is trying to create a journalistic record of war experience with his poetry. Just as Douglas could not have understood how Blunden felt at the outset of World

War II after experiencing the horrors of the First World War, Douglas knows that those who have not experienced war firsthand will not be able to fully process the emotional landscape a soldier must navigate. Therefore, Douglas turned to more factual accounting, events that can be understood by others on a procedural level, even if not on an emotional level. Even as a fifteen-year-old boy, Douglas envisioned what war was like by using modern technological weaponry to see the world through the soldier's eyes in the poem ".303."

Written in 1935 and named after the diameter of a commonly used British rifle cartridge, ".303" is an early foray into the importance of sight, seeing, and, by extension, understanding. The final quatrain of the twelve-line poem reads:

> Through a machine-gun's sights
> I saw men curse, weep, cough, sprawl in their entrails;
> You did not know the gardener in the vales,
>   Only efficiency delights you.
>
>   (lines 9–12)

This excerpt could easily be mistaken for lines drafted by Owen or Sassoon, borrowing heavily from the visceral and bodily horrors of trench lyrics. It holds a particular resonance with a couplet from Wilfred Owen's "Dulce Et Decorum Est" which reads, "In all my dreams before my helpless sight, / He plunges at me, guttering, choking, drowning" (lines 15–16). Douglas's return to pastoral imagery in ".303" is an act of equating the indescribable nature of war in relatable sights. ".303" is a poem in which Douglas postures as a soldier, providing testimony of battle as if they were his own bleak observations. As explained by Shoshana Felman, to "testify—to *vow to tell*, to *promise* and *produce* one's own speech as material evidence for truth—is to accomplish a *speech act,* rather than simply formulate a statement" (Felman and Laub 5). Douglas's vision of a war that finished before he was born is an attempted "speech act," one trying to cultivate an impact through the act of telling. The concluding stanza of ".303" counterbalances the horrific sights of war with the delight of "efficiency" with which violence is committed. The overlapping of these themes of war horrors and the technological ease of killing, as if the center of a Venn diagram, position ".303" as the predecessor to "How to Kill," written before Douglas had the experience to validate his understanding of war.

Just as mechanization, the distance of battle, and technological manipulations of sight were defining aspects of Douglas's World War II experience, so too was the landscape in which it occurred. As the preeminent poet of World War II's desert campaigns, Keith Douglas used the setting of North Africa and the imagery and feeling it provided to create an indelible record of the war in this crucial World War II campaign.

Tactile Landscapes: Sand

On 4 June 1940, British prime minister Winston Churchill addressed the houses of Parliament at a time of increasing fear, trepidation, and concern over the future of Britain amid the advancements of Nazi Germany. His now famous speech crescendoed, "We shall fight on the seas and oceans, we shall fight with growing confidence and growing strength in the air, we shall defend our Island, whatever the cost may be, we shall fight on the beaches, we shall fight on the landing grounds, we shall fight in the fields and in the streets, we shall fight in the hills; we shall never surrender" (Churchill 218). Aside from being a motivational call to defend one's homeland at any cost, Churchill's words remind us of a particularly unique aspect of World War II: the varied locations and landscapes the war encompassed. Keith Douglas made his mark as a witness and participant in one of those unique landscapes, the North African theater. The desert landscape was a characteristic that distinguished Douglas's war poetry from the First World War poets traversing the muddied trenches of the Western Front. While this gritty, hot landscape with minimal foliage looked like a blank canvas in contrast to the serpentine trenches and ruined fields and forests of the First World War, Douglas made the exotic North African landscape feel familiar by translating its features using varied perspectives, imagery of the natural world, and religious allusion.

The bulk of Keith Douglas's war service saw him stationed in Cairo, Palestine, and El Alamein, before being deployed to Normandy for the D-Day invasion ("Keith Douglas"). Douglas acquainted himself with the scorched and monochromatic desert landscapes of Egypt and visualized the war using a landscape vastly different from the damp green English ground he grew up with and the trench systems, no-man's land, and waterlogged fields of mud described by First World War poets. While in North Africa, Douglas either composed or began much of the legacy-building body of poetry for which he is remembered. A three-part poem, "Landscape with Figures" lends a painter's eye to the scenes of a desert war. The first section looks at the desert landscape from above—"Perched on a great fall of air / a pilot or angel looking down"—yet allows the reader to envision this changed perspective as one of three things: a bird, a pilot, or an angel (lines 1–2). Providing these three options gives the reader different frames of reference for the aerial perspective, flight in the natural world, which everyone can comprehend (a bird); flight of the man-made world, which would be more pertinent to the military (a pilot); and flight of the supernatural world (an angel). In order to see the desert landscape, an aerial perspective helps readers to visualize the unreality of war, along with ideas of survival and death in the desert. It is from this view that one would see "crouching on the sand vehicles / squashed dead or still entire, stunned / like beetles" (lines 5–7). Personifying destroyed military vehicles as damaged beetles is easier to picture than what Douglas describes later as steel "torn into fronds / by the lunatic explosive" (lines 13–14). Even in his direct description of the exploded metal structures, he is comparing the shape of the torn metal to "fronds," again relying on the natural world to define the unnatural imagery of vehicles wrenched by bombs into leaf-like shapes. Just months before writing "Landscapes with Figures," Douglas would try this same equation of imagery between weaponry and harmless flora from the natural world in the poem "Cairo Jag." In describing the unreal sites of war, "Cairo Jag" shows "the vegetation is of iron / dead tanks, gun barrels split like celery / the metal brambles have no flowers or berries" (lines 24–26). This method of portraying destroyed iron weaponry as if it were grown naturally from the earth is an attempt to convey the surreal qualities of the imagery of war. Douglas's comparison exemplifies David Kalstone's notion that pastoral imagery, even when used ironically, can be a "clarifying or restorative force" (249). Douglas is aware that what he is trying to describe will appear beyond belief, as he alludes to the biblical episode of the Apostle Thomas not believing in Jesus's resurrection until he could see and feel Jesus's wounds (John 20:24–29). Douglas points out this desire that others have to prove that what he sees is real, writing, "But you who like Thomas come / to poke fingers in the wounds / find monuments" ("Landscape with Figures" lines 9–11). Douglas notes how battle-ravaged vehicles are now tokens of war and proof that the carnage is real, and how memorialization has a propensity for reopening psychological wounds. Monuments are the intersection of memory and trauma, and Douglas abstains from passing judgment by settling for the role of an observer. Douglas observes the intersection of memory and trauma, a familiar experience as someone who came of age as thousands of memorials and monuments were erected to the First World War. While predecessors such as Sassoon critique "Men's biologic urge to readjust" ("At the Cenotaph" line 9), implying that when "discredited ideas revive" (line 6) and people turn back to war out of "pride and power," historical events like war become cyclical (line 8), Douglas's extrospective approach shows the wreckage itself as a monument.

Douglas, in this role of witness to war, shifts the perspective in the second section of "Landscape with Figures" and uses religious allusions to convey war in the desert landscape. Douglas shifts perspective to ground level to heighten awareness of human suffering. "On sand and scrub the dead men wriggle," the second section begins (line 15). With the imagery of the beetles fresh from the first section, the soldiers here are equated with powerless, victimized beings on display. Framing soldiers as helpless alongside the descriptions as if they are performing with stage makeup—"maquillage of these stony actors"—further entrenches the idea of war as theatrical, in which players perform their roles for the entertainment of the civilian viewership (line 27). Douglas equates the desert war to hell by hammering the idea of guilt in the third section, in which the speaker is "the figure burning," though not alone (line 29). In each of these tableaux of war he is present, and by extension so are all who are a part of the war. Douglas is constructing an all-encompassing hellscape in which the war takes place. He sees himself as "all / the aimless pilgrims, the pedants and courtiers" (lines 32–33) and continues:

I am all these and I am the craven
the remorseful the distressed
penitent: not passing from life to life
but all these angels and devils are driven
into my mind like beasts.

(lines 37–41)

Using dichotomies like angels and devils, earth and heaven, and life and death, Douglas is attempting to bridge reality with the seemingly unreal. By conceiving of these disparate ideas as one, or within the same spectrum, Douglas brings the war to the home front through the language of historically high culture mediums such as painting and poetry to capture the devolution of man at war. Describing the desert war requires Douglas to use atypical perspectives and landscapes—aerial views, gnarled metal like flora, and hell—to give his readers a frame of reference for a battlefield that does not reflect the previous generation's waterlogged trenches in any way except for the suffering.

Keith Douglas's journalistic eye for documenting World War II's North African campaign shows the reader what the soldier's experience was like by finding convincing parallels between the abnormality of war he witnessed and more easily accessible images, perspectives, and emotions. Now, eighty years removed from World War II, the world has endured numerous desert wars, and Douglas is among a larger cohort of desert war poets.[6] For Douglas and twenty-first-century desert war poets like Brian Turner, the desert might as well be an hourglass in which the shifting sand counts down the time they have to live, distilling the individual as if frozen in time, and mixing their stories with the centuries of war dead left to rest in foreign landscapes.

A 1939 copy of A Book of Modern Verse that Douglas owned contains a handwritten draft of the first four lines of "Landscapes with Figures" inside the back cover. The phrasing is slightly different between these early drafted lines and the final versions that have been published, such as the line "Perched on a tremendous volume of clear air," which became "Perched on a great fall of air" ("Keith Douglas Marginalia"). Douglas was likely thinking of the legacy of the trench poets he held in his hands with his copy of A Book of Modern Verse as he drafted these lines and thought it appropriate to write of his own landscapes of war. Perhaps changing the word "tremendous" to "great" is a subtle nod to the poets of the "Great War" whose work he had just finished reading, and rereading. Then, on a blank page at the end of the anthology, as if adding his perspective from the desert war to the tradition of landscapes in war poetry, Douglas began documenting his own "Landscapes with Figures."

Poems of Self-Elegy: "Simplify me when I'm dead" and "The Poets"

Lay the coin on my tongue and I will sing
of what the others never set eyes on.

("Desert Flowers" lines 15–16)

I see my feet like stones
underwater. The logical little fish
converge and nip the flesh
imagining I am one of the dead.

("Mersa" lines 21–24)

The soldier poets of World War II anticipated, imagined, and prepared themselves to die at war, a fatalist outlook instilled in them by their First World War poetic predecessors. British poet and critic Vernon Scannell supported the notion that the First World War had an all-encompassing presence in the lives of those who came of age in the interwar years. Born in 1922 and having served in World War II's North Africa campaign, Scannell explained the influence of the First World War in his memoir, *Drums of Morning*:

> I suspect that most, or many, people of my generation—those who were born during or shortly after the war—are haunted by its imagery, its pathos, the waste, the heroism and futility. We were brought up with the echoes of the artillery barrages, the iron stammer of machine guns, the cries of the wounded, the songs and martial music sounding in our ears. There seemed to be pictures of no man's land, of the trenches, the shattered landscape, barbed wire, ruined farms and churches, everywhere we looked. (72–73)

In addition to the pervasive imagery, themes, and difficult lessons learned from the First World War, any British student in the interwar years who had a remote awareness of the poetry of the Great War would know the name Rupert Brooke. By 1930, Rupert Brooke's *Collected Poems* had sold 300,000 copies (Trott 56). Brooke was a handsome, intelligent, and promising young man who died from blood poisoning from an infected mosquito bite en route to Gallipoli (Stallworthy, *Anthem for Doomed Youth* 14). The publication of Brooke's sonnets "The Dead" and "The Soldier" in the *Times Literary Supplement* a month before his death, and his collection *1914 & Other Poems* a month after his death skyrocketed Brooke's reputation as a poet and a symbol of British sacrifice. Brooke's poetry is simultaneously celebrated for its representation of the war effort as a noble, patriotic act, as well as explained for its representation of the mentality of soldiers early in the war, before the deadliest and most morale-crushing battles took place. Nonetheless, Brooke's "The Soldier" has withstood over a century of interrogation and remains one of the most recognized writings to emerge from war, particularly the ambition and pride in the opening lines, "If I should die, think only this of me: / That there's some corner of a foreign field / That is for ever England" ("The Soldier" lines 1–3).[7] This act of the soldier preemptively reclaiming power and control over the narrative of their life would become a sought-after position for war writers amid the bureaucracy of army life. For soldier poet successors like Keith Douglas, this determination to possess some sense of control over the direction of their life was instrumental as the world spun further into the chaos of World War II.

Keith Douglas's concentrated and passionate zest for the excitement of battle, the intensity of intimacy and love, and the characteristic restlessness of youth were a mix that contributed to his literary accomplishment and rogue attraction to danger. If one looks to Douglas's anticipation of war service, he appeared resigned to the inevitability of his death, proclaiming he would "bloody well make my mark in the war" and justifying this certainty by declaring, "For I will not come back" (Graham, *Keith Douglas* 79). Douglas wrote of death not as a probability but a certainty (Waterman 10), and his life was cut short by a nearby shell burst while on a reconnaissance mission in Normandy. It is reported that there was no mark on his body from the blast that killed him (Goldensohn, *Dismantling Glory* 173). Whether fueled by a fatalist or realist frame of mind, Douglas was pragmatic about the possibility he might not survive war. Still, what caused Douglas to possess such willingness and longing to face danger? Why had he preemptively accepted death in his poems? For Keith Douglas, the use of self-elegy in his poetry is a recasting of traditional self-elegies in war poetry, a channeling of fears, and an affirmation of life, existence, and purpose.

Douglas entered World War II with the unique knowledge of that which preceded him, but not yet the experience, an embodiment of T. S. Eliot's response to the idea that "'The dead writers are remote from us because we know so much more than they did'": "Precisely, and they are that which we know" ("Tradition and the Individual Talent" 43). Douglas knew the prevailing lessons and warnings of the First World War poets, and his 1941 poem "Simplify me when I'm dead" recasts Rupert Brooke's "The Soldier," both of which were written in anticipation of combat death. To employ the diction of Adam Piette, World War II ushered in a "redefinition" of poetic genres such as the elegy (13). While both poets are asking to be remembered, a key distinction between these two poems is that Douglas is seeking purpose for his life as an individual through the reduction of the ornamental components of the body, while Brooke is seeking remembrance for his life as a symbol of British sacrifice and purpose. Furthermore, as Vernon Scannell explains, "Though Brooke's 'The Soldier' and Douglas's 'Simplify me when I'm dead' are both self-elegies, Brooke is posing a hypothetical ('If I should die . . . ') while Douglas is certain he will be killed at war ('Simplify me when I'm dead')" (*Not Without Glory* 39).[8] Since Brooke is writing before experiencing battle, his seeming fearlessness contributes to the mythic power of "The Soldier." While "Simplify me when I'm dead" is also written before battle, Douglas knows from the collective knowledge of First World War death tolls and Allied struggles in the early years of World War II that it is conceivable that dying is a likely outcome of deployment. As reinforced by Ted Hughes in the introduction to Douglas's *The Complete Poems*, "To a degree the overall shaping psychological influence on the Second World War was knowledge of the fearful lessons of the First" (xxiii). This distinction between the two poets and generations is what categorizes Brooke's poem as a fearless battle cry and ode to Britain, while Douglas's poem is an introspective seeking of a purpose for one's life.

Despite the mix of bravery and recklessness with which Douglas conducted himself in North Africa, "Simplify me when I'm dead" is a poem written out of the fear that one will not be remembered or understood. It is completely rational that a soldier training in advance of deployment would be thinking of mortality, "particular memories" ("line 13), "the opinions I held" (line 15), and "what I left" (line 16). First World War soldier poets who died in service such as Rupert Brooke, Wilfred Owen, Edward Thomas, and Isaac Rosenberg are remembered in part by their personal and published writings but also in piecemeal fashion by those who knew them. Cognizant of this, Douglas imagines in the fourth stanza how, after he dies, "a learned man will say / 'He was of such a type and intelligence,' no more" (lines 10–11). This speculation over how he will be posthumously remembered boils down to the interactions he had, and the characteristics observed by those who knew him, "but incidents will be no guide" (line 17). Douglas is arguing that the words not the deeds will shape the memory of an individual in the eyes of others. It is through hindsight that Douglas will be remembered in simpler terms, either as "substance or nothing" (line 22), "deserving mention or charitable oblivion" (line 23). This all-or-nothing perspective is again born out of fear of what the war may bring. For Douglas, fear is unlikely to have suppressed his quest for the excitement and ecstasy of engaging in a life-affirming act like war, but rather pushed him to prove himself.

A few years after writing "Simplify me when I'm dead" came Douglas's memoir *Alamein to Zem Zem*, in which he wrote, "To say I thought of the battle of Alamein as an ordeal sounds pompous: but I did think of it as an important test I was interested in passing" (5). Unsurprisingly, Douglas's sentiment about war as a test one longs to pass is a clear echo of what Christopher Isherwood wrote in his 1938 book *Lions and Shadows*. As a major writer, intermittent partner of W. H. Auden, and firsthand observer of Berlin in the late 1920s and early 1930s, Isherwood described an upbringing similar to that of Vernon Scannell in that, "Like most of my generation, I was obsessed by a complex of terrors and longings connected with the idea 'War.' 'War,' in this purely neurotic sense, meant The Test. The Test of your courage, of your maturity, of your sexual prowess" (52). The long shadow of the First World War is pervasive in the psyche of those who came of age afterward or were born in the following generation, making those fortunate to have not experienced war feel they had to prove themselves in its wake. Isherwood continues, "Subconsciously, I believe, I longed to be subjected to this test," but he "dreaded failure so much . . . that, consciously, I denied my longing to be tested" (52). Douglas's use of the same language to describe the same predicament could either be a coincidence or, again, a recasting of earlier influential writers. As someone who grew up largely without the presence of his father, Douglas was determined to prove himself in war, a quest to prove one's masculinity.[9] Rather than being immobilized by these fears of death, purposelessness, and not filling a prescribed role expected of men during wartime, Douglas rushed toward his "call to adventure" and war experience with fear as motivation.

Keith Douglas, while being afraid of "perishing into an ordinary existence," certainly exercised the initiative to avoid such a fate (Douglas, *The Letters* 107). Among the most frequently retold stories of Douglas's wartime escapades is his decision to abandon his post as a camouflage officer, commandeer an army truck, and travel twenty miles to El Alamein to rejoin his regiment in the action at the front (Stallworthy, "Douglas"). Despite these actions being significant breaches of protocol, he was a welcome addition to a squadron desperate for reinforcements after suffering many casualties. Douglas took particular gratification in being told by his driver, "I like you sir. You're shit or bust you are" (Douglas, *Alamein to Zem Zem* 7). While this was a risky decision, Douglas was not content to fall in line with the army's conventions, and this extended to his sense of recasting the role of the poet. In a 1940 poem titled "The Poets," Douglas confronts the embattled reputation of poets, stating, "When we speak, even our words are bad / currency" (lines 8–9) and worrying about how "in a decade or two they'll be extinct" (line 12). The feeling that poetry is becoming a dead language, a no-longer-sufficient medium for a world continually thrust back into armed conflict, is concerning for Douglas.[10] Douglas fears the role of the poet is obsolete, that "we ourselves are already phantoms; / boneless, substanceless, wanderers" equally ineffective to save people (lines 13–14). Though Douglas in this self-elegiac moment is already counting himself and the poets among the dead, he feels poets have a responsibility of persistence, that they "must advance for ever, always belated" (line 18). While the belatedness referenced at the end of the poem is an admission that poetry is always reflective, lacking some measurement of immediacy, he holds firm to the belief that "we must advance," and that there is purpose in adding to the record of history.

In "Simplify me when I'm dead" and "The Poets," Keith Douglas uses self-elegy for the dual purpose of affirming the life of the individual and the purpose of poetry, respectively. Douglas recasts self-elegy to maintain a sense of control over the narrative of soldiers at war. Self-elegy is one way for the individual to transform the fear of death into an excuse to prove oneself. Both Keith Douglas and Christopher Isherwood viewed war as a test one had to pass, a gateway into the world of masculinity and self-worth. This quest for control, self-affirmation, and channeling fears into strengths are in themselves examples of one attempting to mark their position, to create a permanent record of one's existence in the face of perceived death. These efforts by Douglas to preemptively declare one's purpose align with a letter he wrote to friend, J. C. Hall, on 10 August 1943, roughly nine months before his death. Douglas explains the shift in his poetry's prevailing focus, writing, "I never tried to write about war . . . until I had experienced it" (*The Letters* 295). World War II was an undeniable turning point for Douglas, who justified himself to Hall, continuing, "Perhaps all this may make it easier for you to understand why I am writing the way I am and why I shall never go back to the old forms," itself an act of distancing from the past and curating one's own legacy (295). There is solace in knowing one is in control, a rare feeling for individuals in the early 1940s, so even in the anticipation of death Douglas opted to clutch all he could hold and direct his writings and actions with purpose, affirmation, and confidence.

The Presence and Absence of Guilt

How can I live among this gentle
obsolescent breed of heroes, and not weep?

("Aristocrats" lines 9–10)

The burden of guilt, or lack thereof, is one outlet for processing traumatic memory in Keith Douglas's war poems. Considerations of culpability were also present in poetry of the First World War, as seen in Siegfried Sassoon's poems on the corrosive qualities of war and misrepresentations of chivalry, such as a censored draft of his poem "Atrocities," which calls out British soldiers for killing German prisoners. By facetiously remarking in a letter, "But of course these things aren't atrocities when we do them," Sassoon pinpointed the danger of impersonality in wartime, of those who believe their actions can't be judged as those of the enemy would be judged (Alberge). Intrinsic to the reflection prompted by those who write of their war experience are questions of morality. *What is good and evil, and where do I fall on that spectrum? Am I guilty of committing wrongs? Can those wrongs be justified by duty?* In retrospect, these questions were largely quelled after

World War II, both earnestly and facetiously nicknamed "the good war," due to the scale of human atrocity revealed with the discovery of Nazi concentration camps and the extensive bombing of civilian targets. Yet, soldiers still shoulder the weight of their actions, and the presence and absence of guilt is a recurring issue in the poetry of Keith Douglas. Douglas's poems such as "Devils," "How to Kill," and "*Vergissmeinnicht*" confront this internal conflict of whether to carry guilt or act without emotion, revealing moments in which one feels guilt, guiltlessness, and where guilt and sympathy are transposed between soldiers and noncombatants.

While stationed in Egypt in 1942, Keith Douglas wrote "Devils," which begins with a labyrinthine opening sentence that spans the first eight lines of the twenty-line poem. In order to describe "My mind's silence" (line 1), Douglas contrasts it with wood warmed by the "sun's patience" (line 2) awaiting "the arrival of a god" (line 4), before comparing it to a "deceptive quiet" (line 6) like preparing to trap an "idiot crew" (line 8) within a soundless container. Rereading this four-clause sentence is itself like a trap, each word a lynchpin in the construction of syntactical order. The compared and contrasted imagery is ultimately a misdirection that complicates the idea of one's silence, which is inherently an absence. What these disparate comparisons create is the image of one's outer silence and stoicism concealing inner turmoil, as explained in the lines that follow: "Only within they make their noise; / all night, against my sleep, their cries" (lines 9–10). Through the first half of "Devils," readers do not have context for what these troubling thoughts are prompted by, but the second half of the poem invokes imagery of devils inhabiting warfighting spaces, such as "flying in the clouds" (line 12) and "running / on the earth" (lines 12–13). "Devils" continues like a dissection, as if it were possible to traverse the folds of the brain and recognize one's thoughts "imperceptibly spinning / through the black air alive with evils" (lines 13–14). The poem concludes with a separate imperceptibility, that the internal demons "can't hear / the demons talking in the air" (lines 17–18) and that this disconnection could lead to "an alliance of devils" (line 20) if the wall barricading the individual falls. In other words, Douglas is acknowledging the fine line between the evil that one is capable of and the perceived evil of an enemy, the necessity of preventing an "alliance of devils," and maintaining an air of guiltlessness at war.

Although "Devils" remains ambiguous about what specifically has prompted it, Douglas was unafraid to share similar sentiments in his personal letters, such as writing "A conscience is a nuisance" (Graham, *Keith Douglas* 224). This comment was referring to his military service, as Douglas was deciding between serving in a combat-facing role versus being offered a job in military journalism. Douglas felt an obligation to run the same risks as his friends at the front instead of carrying the guilt of maintaining a safer role, writing, "If there seems to be any chance of going into action again I should probably want to go—not that I like action that much, but I don't see why my friends should get blown up while I drop out. . . . I hate fighting but if I stay behind I feel much worse" (224). From Douglas's perspective, either one faces the threat of death or submits to the guilt absorbed from a safe position while one's compatriots are risking their lives.

In contrast to "Devils," Douglas's "How to Kill" is a poem devoid of a mediating impulse. In a complex turn from the binary choice of simple guilt versus guiltlessness, "How to Kill" shows wonder over the ease of murdering another human, and a speaker who has replaced any feeling of guilt with the presumed karma for the actions they take. The amazement the speaker feels over the ease with which one kills at war is encapsulated in the comparisons Douglas makes. In response to making "a man of dust / of a man of flesh" ("How to Kill" lines 13–14), Douglas characterizes this violence as "This sorcery / I do" (lines 14–15). Life transitioning to death, according to Douglas, is as simple as throwing and catching a ball, watching the rise and fall: "Under the parabola of a ball" (line 1) the poem begins, and after "the ball fell in my hand" (line 4) it is a revelation for the speaker: "*Behold a gift designed to kill*" (line 6). The image of a parabola is central to the poem, the symmetrical curve of rising and falling, which the *Oxford English Dictionary* in part defines as "The path of a projectile under the influence of gravity follows a curve of this shape." Not only does the poem track the narrative of one group of soldiers firing on another, having calculated the flight path and aimed accordingly, but the form of the poem does the same. As described by Sebastian Owen, "How to Kill" embodies "parabolic features" such as the "ABCCBA rhyme scheme" (79). While the center couplet of each of the poem's four sestet stanzas is rhyme demarcating a closeness, the mirrored first and sixth lines, and second and fifth lines are like distant echoes, reverberations of a separated oneness. The use of both perfect and imperfect rhymes for these parabolic stanzas echoes the gradients of similarity and difference between similarly situated soldiers from opposing sides.

What a reader may instinctively look for in a poem about killing is a sign of conscience, but does the speaker in "How to Kill" *feel* anything about his actions? If one strips away the childlike wonder over "How easy it is to make a ghost" (line 18), there are two moments of measurable humanity in the poem. The first instance of a suppressed conscience is moments before the kill shot, when the speaker observes how his target "smiles, and moves about in ways / his mother knows" (lines 9–10). By envisioning the enemy combatant as a son, someone whose family is concerned for his safety, the speaker admits to viewing the enemy as human. The second instance of a conscience is after firing the fatal blow, the speaker is sinister in admiration of the violence committed: "Being damned, I am amused / to see the centre of love diffused" (lines 15–16). To self-identify as damned, one has presumably come to terms with wrongdoing, believing repercussions for behavior will be returned at a later moment, like the curve of a parabola returning. The speaker, having killed others, knows that the counterbalance to his actions is that he too will face death. Therefore, the guilt one would ordinarily expect to feel is embedded in the speaker and suppressed, embodiment of the retribution that will eventually come their way.

Two of Keith Douglas's most popular poems, "How to Kill" and "*Vergissmeinnicht*," both implore the reader to "look" (Kendall, *Modern English War Poetry* 154). In both poems, this command directs our attention as if meaning, *don't look away,* as well as offering a conclusive point. Douglas wants his readers to see and, through seeing, understand. This emphasis on showing readers the war was equal parts journalistic impulse and resistance toward the notion that the poets of the First World War had said all that needed to be conveyed about the realities of modern warfare. Gill Plain argues, "Douglas's frustration articulates the fear that the writers of the First World War had somehow had the last word on the horror of war, but this sense of inevitable repetition was accompanied by an equally pervasive sense of obligation" (39). "*Vergissmeinnicht*" is a model distillation of these competing motives. The poem lays bare haunting images of soldier corpses, particularly in the penultimate stanza in which flies crawl over the exposed skin (line 18), the desert has blown dust onto the open eyes (line 19), and "the burst stomach like a cave" (line 20). Douglas is lending his uncensored observational eye to sights of the desert war through unnerving visceral descriptions.

In addition to this sense of obligation toward presenting the war as he experienced it, the desire for poems of World War II to carry weight in the wake of First World War poetry can be found in the subtleties of Douglas's verse. Much of the published analysis of *"Vergissmeinnicht"* focuses on the content of the third stanza until the end of the poem, while the opening lines are often overlooked due to not having as memorable or jarring imagery. What would ordinarily seem like routine scene-setting in the opening two stanzas can be revisited for their subtle thematical depth. *"Vergissmeinnicht"* begins:

> Three weeks gone and the combatants gone
> returning over the nightmare ground
> we found the place again, and found
> the soldier sprawling in the sun.

(lines 1–4)

The first line offers an atypical setting for a poem by an active-duty soldier, the aftermath of the battlefield weeks after the fighting has concluded. A desert battlefield empty except for the human and equipment wreckage positions the poem at a moment of reflection. *"Vergissmeinnicht"* prompts questions of what happens to the spaces of war after the battle concludes, and how the sights of those landscapes can inform opinion of the brutality of war. The deceased soldier "sprawling in the sun" is an anonymous figure at the outset of the poem, yet readers return to these lines with the retrospective knowledge that this soldier had a lover named *"Steffi"* (line 11). Even though death is inevitable in war, the act of humanizing the enemy after death heightens the tragedy of war. This stanza also recasts the desert landscape as a place that has been embedded with new meaning, referring to it as "the nightmare ground." As an extension of how the First World War "changed the way poets approach the pastoral mode," Douglas supplants the wonder and exoticism of North Africa seen from British eyes with a landscape equal to the ruined fields of Flanders now synonymous with war (S. Owen, "When There Are So Many" 113). By repurposing pastoral imagery as deathly landscapes, poets of the First World War subverted the notion of the pastoral, while Douglas's desert battlefields were already wastelands in the traditional sense of the pastoral. *"Vergissmeinnicht"* coincides with the process of grief, a series of reactions outlined by Sandra M. Gilbert in her analysis of First World War poetry: "first, a meditation on the actual scene of dying; second, a preoccupation with the literal body of the dead one; third, a retelling of the details of the past as if to ensure that they have both passed and passed away; and fourth, a resignation that sometimes involves a hopeful (but often sardonically hopeful or fantastic) resolution and sometimes merely a stoic acquiescence in the inevitable" (Gilbert 182–83). Gilbert's steps through the process of grief are mirrored in "*Vergissmeinnicht.*" First, the opening of the poem is a return to the scene of dying, followed by the second step of inspecting the enemy soldier's dead body. Third, Douglas retells the past of the soldier by both describing his last living movements as "he hit my tank . . . / like the entry of a demon" (lines 7–8) and confirming his death through descriptions of the soldier's hardened "equipment" (line 15) and "burst stomach" (line 20). Lastly, Douglas concludes with a "sardonically hopeful" note, to use Gilbert's words, as he categorizes the two identities of the dead soldier, "lover and killer" (line 21), as having become one in death. Describing the deceased soldier as being made whole again, despite being dead, disfigured, and never to be seen again by "*Steffi,*" is a cynical undercutting of any possibility of a hopeful resolution.

Douglas's focus in both "How to Kill" and "*Vergissmeinnicht*" on the casualties of war shows that he does not need to divert the poems to tell the reader what he is thinking or feeling about the actions being described. By extension Douglas frames the steps of processing grief in "*Vergissmeinnicht,*" and the reader can intuit feelings of guilt and sadness without being directly told. Since Douglas's extrospective poetry often refrains from including his personal opinions and emotions, readers are often left to believe Douglas's speaker is an emotionless warrior, an automaton incapable of feeling regret for the acts of violence he commits with wonder and ease. The feelings of guilt are suppressed in "How to Kill," a necessary dampening of one's emotions in order to complete the tasks of the tank crew. The speaker's emotion is absent from "*Vergissmeinnicht*" except for what readers can surmise based on the steps of grief and the recognition of selfhood for the deceased soldier. In both "How to Kill" and "*Vergissmeinnicht,*" the dead enemy soldiers are humanized through their connections to loved ones back at home. Similarly, equating oneself and the enemy through shared traits is the central conceit of "Devils," in which the speaker must acknowledge the potential for all humans to commit evil acts. These poems highlight the necessary compartmentalization a soldier must exact to balance feelings of guilt and sympathy for enemy combatants alongside a duty to one's country when fulfilling a role in the military.

What War Leaves Behind: Lovers, Memories, and Bodies

Throughout his poems before and during war, Keith Douglas counterbalances a longing to be remembered with the fear of being forgotten. With his premonitions from Oxford that he would "bloody well make my mark in this war," Douglas's premonitions of death, writing self-elegiac poems, and drive to have an impact were all attempts to validate his memory and establish a legacy (Graham, *Keith Douglas* 79). The certainty of death Douglas felt was not the only conduit through which he would channel his thoughts, as seen by his engagement with what war leaves in its wake. Particularly in the poems preceding Douglas's deployment, the manifestation of his fear of leaving lovers surfaces, such as in the 1940 poems "Farewell Poem" and "The Prisoner." Also speaking to the remains of war are Douglas's active-service poems like 1943's "Dead Men," in which Douglas again describes human corpses to highlight what lasts of the war dead, both physically and in their emotional wake. Another form of war remnants are the soldiers themselves, as shown in 1942's "I Listen to the Desert Wind" as a speaker longs for the lover who has moved on in his absence. These poems are derived from starkly different perspectives, as they were written preceding and during deployment, yet both perspectives speak to an awareness of what war puts at risk. Using literal separations and metaphorical divisions between people, Douglas exemplifies the emotions of a soldier preparing for war and the importance of replacing those emotions with experiences once one has seen combat.

One literal and metaphorical distance generated by war is the separation between people. While the distance created between a soldier and the loved ones who remain at the home front is a calculable example of spatial separation, the emotional separation that individuals undergo is harder to quantify. In the early years of World War II, when Douglas was still a student at the University of Oxford, his poems speak from the position of a man on the cusp of incontrovertible change. Fears that rising tensions and aggressions would boil over in Europe had been confirmed, and the involved nations were particularly mindful of reenacting the overwhelming loss of life and destruction of nations. Furthermore, European nations were wholly unprepared for this conflict to exceed the First World War in terms of human destruction and damage to cities, infrastructure, and morale. These concerns percolate in poems of the late 1930s and early 1940s, most notably in W. H. Auden's foreboding sentiment "Mismanagement and grief: / We must suffer them all again" ("September 1, 1939" lines 32–33). In 1940, at twenty years old, Douglas wrote poems that tremble with anticipation for his entry to the war and the life he would be departing.

"Farewell Poem" echoes Douglas's "Canoe," both marking moments of serenity before leaving for war. "Farewell Poem" begins with a request for an unnamed "you" to remember their time together: "Please, on a day falling in summer, / recall how being tired, you and I / . . . fell asleep embraced" (lines 1–2, 6). The speaker pleads to be remembered, asking to be validated and mentally memorialized, and therefore kept alive in memory. The undercurrent of this serene scene "among the idle branches by the river" (line 3) is the knowledge that in this moment of innocence the two individuals "had not thought" (line 10) their "day was complete behind us and wiped out" (line 12). Teetering between the naivety of youth and the weight of experience and maturity, the speaker recognizes in retrospect that those carefree days falling asleep by the river are gone, cannot be reclaimed, are "wiped out." Now, the speaker and their companion "are broken apart" (line 13) as each "keep pain prisoner" (line 14). Similarly, in "Canoe," the speaker tries to assure his lover by downplaying the possibility a "sudden fearful fate / can deter my shade wandering next year / from a return" (lines 9–11). Even the ABBA rhyme scheme in "Canoe" across the four-quatrain poem suggests a sending off and return, though the shift from perfect rhymes like "last"/"aghast" and "part"/"art" in the first stanza to near rhymes like "fate"/"boat" in stanza three or "Iffley"/"lightly" in stanza four perhaps imply a speaker who has been changed by his "sudden fearful fate." In both "Farewell Poem" and "Canoe," the companions are discussing being physically separated but also being divorced from an innocent life that cannot be reclaimed, supplanted by the imagery and language of war.

In the second half of "Farewell Poem," Douglas takes umbrage with a question on the unfairness of growing up, asking, "Who is it that is pleased now we are sad," as if someone is directly responsible for the loss of one's youth (line 15). With a rising pessimistic feeling, the speaker believes someone has stripped them of their joy and "has got and has the happiness we had" (line 17), but vindictively takes some relief from believing "soon his misery will start, / for all delight is God's impermanent bluff" (lines 20–21). In the final stanza, the speaker warns of the coming retribution that God will deliver, writing "God is waiting with unexpended pain / and will not bless you my dark afflicted love" (lines 28–29). At this point that readers can glean that Douglas is not just speaking of a karmic balancing but of a looming death wrought from above. It would be difficult to envision this imagery of figures emerging from the air "backed with fires and the red cloud" and not think of bombing raids, particularly given the context of the poem's composition in 1940, the same year the Blitz began (line 26). This imagery of threatening planes bringing death from above was further popularized by T. S. Eliot in "Little Gidding," the final section of *Four Quartets*. Eliot, who served as a fire warden in London during the Blitz, wrote:

> The dove descending breaks the air
> With flame of incandescent terror
> Of which the tongues declare
> The one discharge from sin and error.
> The only hope, or else despair
>   Lies in the choice of pyre or pyre–
>   To be redeemed from fire by fire.

>   (Eliot, "Little Gidding," part IV)

For Eliot, who had read some of Douglas's poetry sent to him by Edmund Blunden, the shared experience of living in England as the country was under attack by Nazi Germany was a galvanizing moment. Such was the case for many civilian poets living in the United Kingdom during this time, such as H.D., who wrote *Trilogy*, and Dylan Thomas, who wrote the poem "A Refusal to Mourn the Death, by Fire, of a Child in London," both of which took inspiration from the Blitz. The fear of death and the surroundings of a destroyed city were pervasive images for poets during the early years of World War II and served as stark reminders of an unfair life that can quickly transition from calm days asleep at the river's edge to anticipating bombs from above.

    Such calm before anticipation of war is also exemplified in "The Prisoner," a poem Douglas wrote after leaving Oxford while at the Royal Military College, before deployment to North Africa. A companion poem to the aforementioned "Farewell Poem" and "Canoe," "The Prisoner" documents the longing for the life one has just left, and the lover who has been left behind. A more overtly autobiographical poem, "The Prisoner" addresses the *you* directly, beginning "Today, Cheng, I touched your face," referring to a woman he fell in love with at Oxford named Yingcheng (line 1). Those familiar with Douglas's later work may recognize her name from the poem "To Kristin Yingcheng Olga Milena," one of Douglas's last poems, written as an ode to the women he had loved in which he will return to them the essences they shared with him. To be done with their memory, Douglas states he will "give back perforce / the sweet wine to the grape" (lines 7–8). In retrospect, Douglas is returning to each woman the memories they have imprinted on him, as if to absolve oneself of attachment.

"The Prisoner" transitions from love poem to one in which the speaker wishes to die to be freed from desire. Shackled by unrequited love from a bygone time, the speaker touches "a mask stretched on the stone– // hard face of death" (lines 12–13). This moment of tactile engagement generates "the urge / to escape the bright flesh and emerge / of the ambitious cruel bone" (lines 13–15). In step with "Farewell Poem," "The Prisoner" shifts from gentleness and love to cruelty and death, the only sure and inevitable resolution to the restlessness felt by the speaker. Vernon Scannell positions Douglas as a counterweight to Owen and Sassoon, determining that Douglas is less concerned with the act of killing and the loss of humanity at war (*Not Without Glory* 49). Yet, based on the preoccupations with dread and the impending horrors to come, Douglas's premonitions of war demonstrate a concern for the loss of peace, youth, and love. While Scannell may be correct that Douglas "does not pretend to feel more pity for war's victims than in fact he does feel" (49), as shown in poems like "How to Kill," the fact that loss, death, and destruction are instrumental to war is not lost on Douglas. Jon Stallworthy posited that war poems move readers to feelings of pity, terror, and fury, and in poems like "The Prisoner" and "Farewell Poem," it is Douglas himself who is moved to these emotions in the lead-up to his own war experience (*Survivors' Songs* 194).

In addition to desire, war also leaves behind corpses. Most of Douglas's most well-known poems—"*Vergissmeinnicht*," "How to Kill," the "Landscape with Figures" triptych, "Simplify me when I'm dead," and "Cairo Jag"— contain or ruminate on the image of a dead body. Tim Kendall states that

"The dead body is, overwhelmingly, the central image in Douglas's work, and each corpse poses new ethical challenges for the poet and the reader" (*Modern English War Poetry* 151). Douglas's 1943 poem "Dead Men" muses on the dead body and how the natural world manipulates one's perception of a corpse. "Tonight the moon inveigles them / to love" the poem begins, as if the dead can still be persuaded, let alone to love (lines 1–2). The poem portrays the corpses in various forms of decoration, first in "white dresses" (line 4), then covered by windswept sand "like dolls" (line 12). These descriptions of revenant bodies mislead the reader into a thought that these victims of war died with grace and dignity, though in reality they have transmogrified into grotesque displays of the body subjected to erosive forces of the natural world. The dead bodies are enacted upon by the blowing sand that coats and covers their bodies and the wild dogs that dig to find "a face or a leg / for food" (lines 16–17). Similar to Douglas's equation of destroyed military equipment to foliage, these examples from "Dead Men" repeat the crossover from pastoral to ruination. Douglas wrote "Dead Men" while recuperating from injuries, and it channels imagery used by Wilfred Owen in "Miners" to echo Owen's ruminations on time, death, and sacrificial youth (Graham, *Keith Douglas* 184–85). The similarities of imagery and sentiment in lines of Douglas's "Dead Men," such as "you see your own mind burning yet / and till you stifle in the ground will go on / burning the economical coal of your dreams" (lines 22–24), are difficult to ignore alongside the "sigh of the coal" (line 2) in Owen's "Miners":

> The centuries will burn rich loads
>   With which we groaned,
> Whose warmth shall lull their dreaming lids,
>   While songs are crooned;
> But they will not dream of us poor lads
>   Left in the ground.

> (lines 29–34)

Variations of coal, burning, dreams, the ground, and unacknowledged voices in death are parallels between these poems, Douglas even alluding to Owen's "Miners" by writing, "Then leave the dead in the earth, an organism / not capable of resurrection, like mines" ("Dead Men" lines 25–26). Despite this borrowed imagery, the intended function in each poem is significantly different.

Whereas Owen equates the imagery of 156 miners who died in the 1918 Minnie Pit Disaster in Staffordshire to a generation of dead soldiers, both as a sacrificial and unremembered cost, Douglas is distinctly not trying to make a symbol of the dead (Cooke 213). Both poets are using the literal act of mining the earth for resources, whether coal or shelter, and figurative implications of mining one's mind for memories. Owen acknowledged this extended metaphor by personifying coal as suffering soldiers "Writhing for air," as they would amid poison gas attacks or drowning in mud ("Miners" line 16), when he wrote of "Miners" that he got "mixed up with the War at the end" of the poem (Silkin 217). Owen is concerned with collective memory, suggesting "few remember" (line 20) the charred hearts of those who served and those who "died" (line 22). In exchange for the countless men who died digging into the earth, civilians' lives will prosper, as "The centuries will burn rich loads / With which we groaned" (lines 29–30). Owen's frustration is twofold, an anger toward war causing the unheroic deaths of soldiers, and the absence of recognition for soldiers' sacrifice by those who "will not dream of us poor lads / Lost in the ground" (lines 33–34). Concerned that the death of soldiers is an unacknowledged consequence of war, Owen believes men's lives are thrown into war like coals to a fire, sacrificed for the comfort of others. To Douglas, the war dead are just that, dead, and their concerns are no longer of consequence. Unflinchingly presented, Douglas describes the dead body as something to be acknowledged without a need for symbolic amplification. For example, the poem "Cairo Jag" concludes with the unsettling and dissonant image of "a man with no head" (line 29) left clinging to sweet and memorable reminders of life: "a packet of chocolate and souvenir of Tripoli" (30). In a further attempt for the death of others to occupy some substantive purpose, the final stanza of "Dead Men" philosophizes its way to the same conclusion as "*Vergissmeinnicht*" and "How to Kill," that it is the survivors who must confront what the loss means, the loved ones of the deceased who must carry their grief. Douglas concludes "Dead Men" by arguing, "The prudent mind resolves / on the lover's or the dog's attitude for ever" (lines 35–36). In other words, the forward-thinking individual will transition to those still living, the lover left behind and the wild dog scrounging for food, leaving the dead men of war as remnants of the past.

Douglas also viewed the deployed soldier's former life and loves as things left behind. While stationed between Alexandria and Cairo in the northern Egyptian town of Wadi Natrun, Douglas wrote the poem "I Listen to the Desert Wind" about longing for a former lover. Though desire and pain are the engines of the poem, these feelings are heightened by the secluded desert landscape. The poem begins with a rumination on the staying power of a lover in the mind of a deployed soldier: "I listen to the desert wind / that will not blow her from my mind" (lines 1–2). War introduces a host of new experiences that find their way into the writings of soldiers stationed abroad, yet the extreme experience of combat does not prevent ordinary people from longing for companionship. Douglas compares "the reflection of her face" (line 8) to the way the moon moves "by clouds and cruel tracts of space" (line 6). It is difficult enough to feel alone and unloved, but the speaker's feelings are magnified by being physically secluded for miles in every direction from people and the possibility of new love. He is "sleepless," his mind wanders "Like a bird" who "skims the sands" as he searches for her, or the memory of her (lines 9–10). Resigned to solitude after losing the lover to someone else, Douglas concludes the poem with parallel motions: the lover who will "turn in the dark bed again / and give to him what once was mine" (lines 17–18), and he who will "turn as you turn / and kiss my swarthy mistress pain" (lines 19–20). As much as this poem tackles the familiar longing of love and intimacy, Douglas is equally passing judgment on the distance that war takes individuals from the people and places they love. Unique to Douglas's war poetry is how these relatable themes are cast through the spectrum of desert conflict, and how the bleak landscape of sand, wind-sculpted dunes, and oppressive sunlight is a barrage on the senses. The opposite of the brutal cold captured by war poems such as Wilfred Owen's "Exposure" and Louis Simpson's "The Battle," Douglas is writing of an equally harsh and deadly landscape climate where heat, dehydration, and exposure to the elements are daily threats. Yet, for a poem like "I Listen to the Desert Wind" in which heartbreak seems as dangerous as the elements, the image of a man trying to sleep in the desert, tossing and turning from insomniac visions of his former lover with a new beau, is heightened by the Egyptian desert in which this secluded soul feels exponentially removed from the life he left behind.

Douglas's poems of transition are noteworthy given the transitory rhetoric during the war by major literary and political figures. For example, American poet T.S. Eliot, who had become a British citizen in 1927 and who lived in London throughout the war years, spoke of transitory moments in some of his greatest works. Eliot's return to writing poetry in the late 1930s and early 1940s was with the incremental publication of *Four Quartets,* arguably the most popular poem of the World War II era. The second section of this poem, "East Coker," was published in 1940 and is bookended by the lines "In my beginning is my end" (line 1) and "In my end is my beginning" (line 211). The ideas of end and beginning, death and rebirth, and war and peace are woven throughout the poem. Exploring these dichotomies appealed to many who sought a life beyond war, or salvation beyond the perilous state of their lives during wartime. Poetry readers during this era would no doubt find parallels in a speech delivered by Winston Churchill on 10 November 1942, in which he proclaimed, "Now this is not the end. It is not even the beginning of the end. But it is, perhaps, the end of the beginning" (Churchill 342). Perhaps it is of little coincidence that Churchill delivered these remarks on the eve of the First World War's armistice anniversary. To renew a sense of purpose and the political and military will to continue the war against the emboldened Nazis, Churchill invokes the same rhetorical construction of Eliot's argument that humankind has reached a decisive moment in history in which they must make a choice about their direction forward. In contrast to using this end-of-days approach of Eliot and Churchill, Douglas is speaking of specific ends and beginnings to capture the enormity of the moment. Douglas highlights the end of his youth and young love, leaving behind the peaceful and innocent prewar life; and he ushers in direct exposure to corpses and the worst of what war offers. Douglas's imagery of corpses and the losses of war falls in line with his ideas of needing to write journalistic and "extrospective" poetry. For Douglas, there is simply too much at stake to be writing in vague, philosophical ruminations, and so he turns toward poetry that will serve as a historical record.

Keith Douglas did not intend for his brand of poetic reportage to avoid emotion but rather to "find different ways of provoking it" (Kendall, *Modern English War Poetry* 160). Douglas is portraying images of dead bodies in disgraced situations (eaten by dogs in "Dead Men" and teased for a rigor mortis–induced erection in "*Vergissmeinnicht*") without providing an emotionally driven commentary. Such imagery allows the reader to fill in the emotional gaps, to make deductions about the nature of war and whether nations sacrifice too much humanity by sending generations away to kill and be killed. Poems such as "Farewell Poem," "The Prisoner," and "Dead Men" paint a fuller picture of Douglas before and after his transition to military service. These poems show the emotions he felt anticipating war, and the emotionally callous soldier who believed showing the war as it was would be more impactful than trying to tell an audience how they should feel about a dead body. What defines the early 1940s for Douglas, what would be his final years of life, are the things war leaves behind: lovers and the memories they created on the banks of tranquil rivers, their touch, their youth, and the bodies of soldiers and civilians. Each abandoned body is proof of having lived, and leaves the reader in a limbo, aware that the only guarantee of armed conflict is sacrificed life.

■ ■ ■

Since no soldier poet received critical acclaim during World War II in the way that famous trench poets had from the First World War, Douglas projected in a 1943 essay "Poets in This War": "it seems to me that the whole body of English war poetry of this war, civil and military, will be created after war is over" (*The Letters* 353). While Douglas was largely correct, in that much of the poetry published on the war, and that is being advocated here, was not written until after the war, there are notable exceptions. In addition to poets such as Randall Jarrell, Karl Shapiro, and soldiers who died in service such as Alun Lewis, Keith Douglas himself was a poet who published during World War II and is an invaluable figure for transcribing aspects of the North African theater through a unique, individual perspective. Despite this body of diverse and innovative work, opinions persist by critics such as William Logan, who believe "It's shameful to find almost nothing in Keith Douglas or Sidney Keyes, or Louis Simpson or Lincoln Kirstein worth reading now" (196). While Logan may be attempting to be intentionally incendiary by discrediting the aforementioned war poets, his argument that a new World War II poetry canon should include Eliot's "Little Gidding" and the writings of civilians entirely misses the reality that the established canon of World War II poetry *is* overwhelmingly comprised of civilian poetry, and the likes of Eliot (186). Logan plays both sides of the argument, though, admitting that "Perhaps it's time to reexamine the old prejudice" against World War II poems compared to those of the First

(106). While brilliant works by civilians such as Eliot, Auden, and Miłosz give unique perspectives of the war, so too does work by combatants who saw the war firsthand. Douglas's war poetry demonstrates his extrospective approach by elevating sensory and emotional engagement with conceptions of distance and traumatic memory. Keith Douglas's poetry is an ideal example of Catharine Savage Brosman's explanation of the functions of war literature, efforts that reflect "the fundamental drive to life and its contrary, the fear and fascination of death, ever-present and universal" (96). By tackling issues of distance and mechanization, transmitting desert landscapes, writing self-elegies, exploring the presence and absence of guilt, and lamenting that which war leaves behind, Douglas provides an indelible testimonial on the North African campaign and the psyche of the soldier at war.

3

RICHARD HUGO

REVISITING THE SITES
OF TRAUMA

> You know the mind, how it comes on the scene again
> and makes tiny histories of things . . .
> And we return to the field of our first games where
> when we find it again, we look hard for the broken toy,
> the rock we called home plate, evidence to support our claim
> our lives really happened.
>
> —RICHARD HUGO, "Letter to Matthews from Barton Street Flats"

Of the five poets concentrated on in this body of research, Richard Hugo is undoubtedly the war poet least recognized as such. As evidenced by scarce representation in anthologies, critical analyses, and broader cultural recognition, Hugo's war poetry has garnered little literary and cultural attention relative to that of other soldier poets. In her essay "War Poetry in the USA," Margot Norris criticizes one of the only anthologies that identifies Hugo as a war poet, Harvey Shapiro's *Poets of World War II*. Norris writes, "Taken as a whole, these poems exemplify another reason why their response to World War II has not achieved the same public visibility and cultural significance as the poetry of the Great War" (43), and she describes Hugo's poetry as exhibiting innocence as a response "to violence and endangerment" (47). While Norris elaborates using World War II poetry's thematic and formal diversity as an example of the differentiation between the world war generations, this line of argument reinforces stereotypes and expectations of what a war poem *should* be rather than being open to what a war poem *can* be. Literature, like all forms of art and expression, evolves over time, and one cannot expect war poetry to remain in a singular mode, particularly when war itself evolves. Norris's suggestion that World War II poetry suffers in popularity because of its stylistic diversity, while one possible explanation, casts a broad range of experience and style as a weakness rather than seeing limitless possibility as a strength. Hugo's war poetry embodies intellectual engagement with the past by spelunking the caverns of the mind and serves as an argument that war is too world-changing an event not to learn anything from.

Hugo is nearly universally omitted from anthologies as a war poet and is only marginally recognized as such by modern scholars of war writing. Harvey Shapiro's anthology *Poets of World War II* (2003), Leon Stokesbury's *Articles of War: A Collection of Poetry about World War II* (1990), and Lorrie Goldensohn's *American War Poetry* (2006) are the only major anthologies of war poetry in which Hugo appears. Shapiro features "Where We Crashed," "Spinazzola: *Quella Cantina La*," and "Note from Capri to Richard Ryan on the Adriatic Floor," and Stokesbury features "Where We Crashed" and "Mission to Linz." Goldensohn's *American War Poetry* anthology includes one poem by Hugo, "On Hearing a New Escalation," a 1975 poem from his collection *What Thou Lovest Well Remains American*. Yet, this last poem is in response to the Vietnam War, which Goldensohn categorizes as such, meaning his World War II poems are omitted altogether from the anthology. Goldensohn includes a biographical note acknowledging Hugo's World War II experience flying "many bombing campaigns over the Balkans" and how his postwar returns to Europe produced "several moving poems . . . about war's aftermath," but she does not include them in the anthology (382). Such widespread absence and omission of Hugo's World War II poetry from anthologies means forfeiting the insight that can be gained about the external and internal landscapes of war to which Hugo is an expert witness. Through testimony of memory and delayed returns to the locations of his deployment, Hugo highlights the psychological repercussions and societal ramifications of war's destructiveness. Hugo wrote the majority of his World War II poems retrospectively in the 1960s, notably in the 1969 collection *Good Luck in Cracked Italian,* which contains Hugo's largest concentration of poems either directly or tangentially related to the war. Critics did not wait through this period of postwar decompression before cementing the poetic legacy of the World War II generation. The lack of revision to that legacy in recent decades largely bypasses those whose traumatic stress created a fissure between the war they endured and the ability to confront it in their writing.

Hugo's autobiography is often simplified by reference to a broken home in which he was raised by abusive grandparents, his parents having divorced and been largely absent from his life (Hugo did not meet his father until he was thirty years old) (Hugo, *Real West* 5). In conjunction with an adulthood saddled with depression, a mental breakdown, and alcoholism, Hugo had ample dark inspiration for his poetry even before deploying for service in World War II. Born as Richard Franklin Hogan in 1923, he legally took his stepfather's surname, Hugo, in 1942, volunteered for war service in 1943, deployed in 1944, was officially discharged in 1948, worked as a technical writer for Boeing before becoming a poet and professor, and died of leukemia in 1982 ("Richard Hugo, 1923–1982"). Despite experiencing a number of impressionable life events in the thirty-four years he lived after leaving the military, Hugo and his writing reverberated for decades with the war he experienced in his early twenties.

Hugo's poetic legacy is chiefly as a regionalist representing life in the Pacific Northwest and Northern Plains of America, stemming from his studies at the University of Washington, where he absorbed influence from his professor, poet Theodore Roethke. While some writers bristle at the notion of being categorized as a regionalist, Peter Stitt delineates that a "regionalist writes *out of* a given locale; the local colorist writes only *of* that locale. The regionalist gives an accurate portrayal of the locale but is not limited by it" ("West of Your City" 46). Stitt adds that Hugo has "established himself as the preeminent poet of the Pacific Northwest" and praises his poetry of both physical and psychological landscapes (48). Beyond literary criticism, historians of the Pacific Northwest such as Raymond Gastil and Barnett Singer also claim Hugo as one of their own, categorizing him as "a Northwest poet" who "emphasized the regional landscape" (167). Frances McCue, the poet and former director of the Richard Hugo House, a literary arts center in Seattle, published a book, *The Car That Brought You Here,* retracing Hugo's steps to small towns in the Northwest to better understand the places that inspired Hugo, and into which Hugo breathed life. Hugo's years spent teaching at the University of Montana have also left him with the reputation of being the most famous "Montana poet" (Bolin).

A number of factors have contributed to the canonical neglect of Hugo's World War II poems, including (1) the decentralized landscape imagery of World War II in which air, sea, and land battles were fought, compared to the primarily centralized trench warfare of the Western Front in the First World War; (2) the delayed writing and publication of Hugo's war poems (Hugo published his first collection of poems, *A Run of Jacks,* in 1961, fifteen years after the war's end); (3) a cultural shift toward film as a narrative medium; (4) Hugo's war poems being rarely about battle itself, in favor of the psychological implications and repercussions of war; (5) Hugo's poetic reputation and legacy having primarily been shaped by identifying him as a regionalist whose muse is the Pacific Northwest; and (6) the persistent misconception that World War II produced little poetry of note. While Hugo's regionalist poetry is not in dispute, it is too limiting to assume his poems about fishing, failing mill towns, and rural desolation were his only contribution to twentieth-century poetry.

Hugo's regionalist tendencies extend to his war poems, using landscapes as canvases, such as the airfields and surrounding farms and villages in rural Italy where he was stationed for his thirty-five bombing missions. Hugo used the dichotomy of ground and air to explore the real and mystical, security and danger, internal and external, and sense and the unknowable. Richard Hugo's legacy is chiefly defined by spaces, such as the landscapes of his upbringing in the Pacific Northwest, his war service in Italy and his postwar return to Europe, the small towns scattered between open stretches of Montana, the Scottish Highlands and islands where he lived briefly, and his eventual return home to Seattle. Hugo's military service as a U.S. Army Air Force bombardier formed irrepressible, troubling, and invasive memories marked by the literal distance traversed between the bomber and his targets miles below. For decades after the war, Hugo carried the memory of the skyscapes he navigated and the landscapes where he was stationed. The time needed for Hugo to put words to the events that shaped his life stretched decades, each era of his life becoming more easily distinguishable as time passes. As Hugo suggested about William Stafford, a landscape poet is one "who uses places and experiences in those places as starting points for poems. For such a poet . . . there are two landscapes, one external and one internal" ("Problems with Landscapes" 33). Hugo's poetry uses the external and internal as coequal landscapes, one used to translate the experience of the other.

This balance between the external and internal landscapes is an apt parallel to the ways Hugo responds to issues of distance and traumatic memory throughout his poetic output on the war. As a bombardier in the Fifteenth Air Force's B-24 Flying Fortresses, Hugo perceived the war much differently from the ground combat experiences of Louis Simpson and Keith Douglas. While the infantryman Simpson and tank commander Douglas noted the distances between combatants compared to descriptions of trench warfare by their First World War predecessors, war felt like a new concept altogether for bombardiers, separated from their targets by miles and infrequently seeing up close the damage of their actions. Although Hugo described himself as the "world's worst" bomber, he developed empathy for civilians who would be on the receiving end of his bombs (*Real West* 106). Hugo's internal struggles and empathy for others amplified with return visits to Italy and Sarajevo decades after the war. In an attempt to reclaim himself from the past and give meaning and purpose to the psychological grip the war had on his mind, Hugo placed immense value on refinding the locations of his war service as if returning to them would make whole a broken set of memories.

In addition to analyzing Hugo's use of distance as a thematic keystone to his work, this chapter will also outline Hugo's confrontation with traumatic memory in his poems. Hugo revisited the sites of his traumatic war experience later in life to try to ease the war memories that haunted him, to compare his memory to the changed places decades later, and to attempt to give meaning to unexplainable feelings and experiences of the war. Furthermore, Hugo turns to ekphrastic poetry to describe artistic creations that serve as channels for the recognition and confrontation of war guilt. Notably, this process leads to different outcomes than those of Keith Douglas. While both Douglas and Hugo explore the nature and prominence of guilt as an engine for reflection, Douglas refrains from overtly accepting or expressing guilt, and Hugo admits culpability even when acknowledging his actions were part of a larger moral mission of peace. Richard Hugo is a testament to the need to revisit World War II poetry and to evolve and more fully recognize work written in the aftermath of war.

The Evolution of Testimonial War Poetry from First World War Sympathy for Soldiers to Hugo's Empathy for World War II Civilians

As posited by Antony Rowland in *Poetry as Testimony*, poetry on war and other traumatic events has historically served the purpose of testimonial writing (1).[1] The literature of war and "near-universality of war" as a subject of storytelling has worn many faces, starting with grand narratives glorifying battle, heroism, and the change of power through physical domination (Brosman 85). Though there are many literary examples expressing caution toward the brutality of men at war, the poem as a method of challenging conventional thought toward war was particularly notable during the First World War. In *Coming out of War*, Janis P. Stout identifies six characteristics of a new style of poetry after the midpoint of the First World War, which include "Irony . . . Bluntness of visual details . . . A reluctance to use marching rhythms . . . Ambiguity and disorder . . . sadness and misery . . . Ruined landscapes" (40–41). The importance of "bluntness of visual details," or realism, can be tracked in the evolution of world war poetry. The poetry of Wilfred Owen and Siegfried Sassoon conveyed stark realities of war brutality in direct contradiction to the propaganda efforts of the British government and media. The environmental stressors and trauma of trench warfare experienced by Owen and Sassoon directly influenced their shift from unencumbered duty to generating sympathy for conflicted combatants. These competing narratives were reengaged a quarter century later when Richard Hugo inherited this precedent of realist truth-telling by conveying the ambivalence and guilt of his World War II participation, resulting in greater empathy toward civilians during wartime.

In Britain, the First World War dichotomized public opinion of war and presented "a profound challenge to accepted national values" (Hobsbawm 29). To encourage British men to enlist and join the First World War, Jessie Pope's jingoist poem "The Call" exudes patriotism and implies that reluctance to fight is a show of cowardice. Pope begins with a call to arms, writing, "Who's for the trench— / Are you, my laddie?" (lines 1–2). Challenging Pope's cheery call, Wilfred Owen depicted the horror of poison gas attacks and conveyed the traumatic resonance of images of "guttering, choking, drowning" soldiers that haunt his dreams ("Dulce Et Decorum Est" line 16). James Anderson Winn declared that the role of war poetry is to "counter the mindless simplifications of war propaganda," and Wilfred

Owen's "Dulce Et Decorum Est" is a prime example of this resistance in practice (Winn 4). "Dulce Et Decorum Est" supplants Pope's call by imploring readers to envision a scene of war that precipitates Pope's vision of victory marches: "If you could hear, at every jolt, the blood / Come gargling from the froth-corrupted lungs" (lines 21–22). Owen wants his readers to visualize the visceral suffering of soldiers, and this new style of war progressively erased the chivalric conceptions of battle that Pope was invoking, alluding to previous wars in which fighting occurred at arm's length. Owen concludes "Dulce Et Decorum Est" with biting sarcasm, addressing Pope and all those who promoted the war effort without concern for the cost of soldiers' lives:

> My friend, you would not tell with such high zest
> To children ardent for some desperate glory,
> The old Lie: *Dulce et decorum est*
> *Pro patria mori.*
>
> (lines 25–28)

Quoting Horace's Latin phrase after which the poem is named, "Dulce et decorum est / Pro patria mori" translates to, "How sweet and honorable it is to die for one's country" (Cassidy 1). Owen ironically repurposes this "old lie" to end the poem, at which point it is clear after the suffering he has outlined that "sweet" and "honorable" are opposites to the horrific and undignified deaths of soldiers in the trenches.[2] Similarly, optimism also eroded for Siegfried Sassoon as the First World War devolved into a war of attrition, as evidenced by blunt observations such as, "O German mother dreaming by the fire, / While you are knitting socks to send to your son, / His face is trodden deeper in the mud" ("Glory of Women" lines 12–14). The change in sentiment exemplified in the poetry of Wilfred Owen and Siegfried Sassoon sympathized with the plight of soldiers in the squalor of the trenches. Though Richard Hugo was among the apprehensive voices of World War II who wrote poetry rooted in realism, his poem "Letter to Simic from Boulder" shifts focus from pity and sympathy for soldiers to expressing guilt and empathy for the civilians killed or traumatized by war.

At a literary gathering in San Francisco in the 1970s, Hugo met Serbian American poet Charles Simic. As the two spoke, Simic recalled his experience as a five-year-old in Belgrade, Serbia, where he survived a 1943 bombing campaign by the United States, who were attempting to cut off Nazi movement by destroying bridges over the Danube River. In a moment of great coincidence, Hugo recognized that he was also present in Simic's story because he was one of the airmen who was dropping those bombs. Hugo was among the fleet whose bombs narrowly avoided Simic, including an unexploded bomb outside of his house. This realization humbled an apologetic Hugo, who later addressed this moment in a direct, autobiographical poem titled "Letter to Simic from Boulder." Hugo's stance that American military involvement in World War II was simply a job that needed to be done is captured in the lines, "I was interested mainly in staying alive, that moment / the plane jumped free from the weight of bombs and we went home" (lines 12–13). Hugo would later write in his autobiography, *The Real West Marginal Way,* that the insane contradictions of war, such as bombing for peace, are even more apparent "when a war is as close to being 'justified' as was World War II" (95). Though clouded by the threat of death, Hugo treats the mission as if he is a factory worker who punches the clock, works, and punches out, anxious to get home. The impersonality of Hugo's war service is clear when he recalls the emotional distance present when "our bomb bays empty, the target forgotten, / the enemy ignored" (lines 33–34). The most telling moment of "Letter to Simic from Boulder" is also its most direct, as Hugo broadens his scope to ruminate on his role in the war, war itself, and the failure to learn from history:

> I don't apologize for the war, or what I was. I was
> willingly confused by the times. I think I even believed
> in heroics (for others, not for me). I believed the necessity
> of that suffering world, hoping it would learn not to do
> it again. But I was young. The world never learns. History
> has a way of making the past palatable, the dead
> a dream.

> (lines 18–24)

Here, Hugo admits confusion over the circumstance of war, suspends belief that one's actions are heroic, and ruminates on the notion that the world's suffering is a "necessity" to learn from historical ills. Ultimately, he realizes that "The world never learns" and that even the most egregious lapses of a collective humanity are not enough to protect against evil and its repetition. Hugo became resigned to these facts and "accepted without question a world where events defied explanation" (*Real West* 97).

Though the form of Hugo's poem is that of a literal letter, beginning with "Dear Charles" ("Letter to Simic from Boulder" line 1) and ending with "Your friend, Dick" (line 39), the direct language and absence of comparisons or allusions that would serve the purpose of masking or layering intent are acts of reportage. Similarly to Owen's interjection of "Gas! GAS! Quick, boys!" in "Dulce Et Decorum Est" (line 9), a literal battlefield intrusion of warning rather than observing and interpreting a scene, Hugo's reflection on the war deliberately recalls feelings of indecision, optimism replaced by realism, and a degree of resignation that "The world never learns. History / has a way of making the past palatable, the dead / a dream" ("Letter to Simic" lines 22–24). This feeling of resignation is not exclusive to World War II, as seen in Siegfried Sassoon's "The Hero," in which a fellow soldier is "Blown to small bits," and yet, "no one seemed to care" (line 17). A notable difference between Sassoon's "The Hero" and Hugo's "Letter to Simic from Boulder" is that though Hugo does not feel guilty for participating in the war, he expresses empathy for those affected by his actions. Contrary to Keith Douglas's aims of writing extrospective poetry, Hugo's introspective poems are intended to cultivate empathy and acknowledge guilt. Now that Hugo has, in Simic, a face to associate with the once anonymous collateral damage of a bombing campaign, the "mindless hate" that drove the war feels trivial ("Letter to Simic" line 35). Interactions like this conversation with Simic further drove a wedge between Hugo and the self-sympathetic writers of the First World War. "I've never been able to tolerate those British war novels that see war as an adhesive force binding us all together in our common cause," Hugo wrote, speaking to the dissolution of a united front of soldiers, and instead implies that both soldier and civilian, all of humanity, suffer equally at the hands of war (*Real West* 113). Furthermore, as Dominick LaCapra suggests, "Testimonies serve to bring theoretical concerns in sustained contact with the experience of people who lived through events and suffered often devastating losses" (xiv). The imagery used to convey such suffering evolved with war, from the trench lyrics of defiled pastoral landscapes in the First World War to the decentralized skyscapes of air combat in World War II.

From First World War Mudscapes to World War II Skyscapes

The Somme, Verdun, Passchendaele, and other major First World War battles share the feature of earthen landscapes degraded by shellfire, trenches, and heavy rain. No matter the time of year, these battles were fought in muddied trenches where the water was deep enough to drown in or on frozen earth impenetrable to digging. To develop familiarity or a sense of home away from home, First World War trenches were often identified using popular street and location names from Britain, such as "Piccadilly," "Regent Street," "Strand," "Hyde Park Corner," and "Marble Arch" (Fussell, *The Great War and Modern Memory* 42–43). Yet, in the poetry of Siegfried Sassoon and Wilfred Owen, mud is as common a character as the soldiers themselves and serves a multitude of purposes in conveying the trench warfare experience. Oppressive, treacherous, and deadly, for Sassoon's speaker in "Memorial Tablet" "Into the bottomless mud" is where he "lost the light" (line 6), a sharp pivot from the early optimism of Sassoon's war poetry in which a speaker tells his brother he will emerge victorious and "win the light" ("To My Brother" line 8). For Owen, mud is multifaceted. In "Apologia pro Poemate Meo," mud is the veneer through which he attempts to find beauty, writing, "I, too, saw God through mud" (line 1) and "The mud cracked on cheeks when wretches smiled" (line 2). In contrast, mud is also the final indignity for soldiers to endure in Owen's "The Last Laugh" in which a soldier's death is observed: "Till slowly lowered, his whole face kissed the mud" (line 12). For women poets of the First World War such as Mary Borden and Helen Saunders, mud is "equally obscene and putrid," and like war itself it is responsible for "swallowing a generation" (McLoughlin, "Beyond the Trenches" line 31). According to anthropologist Matthew Leonard, "The mud of the Western Front is mentioned in the literature, art, poetry, memoirs and memories of the time perhaps more than any other object of the war." Even for those in the successive generation who fought in World War II, images of mud withstood time and registered in their own war memory. Richard Hugo, in his poem "The Yards of Sarajevo," reflected on the locations and landscapes of World War II in a return to Sarajevo roughly twenty-five years after he had dropped bombs on the city:

> One war started here. The coal smoke
> of our dirty train compounds the gloom.

The past is always dim. A plot. A gun.
The Archduke falling. A world gone
back to mud.

(lines 8–12)

The return to war and destruction of mankind is represented in a return
to the foundational elements of the natural world. For Hugo, mud is synonymous with chaos, destruction, and the devolution of man. While Hugo
acknowledges the resonance of mud as representative of war, his poetry
turns to the skyscapes of World War II bombing runs to alter the perspective of battle and complicate his level of emotional engagement with those
impacted by the missions he conducted.

Though facets of the First World War relied on aerial efforts, such as
the distribution of propaganda and zeppelin bombing runs, the rapid technological advancements between the First and Second World War dramatically shaped the course of air combat during the 1939–45 conflict (Wilkin).
The presence of planes in literature of the First World War is uncommon,
since not only was it not the primary method of combat, but it was not a
primary method of transportation either, as trains, ships, vehicles, horses,
and travel by foot were the most utilized modes of troop movement and
combat (Whitmore). In contrast, many prominent battles, attacks, and
shifts of momentum in World War II were air strikes, such as the bombing of Warsaw, the Blitz and Battle of Britain, the attack on Pearl Harbor,
the firebombing of Dresden, and the dropping of the atomic bombs on Hiroshima and Nagasaki. While soldier poets like Louis Simpson and Keith
Douglas gave poetic and memoir accounts of the ground war, bombardier
Richard Hugo, pilot Howard Nemerov, and celestial navigation instructor
Randall Jarrell all spoke of the war in the air, serving as conduits of their
experience.

Since Hugo was a poet of the air war tasked with striking specific targets
and had a reputation as "his era's arch-regionalist" and "a landscape poet," it
is unsurprising that his recollections of war experience are linked to precise
locations (Wojahn 116). Using poem titles alone, location naming is crucial to Hugo's attempt to create a public record of his personal experience:
"Centuries near Spinnazola," "Mission to Linz," "Napoli Again," "G.I. Graves
in Tuscany," "A View from Cortana," "The Yards of Sarajevo," and many

others. As Frederick Garber posits, "The landscape where things happen to Hugo goes as far into his mind as it goes outside of it," suggesting that Hugo's poems hinge on the contiguous plane that connects external landscapes with the internal landscapes of the mind (58). Michael Dobberstein bolsters this idea by describing Hugo's poems of the American Northwest as a coexistence of "two separate but connected locations: in the derelict, broken-down place—house, bar, street, town, etc.—and in the damaged self that is a product, inhabitant, and observer of that place" (417). As a soldier who returned to the sites of his war experience decades after the war, Hugo seeks comfort by identifying and retreading the details of an otherwise untranslatable experience, as if being able to name these sites means being able to understand them or exert control over what occurred there. The skyscapes, landscapes, and place-names in Hugo's poems "Mission to Linz," "Tretitoli, Where the Bomb Group Was," and "Where We Crashed" are used to establish a stable narrative of his war experience, both for himself and his readers, even if he himself struggles to make sense of the events.

Hugo's "Mission to Linz" embodies what poet-critic William Heyen suggested about Hugo, that "our landscapes choose us and writing poems is a momentary burst of self acceptance [sic] in alien country" (126). In "Mission to Linz," Hugo displays a degree of powerlessness over his role in the war, the war itself, and, to a broader extent, life. In trying to explain the movement of flight, the scenes of different cloud colors over mountain ranges, Hugo remarks of the desire to be in the cold ozone, "It must seem weird, incommunicable" (line 15). The difficulty in explaining what flight is like extends to other perceptions, including time, as Hugo declares, "The air / is ten centuries of waiting" (lines 70–71). An effort to bridge the gap between the mind's landscape and the landscape of air combat appears in the third section of "Mission to Linz," when Hugo gives subdued description to replace the fear of being shot down and plummeting to earth:

> And the moment
> when the sky split open, allowed
> the lazy tons of yellow-banded children
> to fall in forty-second wonder, converge
> in a giant funnel. Now you
> who, so high, can only see
> the puff like a penny dropped in dust

at your toe on a country road, rack up
and out, down with a speed
that strains the blueprint—until
noiselessness, the level back
into clean sky.

(lines 123–34)

This comparatively microscopic shift—the explosion of a plane being shot down and hitting the ground equated to the size of a puff of dust made by a penny dropped on a dirt road—is an attempted translation of a unique moment to the imagery of an ordinary equivalent, a penny notably being an object of relative insignificance. One could argue that this attempt is the role of any poet, to interpret a complex world in language that readers can relate to, but that is not the only function. Hugo simultaneously retells his experience while negotiating the fear and bewilderment of the experience into manageable avenues of questioning and processing. As Hugo explained in his poetic craft book *The Triggering Town*, "I suspect that the true or valid triggering subject is one in which physical characteristics or details correspond to attitudes the poet has toward the world and himself" (5). Simply put, if the subject of the poem is a conduit for the feelings of the poet, "Mission to Linz" is a poem about managing fear. Though Hugo is resigned to the statistic that on average three planes of the fleet will not return from a bombing run, he is able to find calm in flight (lines 86–88). Hugo comes to peace with the dangerous possibilities war affords because it is through the air that he can transport himself back to safety:

If you think about it for a long time
the mind, like engines, will sing
you to the home of men,
where concerts carry
fast in summer wind.

(lines 165–69)

While any allusion to the German song "Der Sommerwind" is likely coincidental,[3] "Mission to Linz" concludes with the promise of returning to mental calm, an understandable desire in mid-1960s America in the aftermath of the assassination of President Kennedy, the civil rights movement amid a divided country, and the worsening reality of the Vietnam War. Hugo's "Mission to Linz" ends with a vision of peace, calm, and normalcy, a tight bookend to the opening stanza that assures the reader that there is more beyond the limitations of what can be perceived:

> If you look at the sky
> . . . .
> you might suddenly know this:
> that the sky where it ends does not end
> and you will pass its horizons.

> (lines 1, 5–7)

Whether searching for a reprieve from battle or trying to settle one's mind long after war has ended, Hugo is banking on the belief that there is life beyond the life-threatening days of war. Searching for reassurance, as if reciting a prayer, Hugo describes the skyscape as a duality of freedom and danger, seen and unseen, life and death.[4]

Just as Hugo's war poems express dualities of mental and physical observation, his war poems transform the way we think about setting because they are the intersection of landscape and skyscape. Aside from the sun, moon, stars, clouds, and a gradient of colors depending on location, time, and weather, there are comparatively fewer things to describe in a skyscape than a landscape. Creative interpretations of this issue lead us to two characteristics of Hugo's war poems that make them notable: perspective and the intersection of landscape and skyscape. Hugo is considered "more typically a Romantic than he is a Realist," and one such intersection of these two modes is the natural presence of wind in Hugo's poems, a feature of the natural world that would be visually imperceptible if not for the objects on which it exerts itself (Wojahn 117). In Hugo's poems, wind is *seen* bending grass and branches, lifting dust, and through the senses of touch and sound.[5] Though wind is a sensory experience unsurprisingly found in poetry, it is more notably a practical concern for the day-to-day operations of a bombardier because its presence and power can influence flight paths and bombing accuracy. Therefore, Hugo's sensory experience of wind is equally noted as a force that can be seen by what it pushes, felt in the resistance of flight, and heard in the tunnel-like fuselage of a B-24. In "Tretitoli, Where the Bomb Group Was," Hugo returns to where he was stationed in Italy decades after the war, to see "Windy hunks of light . . . bend / the green grain no one tried to grow twenty years ago" (lines 1–3). Life has returned to the airfield now that the war is over, and the grown grass appears in its place almost like overgrowth on abandoned buildings. Now in the space where the runway once was, he sees "nuns and shepherds try to soar by running, / arms stuck out for wings against the air, / and wind is lit in squadrons by the grain" (lines 39–41). Time has passed, and the landscape has reverted to its natural state, yet the history of the airfield remains for locals who try to imagine the thrill of flight.

One of Hugo's only anthologized war poems is "Where We Crashed," a poem in which each line is between one and four words. This form pulls the eye down the page, mimicking the internal monologue and vocalized outbursts of the pilot of a free-falling airplane that has been hit, a dangerous departure from Hugo dropping bombs over ground targets. This frantic form links "Syntax and logic" in a rare intersection of form and content in Hugo's poetry (Vaughan 140). Not only is the speaker a panicked pilot, but fear is born out of the threat of a literal transfer from skyscape to landscape and the imminent death of the bomber crew. The opening two lines of "Where We Crashed" oscillate between procedure and panic—"I was calling airspeed / christ" (lines 1–2)—and fear makes each moment appear to go in slow motion:

slow dream
breaking
slow
sliding
gas and bombs
sliding
you end
now
here.

(lines 7–15)

Even amid frantically troubleshooting a crash landing, the speaker locates his fellow soldiers both in the immediate scene and by their place of origin. As the crew members run from the crash-landed plane, not wanting to be caught in an explosion of the gas and bombs it carries, the speaker sees "running / Stewart / . . . Klamath Falls" (lines 94–95, 97), while "O'Brien / L.A." is limping away on a broken foot (lines 103–4). In this moment of unexpected survival, Hugo creates a record that these men belong to a place, apportioning an emotional weight to their survival by associating them with a hometown, places likely easier to envision than a wartime landscape where a bomber has crash landed. By bringing the skyscape to the landscape, Hugo gives the perspective of a bomber team falling to earth and in doing so tries to isolate the rapid-fire emotions and thought process of a panicked airman. By guiding his reader through the emotional landscape of this crash, he is able to convey an otherwise unrelatable experience.

With the rush of a crash landing, the return to a former airfield, and a bombing mission itself, each of these poems by Hugo offers a perspective unique to the skies as his planes repel and are attracted to the land like magnets. For Hugo, the sound, vision, and touch of the wind have transformative properties, alerting him to the way history, memory, and time interplay. During Hugo's return to Italy after the war, he seeks out a field in which he had found respite from the war in the poem "Spinazzola: Quella Cantina La": "A field of wind gave license for defeat. / I can't explain. The grass bent. The wind / seemed full of men but without hate or fame" (lines 1–3). This innocuous field in rural Italy may mean little to the world, but it "becomes 'vital' to Richard Hugo—past and present, boy and man—even as the war (perhaps both the literal one in the past and the mental one in the present) 'went on absurd'" (Davis 66). The wind in this field carries with it memories of the war, the quiet legacy of the individuals who served, and the unanswerable feelings that he has carried with him since. Returning to the locations of his greatest emotional connections to the war was a profound spark for Hugo, as demonstrated by his collection *Good Luck in Cracked Italian*. This collection confronts traumatic memory by retreading the locations of Hugo's deployment, as he believes he can find some form of solace and closure by returning to the physical spaces of his psychological disruption.

Revisiting the Sites of Trauma

Processing memory and historical events often relies on the perspective generated from one's sense of place. Before monuments and memorials are erected, the prevailing memories of a war and the events of monumental and often catastrophic change are first captured in place-names. Cities, towns, rivers, hills, beaches, and other geographical landmarks have become synonymous with victory, devastation, horror, and inhumanity. Unshakable from the collective memory of the world wars are names like "the Western Front," "Verdun," "the Somme," "Passchendaele," "Mametz Wood," "Pearl Harbor," "Normandy," "Auschwitz," "Hiroshima," "Iwo Jima," and countless others. Trauma theorists have studied the connection between a traumatic event and where it took place, both as a source of continued stress and a potential opportunity for healing and closure. Although the field of trauma studies has been evolving since the nineteenth century, one could argue it had not received vital attention and exploration until the mid- to late twentieth century.[6] Despite the once-underdeveloped awareness and methodology of treatment for war trauma, the recognition of the psychological damage found in survivors of war has gained traction over time.[7] Prior to the 1980 introduction of the term "post-traumatic stress disorder," or PTSD, physical, emotional, and psychological repercussions from exposure to war and traumatic experiences were diagnosed as "neurasthenia," "shell shock," and, later, "battle fatigue," designations intended to serve as the male equivalents of "hysteria" for women (Alexander). Beyond the dismissive attitudes and obvious gender bias in the discrepancy of these early evaluations, there was an underdeveloped understanding of the fundamental issues faced by the traumatized soldiers and civilians affected by war. War poetry routinely links traumatized soldiers to the sites where their trauma originated. Based on an evaluation of the Ehlers and Clark Cognitive Theory, key functions in the visiting of traumatic sites include (1) then-now discrimination, (2) memory updates, (3) belief change, and (4) behavioral experiments (Murray et al. 422). Revisiting the place of a traumatic event allows for "then-now discrimination," which is comparing and contrasting the appearance of a location in one's memory versus its current appearance. Distinguishing a changed version of a place from one's memory of the place at the time of the traumatic event can benefit the individual in compartmentalizing an event as existing in an isolated past, separate from their present. In Richard Hugo's poetry, the act of returning to the site of traumatic war experience engages the memories that had haunted him. With particularly regard to commemorating loss, "traditional forms in social and cultural life, in art, poetry, and ritual" are effective because they can assist in mediating bereavement (Winter 5). Hugo's poems on his returns to sites of traumatic memory affirm anger, demonstrate an attempt to cope by uncovering previously inaccessible memories, and allow for accepting responsibility for actions that caused human suffering.

As a poetic voice of America's Pacific Northwest, Richard Hugo is known for poems that have an inseparable relationship to place. Hugo believed that a poet's "vocabulary is limited by [one's] obsessions" and noted his own frequent use of words like "stone," "wind," and "gray" (*The Triggering Town* 15). Hugo aligned himself with arguably the most recognizable American poet of place, New Englander Robert Frost, by saying he believed Frost understood that trying "to make every poem as different as possible from the last one is a way of saying . . . it couldn't be" (15). Having drawn upon the rural landscapes of Washington and Montana in much of his work, Hugo initially stowed away his wartime experience before writing retrospective works in delayed response. Hugo's 1969 collection *Good Luck in Cracked Italian* was his first poetry collection that extensively explored his war memories, and Hugo's posthumously published autobiography *The Real West Marginal Way* provides insights into a few of these war poems. In doing so, Hugo reveals a reckoning over the negotiation between one's memory and evolving locations that bring both clarity and dismay to the survivor's attempts at coping. Some of Hugo's most poignant poems about his wartime experience come from reflecting on his service as he returned to the Mediterranean sites of his traumatic experiences in World War II.

The poems in Hugo's *Good Luck in Cracked Italian* chronicle his 1963 and 1968 returns to postwar Europe, with poems retracing his steps in Italy and the former Yugoslavia. As Hugo explained in a 1977 interview, he felt the need to return to the Italian sites of his World War II experience "in order to validate and reclaim my past" (Dillon and Hugo 107). This sentiment reflects the notion that war writing is "a way of resolving, or attempting to resolve, war experiences whose recurring trauma must be relived, reexamined, and through an apparent catharsis, accepted" (Brosman 90). Fresh to the feelings of rediscovery, in "Napoli Again" Hugo announces, "I am back" (line 3) before pointing out landmarks he recalls from his service, such as "That dock I sailed from eighteen years ago. / This bay had a fleet of half-sunk ships" (lines 4–5). In Hugo's memory of Napoli from more than twenty years earlier:

Fountains didn't work. I remember stink.
Streets and buildings all seemed brown.
Romans hate such recent ruins,
bombed-out houses you do not repair.

(lines 8–11)

It is not the people that have changed in Hugo's mind, for he is trying to "Forget the innocent cut down" (line 13), but it is the absence of the ruins he remembers that jars him. The reconstructed "*galleria* roofs, / *cappuccino* too high priced" (lines 16–17) are hallmarks of the new Napoli, a far cry from his memory of the prostitutes whose services were paid for in food. Now, years later, he is paying for food at a restaurant and believes he is being taken advantage of with a menu with higher prices given specifically to foreigners. This paranoia of being exploited causes Hugo to wonder if he is remembered there by "My wings? / The silver target and the silver bomb?" (lines 22–23). Yet, Hugo acknowledges that even if being an American and a tourist was the reason for his upcharge, the extra money is something he can afford to give to a place he once helped destroy in a bombing campaign. "Take the extra coin," Hugo writes, "I only came / to see you living and the fountains run" (lines 24–25). Lidija Davidovska describes this reciprocity of feeling as a "Subject-Object relation" in which the speaker projects "emotions upon the encountered locations and their inhabitants" and "the encountered locations and their inhabitants" trigger "emotions in the speaker which make his perceptions subjective" (117). From his memory of a ruined city, Hugo's guilt softens by seeing that the destruction he perpetrated was not permanent, and though the repercussions of the war persist, some of the aesthetic qualities marred by war were not irreparable.

Similar to "Napoli Again," Hugo demonstrates the Ehlers and Clark concept of discriminating between then and now in the poem "Galleria Umberto I" by identifying the differences of a place of traumatic memory, this time in observation of a revamped shopping gallery "where soldiers and Neapolitans congregate to engage in all manner of illicit transactions" (Samet 125). "Now it's clean," the poem begins, referring to both civilians and locales by noting "The whores seem healthy / and the bombed-out panes have been replaced" ("Galleria Umberto I" lines 1–2). These observations are in stark contrast to the second stanza, in which Hugo reflects on his "forlorn" (line 9) memory of the place, its "roof glass gone" (line 10) and "pathetic faces / crying for ten lire" (lines 11–12). Hugo was incapable of digesting these sights of struggle without them leaving an indelible mark on him:

> There were faces
> broken by the war, and faces warped
> by cruelty they'd learned, and faces gone.
> I kept my face by turning it away.
>
> (lines 12–15)

Hugo is using external, physical descriptions of the face in order to convey the internal wrenching of the psyche. Hugo describes the faces of civilians as "broken" and "warped" by war and the "cruelty they'd learned," as if suffering the cruelty of others is learned behavior. The unspoken implication in this line is that committing cruelty against humans is also a learned behavior. Both victim and perpetrator, the civilians and soldiers, are exuding man's capability both to endure and to commit inhumane acts. In an attempt to make sense of this suffering and his insufficient response, the third stanza of "Galleria Umberto I" takes another step toward the retrospective as Hugo writes, "There's no metaphor for pain, despair. / It's just there. You live with it" (lines 20–21). Twenty years have passed since the war, but Hugo is admitting that the consequences of what he participated in and witnessed in war cling to him. Through the poem Hugo wrestles with what he tells himself to cope and what he would tell himself if he is being honest:

> In all our years, we come to only this:
> capacity to harm, to starve, to claim
> I'm not myself. I didn't do these things.

I did lots of things and I'm myself
to live with, bad as any German.
It's a place to start undoing.

(lines 27–32)

Guilt-stricken, Hugo is coming to terms with his actions and sees that his own "capacity to harm" has forced him to an irreconcilable crossroad. Hugo recasts an understanding of who he is as he passes the threshold of evil he thinks he is capable of. The enjambment of "to claim / I'm not myself" gives two possible readings: if pausing with the line break, "to claim" can be read as an act of conquest, while to read the sentence as it is syntactically constructed, "to claim I'm not myself," is an attempt to excuse one's actions by trying to distinguish oneself as an individual from one's behavior. Furthermore, a poem reflecting on the damage of war which employs the concept of "undoing" echoes T. S. Eliot's *The Waste Land,* a poem that is, in part, a reaction to the First World War, and the disbelief of one speaker who remarks, "I had not thought death had undone so many," itself an allusion to Dante (*The Waste Land* 63). Dante's "disfatta," Eliot's "undone," and Hugo's "undoing" are each remarks on the shortcomings of humanity, and Hugo is using such disappointment as an equalizer between once-warring nations. By setting aside Allied and Axis forces and isolating the behavior of the individual, Hugo struggles with the notion that killing in war is still killing, and that his actions were just as "bad as any German." Therefore, just as the earlier noted civilians are forever changed by war, so too are soldiers.

Just as in "Napoli Again," Hugo's "Galleria Umberto I" pays penance for the wrongs committed in the name of war. In a way, these speakers accept the endured trauma as punishment for acts of war. Addressing this self-reflection, Jiri Flajšar argues that "In the poetic metamorphosis of his 1960s trips to the Mediterranean, Hugo reenacts his suffering to pose as a victim of traumatic memories and, having established this stance, he hopes to be rid of guilt for his war actions" (53). Yet, in these poems it is difficult to envision Hugo's speaker positioning himself as a victim. Rather, the speaker recognizes that despite his role of fighting in the war, his world has not been torn apart in the way that it has been for civilians living where the war was fought. Hugo is not playing the role of the victim but instead accepts the prolonged trauma of war as a fair share of suffering. After all, the speaker of "Galleria Umberto I" admits, "I did lots of things and I'm myself / to live with" and that if there is any healing to be found, it is in recognizing one's own role in the greater scope of human suffering, one's "place to start undoing."

In other episodes of Hugo's returns to Italy, he relives the immense loss of life as he walks through "the uniform lines / of white crosses" ("G.I. Graves in Tuscany"), recalls the youthful ignorance of American GIs ignoring the beauty of Italian architecture as they liberate a town ("A View from Cortona"), endures an inadequate ceremony for a plaque and wreath-laying for those who defended Cortona from the Germans ("Viva La Resistenza"), observes the changing landscape of the airfield that is now farmland ("Tretitoli, Where the Bomb Group Was"), thinks of a field in rural Italy where he got lost and had an existential moment away from the war ("Centuries near Spinnazola" from Hugo's first poetry collection, *A Run of Jacks*), and locates that same field more than twenty years later ("Spinazzola: *Quella Cantina La*"). Although many of these internalized reflections prompted by revisiting the sites of war are impactful for Hugo, memories are also elicited by thinking of the people who have become synonymous with these places.

One such poem that links place, people, and memory is "Note from Capri to Richard Ryan on the Adriatic Floor," a letter to a dead friend written from the rocks they sat on in Capri during the war. In the poem, Hugo drinks and imagines the decay of his friend's body, sunk to the sea floor after crashing. Hugo writes as if Richard Ryan is still alive, "Dick, I went back to those rocks today, / the ones we ate on nineteen years ago" (lines 1–2). Though Hugo grudgingly blames Ryan for being "a damn fool" (line 3) and taking risks while flying, his attention is more fixated on the landscape, how "The rocks have changed" (line 7) from "years / of wave and storm" (lines 7–8), and presumably like Hugo himself have taken on "rough edges" (line 9) from the years of erosion. In an uncharacteristic shift, Hugo invokes grotesque imagery as he imagines the state of Ryan's body in the sea, with "slow eels / sliding through your eyes" (lines 14–15) and barnacles accruing on his bones. The vowel sounds of "slow eels / sliding through your eyes" (phonetically: sloʊ iːlz ˈslaɪdɪŋ θruː jʊr ˈaɪz) mimic the slow coiling penetration of the eels. This phrase forces the reader to slow down as each word shifts the mouth to a different shape, transitioning from "oh" to "ee" to "i" to "ooh" to "oh" to "i." This deceleration coincides with the pensiveness in the poem, a speaker slowing time down and pausing to reflect on the past. Ultimately, though, the physical change to Richard Ryan's body is not the focal point for Hugo, but it is the persistence of wartime memory, and how a formerly positive memory of Capri is now forever marked by tragedy. "Dick," Hugo concludes, "I went back to those rocks today, / and sat there, glaring at the sea" (lines 21–22). By revisiting a site linked to traumatic memory, Hugo must endure the pain that comes with remembering a dead friend. The final image of Hugo "glaring at the sea" suggests anger or resentment either toward Ryan, whose recklessness resulted in his death, or at the sea and the circumstances of war that have taken Ryan. Still, there is a faint glimmer of Capri being a location in which the memory of Richard Ryan survives. Here, Hugo is writing "about the war in order to sustain a memory of its tragic dimensions and the tortuous experience . . . endured" (Bodnar 59), and since many World War II memorials did not contain the names of the dead, this act of grieving is a reminder that "talk of victory and the 'good war' could never compensate them for what they felt they had lost" (129). By retracing his steps, Hugo revives the memory of the lost so that they may live again.

Just after "Note from Capri to Richard Ryan on the Adriatic Floor" in Hugo's collection *Good Luck in Cracked Italian* is "The Yards of Sarajevo," which, like many of Hugo's poems about revisiting sites of war, confronts the place and people who were subjected to a bombing campaign Hugo conducted during the war. What distinguishes "The Yards of Sarajevo" from his Italy poems is that this train yard was a target the Allies attempted to hit from the air, but it was not a place he had previously set foot in. As his train arrives in the station, among his first thoughts are "These people, tracks and cars were what / we came to bomb nineteen years ago" ("The Yards of Sarajevo" lines 5–6). Hugo equates the low visibility he had when trying to strategically bomb the train yard to the lack of foresight people have in the wake of great historical ills: "The past is always dim. A plot. A gun. / The Archduke falling. A world gone / back to mud" (lines 10–12). Hugo extends the historical scope of the poem to link the unknowable destruction brought on by the assassination of Archduke Franz Ferdinand and the onset of the First World War. Channeling imagery of trench warfare in the First World War by noting "A world gone back to mud," Hugo is critiquing war as a devolution of man, returning to an early evolutionary state of elements. Furthermore, decisions that are made in the past are seen as "dim" (appropriately, both the absence of light, and slang for stupid), as though time sheds light on our histories so that we may understand them with greater context. This regression triggers a chain reaction of events that would unfurl into World War II and is implied with recurring images of short-sightedness and impaired vision throughout this three-stanza, twenty-two-line poem. Hugo's attempts to bomb the station "through blinding clouds" (line 7), as the train arrives "The coal smoke" (line 8) reduces visibility like the dim past, and now in the "rebuilt / and modern" (lines 21–22) train station "Only the lighting" is "bad" (line 22). Wars are fought over concerns of the past, present, and future, and Hugo is pointing out the inherent blindness with which countries enter armed conflict, unable to predict the outcome, losses, and consequences. For a bomber five miles above ground the target is just a cross-section of coordinates, and Hugo, who is seeing that missed target on the ground by literally putting himself in the once-intended blast zone, erases any ignorance he may have about the place and people who would be directly affected by such an action. Hugo is not trying to take back his actions or apologize for what he did during the war, opting instead to envision more intimately the human cost and cultural ramifications of war and recontextualize his guilt.

In each of the aforementioned poems from *Good Luck in Cracked Italian*, Hugo revisits a site he associates with traumatic war experience. In doing so, his memories are confronted with the reality that the world has changed, those memories must be updated to accommodate these changes, and through exposure he may be able to "overcome anxiety associated with the event" (Murray et al. 421). The sites of traumatic memory for Hugo have changed through rebuilding, repopulation, erosion, and, in some cases, have taken a modernized shape. Though these places are sometimes cheap reproductions of the original, Hugo accepts responsibility that he may have contributed to the deconstruction and evolution of a culture by means of war. Hugo repurposes his observations of landscape in the postwar European visit poems of *Good Luck in Cracked Italian* to measure the change of places and people, and to calibrate his own guilt and trauma in relation to the suffering of civilians and the deaths of fellow soldiers. It is unclear whether revisiting these sites of Hugo's wartime experience helped to alleviate the stress of coping with sustained traumatic damage, as would be suggested by the Ehlers and Clark Cognitive Theory. Though Hugo carried pain and despair from the war back to these sites of traumatic memory, resigned to idea that "It's just there. You live with it," he worked to reconcile his memory of a fractured past with an incongruent present.

Richard Hugo's return to sites of traumatic experience is an invaluable component of the veteran experience of World War II, just as it was for his predecessors. First World War poets have been recognized for their acts of reflection, including Siegfried Sassoon's return to Ypres to find the Menin Gate Memorial, an enormous stone monument overshadowing his memory of the muddy, cratered hellscape. As he observed the influx of monuments that brought reminders of the war back to him, these only served to further fuel his distaste for commemorations and honors that felt both insufficient and disingenuous. By returning to the physical site of traumatic memory, Sassoon believed the dead were being "Paid, with a pile of peace-complacent stone" ("On Passing the New Menin Gate" line 7), a monument meant to stand in the place of the thousands who "endured that sullen swamp" (line 8) and "struggled in the slime" (line 13).[8] Similar to Hugo's process of "then-now discrimination," Edmund Blunden's returns to Flanders and reflections on the war also generated feelings of dismay. Driven by his inability to leave the war in the past, Blunden struggled to negotiate the unreality of Passchendaele and the Somme with the same peaceful fields he later visited with his wife.[9] As someone who literally and figuratively "revisited the Flanders battlefields" of the First World War throughout his life, Blunden reflects on those landscapes a half century after the conflict in the 1966 poem "Ancre Sunshine" (Egremont 251). It was here where he sensed "old terrors behind the now peaceful scene" and felt dismayed by the land he saw before him vastly different than he remembered (Egremont 259). Blunden is unable to draw the fissure of past and present back together, for only his wife, Claire, is able "to witness, with no cold surprise, / In one of those moments when nothing dies" ("Ancre Sunshine" lines 23–24). Despite fifty years passing since the First World War, grass growing in the once-cratered landscape of the battlefield, and a Europe at relative peace, it is not enough to keep Blunden from reliving the war each day. Shortly before his death, Blunden remarked, "My experiences in the First World War have haunted me all my life and for many days I have, it seemed, lived in that world rather than this" (Gibson 37). Trauma is embedded in these veterans, and according to the Ehlers and Clark Cognitive Theory, the fear of a persistent threat is a key factor contributing to the ongoing effects of trauma (Ehlers and Clark 9). Each of these poets felt compelled to return to the sites of their war-induced trauma, and the now peaceful battlefield is proof that the threat of the war they survived is no longer active. In his return to the sites of his Mediterranean bombing runs, Richard Hugo found changed places and was reminded of the guilt a surviving member of the armed services bears, as places were reconstructed and are forever changed after the damage he inflicted.

Hugo's return trips to Europe came before substantial developments in the field of trauma studies and a true recognition of the mental cost of PTSD on veterans. Yet, there is little doubt that Sassoon, Blunden, and Hugo possessed at least a momentary feeling of completeness by returning to, arguably, the most influential locations of their lives. By actively engaging in then-now discrimination, these poets revisited the sites of traumatic experience, and these places brought out a justified anger over memorialization, an opportunity to heal by recognizing the incongruity of the past and present, and an acceptance of blame for the participation in actions that led to the suffering of others. Hugo's attachment to place is evident by revisiting locations of traumatic experience in an effort to heal. As locations brought World War II back to life in Hugo's mind, so too did the works of art Hugo viewed in European museums and galleries during those return visits.

Exploring Guilt through Ekphrasis

Throughout the collection *Good Luck in Cracked Italian,* Richard Hugo's poems read like a travel diary with pockets of deeper moments of introspection. In addition to revisiting the locations of Hugo's Mediterranean war service, these poems note works of art and culture that provoke introspection on war guilt. Hugo writes a series of ekphrastic poems that analyze artworks and objects of cultural significance housed in various Italian galleries, churches, and museums. James Heffernan defines ekphrasis as "*the verbal representation of graphic representation*" (299) and believes poets have used ekphrasis to "reveal the ultimate inadequacy of all representation" (312). Emma Kimberley expands on the role of ekphrasis in contemporary poetry by positing that ekphrasis is "a technique for getting beneath the skin of the ideas that are most difficult to express: the idea of representing nothing, the idea of non-being, of the spiritual without a god, of the almost seen and almost understood" (218–19). Hugo's ekphrastic poems wrestle with representation and his attempts to mediate memory and war guilt. Hugo's knowledge of war, political turmoil, and human destruction subvert what would ordinarily be a peaceful trip to Venetian churches, Roman art museums, and galleries in Padua: totems of peace, beauty, art, and culture. Counterintuitively, in 1963 Hugo wanted to return to the "brown and gray and lifeless" Italy he had known in 1944 (Hugo, *Real West* 107). Though he expresses shame over hoping this is what he would find in Italy when he returned, he felt an attachment to this "sad early Italy" because for an airman even a bleak Italy represented earth and safety, and "On earth, you can say goodbye" (107). While poems such as "The Bridge of Sighs," "Galileo's Chair," and "Brueghel in the Doria" show a tourist's approach to Italy as opposed to the perspective of a war veteran, these ekphrastic poems contain an undercurrent of traumatic memory prompted by the resurfacing of Hugo's war experience.

On the surface, "The Bridge of Sighs" is a poem that could be about any couple traveling through Venice who observe the Bridge of Sighs arching over the "green canal" (line 1) and the "Tintoretto mural" in the Madonna dell'Orto church (line 4). Yet, by the end of the first stanza, the speaker sees himself as if he is one of the figures in Tintoretto's mural *The Last Judgment*, a fifteen-foot-tall painting depicting a mass of heavenly and earthly figures deluged by flood and violence. This act of heavenly terror is a cleansing or retribution for the violence and sin committed by man, but for the poem's speaker the image reflects quotidian life. The judgment cast upon the overcrowded and manic space of figures in the painting is equated to modern-day imprisonment, where "Jails today have thinner walls / and better air," though one key similarity remains: "Judges are the same" (lines 7–8). The poem's speaker continues by constructing an argument that people play their role by writing, "Giants paint what kings require" (line 16), and that history moves forward in lines of royal succession: "This son took the throne and so on" (line 20). Ultimately, the poem affirms monarchical succession, yet desires an outcome in which the roles are reversed and "a king still begs for food" (line 23) from a dungeon where he will "age, but never die" (line 25). While the poem can sustain itself as a rumination on duty and judgment, these notions reverberate with added depth when acknowledging Hugo's experience in World War II. Hugo implies parallels between those in servitude to the Lord in the painting and those serving in the military. Soldiers are painting the outcome their generals require,

"Uniforms ablaze" in the "Glory of our time" (line 17). Now, new national sons have ascended to the thrones of their respective countries and proclaim, "we've won" (line 22), while those who fought the war remain "white with pain" (line 21). "The Bridge of Sighs" is a poem about judgment and guilt, the perceived imprisonment of those who are guilty of committing violence on earth.[10] While Hugo is not physically imprisoned, he is writing from the perspective of an individual who accepts the penance of guilt for his actions, a mental imprisonment to the past. In a 1981 interview, Hugo explained a habit he believes many writers possess of "dwelling over and over on the same thing . . . replaying incidents in one's life that are very painful. The hope is that one time I'll play it out and the pain will be gone" (Gardner and Hugo 143). By channeling war guilt through Tintoretto's mural, Hugo is caught in a cycle of self-blame, "an attempt at 'belated mastery'" as one incarcerates themselves with their "own sensibilities, and the poem is a kind of release, a kind of parole we earn" (143). Hugo turns to poetry as a temporary escape from the darkest moments of his life. Similarly seeking solace from one's past, the speaker in "The Bridge of Sighs," like the warriors in the painting, longs for the "Sweet ax" (line 18) to "come down and save the state from shame" (line 19). Images in "The Bridge of Sighs" shift from light to dark, beginning with the outdoor "green canal" (line 1) and ending in a "dungeon" (line 23) where the gray color of the stone walls of the jail can only be made by mixing "black with black" (line 24). This shift toward darkness mimics the movement of the eye observing Tintoretto's *The Last Judgment* as the lightness of the heavens drops down into the darkness below. For Hugo's speaker, *The Last Judgment* is a visual representation of the guilt he possesses and judgment he anticipates.

Hugo makes a similar shift from light to dark in another ekphrastic poem considering relative guilt, "Galileo's Chair." On display "In golden light" (line 1) behind a "velvet chain" (line 2) are items belonging to Galileo, such as his chair and telescope. The poem spends equal time alluding to Galileo's scientific and philosophical theories, and the resistance he faced in the form of "Roman hate" (line 14) and how "No pope honors proof / we move about the sun" (lines 15–16). Similar to "The Bridge of Sighs," the progression from lightness to darkness exists on a literal and figurative plane. In "Galileo's Chair" darkness envelops light from the illuminated display at the outset of the poem, to the halls that turn "a darker brown / each year" (lines 22–23) and again in the final stanza in which the speaker wonders about Galileo's imprisonment: "Was the dungeon black?" (line 31). The figurative fight between lightness and darkness is exacted through the conflict of Galileo's worldly knowledge against the resistance of religious belief.[11] Even if unintentional, a parallel between Galileo and Hugo's speaker is created: Galileo is seen as an intellectual outsider, the speaker in "Galileo's Chair" as an emotional outsider. Both individuals possess knowledge that their respective communities lack: Galileo's knowledge of heliocentrism and Hugo's experience of war that others cannot comprehend. "Galileo's Chair" uses the common metaphorical structure of light representing recognition and learning, such as a light bulb being turned on as an illumination of knowledge, posited against the metaphor of darkness as ignorance, one figuratively being left in the dark. This dichotomy is exemplified in the final lines: "Was the dungeon black? The one he went to / when he'd lied to God, and where he said / *eppur si muove* and it did" (lines 31–33). According to *Merriam-Webster's Collegiate Dictionary,* the Italian expression quoted from Galileo, "eppur si muove," translates to, "and yet it does move," which is "attributed to Galileo after being forced to recant his assertion that the earth moves around the sun." This rebuttal calls attention to indisputable facts in spite of religious belief. In "Galileo's Chair," the Catholic Church recognizes Galileo as one who had "lied to God," yet the poem's speaker knows Galileo was right for saying the Earth moved, "and it did" (line 33). Ultimately, this is a poem of light against dark, knowledge against ignorance, and combating one's feelings about a situation with its reality. Conflicts like these are moving opportunities for reflection for Hugo because, as with many of the poems in *Good Luck in Cracked Italian,* the individual must challenge and revisit his feelings and memories against the concreteness of the present and the compartmentalization of admitting that memories are the past, a different time.

In close succession to "The Bridge of Sighs" and "Galileo's Chair" in *Good Luck in Cracked Italian* is the ekphrastic poem "Brueghel in the Doria," a poem describing Pieter Brueghel the Elder's painting *Battle in the Bay of Naples,* on display at the Palazzo Doria Pamphilj in Rome. The poem begins with the observation "It's a rare Brueghel without people" (line 1) and the conjecture that "Perhaps they cower on the maindeck / as the cannons bang" (lines 2–3). Brueghel's painting of a battle is in stark contrast to the war imagery that Hugo experienced: bombed cities reduced to rubble, gaunt victims stacked like cord wood. Hugo's speaker is struck by the absence of people in a painting depicting war, with the inviting city of Naples in the background, whose docks are splayed out "as the two arms" (line 20). An attraction to a scene where the sea meets the land is familiar to Hugo, whose upbringing in the Pacific Northwest made him feel he "was near the edge of civilization" with "the civilized world" on one side and where "the ocean opens forever to nothing" on the other (Gardner and Hugo 152). Were it not for the painted plumes of smoke denoting the firing cannons, Brueghel's scene would appear to be an ordinary landscape of city meeting sea. Such a surreal vision of war creates a distance between the bombers and their targets, as Hugo explained in his memoir:

> I remember once a friend criticized a long bombing mission poem I'd written because he said I showed no awareness I was bombing people, and in a rare burst of intellectual superiority I said that's exactly the point. We were not bombing people. Towns looked as real as maps. Bomb impacts were minute puffs of silent smoke. The first time I saw "the enemy" was after I returned to America where German POWs were waiting on us in the mess hall at Camp Patrick Henry, Virginia. Somehow they didn't look like the enemy. (*Real West* 98)

The distance between oppositional forces creates a traumatic buffer from which the imagination and later accounts of the war pose a stronger influence in shaping one's relationship with the death and destruction to which they contributed.

This precise act of turning away from reality and the suffering of others was expressed in another ekphrastic poem about a Brueghel painting published thirty years earlier, W. H. Auden's "Musée des Beaux Arts." Beginning with the declaration, "About suffering they were never wrong, / The old Masters," Auden describes the scene painted in Brueghel's *The Fall of Icarus* (lines 1–2). Auden's poem critiques the ease with which people find the capacity to turn away from suffering, like the ploughman in Brueghel's painting who "may / Have heard the splash, the forsaken cry" (lines 15–16) of Icarus falling into the sea, and the sailors who may have seen "a boy falling out of the sky" (line 20) but carry on sailing because they "Had somewhere to get to" (line 21).[12] Like quiet quotidian suffering in Auden's poem or the bombing runs Hugo flew, Brueghel's paintings show danger from a distanced perspective, making the grim reality of war death unspecific. This relative ambiguity prompts Hugo's speaker to ask, "What war was this? The ships seem grimly similar" ("Brueghel in the Doria" lines 6–7), before adding contemplative depth with the rhetorical question, "or did Brueghel know / when war begins the enemy dissolves?" (lines 7–8). Such a subtle interjection of perspective mirrors the emotional investment someone in Hugo's role of bombardier would have toward war, that from miles above the earth "the enemy dissolves" in place of a target, a mission, an objective. Like the internal conflicts evoked by Tintoretto's mural, Hugo's speaker points to Brueghel's *Battle in the Bay of Naples* as if it were his own con- sciousness, where "the old boats inside him playing out / the war he must not win" (lines 23–24). Like war memories firing damaging shots within the mind, the speaker sees these battling fleets as if they were one's post- war landscape of the mind. The "strangers / on the dock" (lines 24–25) with the speaker's "money in their eyes" (line 25) are welcoming him ashore, inviting him back to a place of danger. Traumatic memory resurfaces while viewing a painting from 1560 depicting a battle in Italy, connecting across time Brueghel's aesthetic insight with something Hugo would experience himself nearly four hundred years later. For Hugo's speaker, this recur- rence of war is so cyclical that the enemy is inconsequential and dissolves from historical memory.

In "The Bridge of Sighs," "Galileo's Chair," and "Brueghel in the Doria," Hugo uses ekphrasis to channel feelings of personal guilt and judgment, conflicts of the past and present, and the persistence of war and the trau- matic memories generated by it. While many poems in *Good Luck in Cracked Italian* chronicle Hugo's returns to the sites of his war service and trau- matic experience, Hugo's ekphrastic poems show the pervasiveness of war memory. In observation of these paintings and artifacts, the speaker in each poem interprets their meaning and relevance through the identity of a war veteran. Questions of guilt and eternal judgment, the blurring of past and present, feelings versus reality, and the recursive nature of war and the anonymization of enemies are all prompted by these works of art and cultural significance. Doomed like Sisyphus, Hugo is forced to relive his war experience (Flajšar 51). Seeping into his dreams are feelings of guilt, obligation, and being sentenced to atone for his actions, such as in the poem "In Your War Dream" in which Hugo must fly his "35 missions again" (line 1). For even in those interrupted dreams, Hugo is held captive to the traumatic memory of war. Hugo succumbs to the same alarming reactions as Simpson and Graves, who both suffered from PTSD after the war: "Nights I went to bed sober right after the war, bad dreams exploded me awake. Even a slight sound would bring me wide awake up from the bed. A car horn in the streets made me flinch and jump" (*Real West* 70). For Hugo, these works of art and symbols of human refinement and progression are ironic in the sense that, for all their beauty and cultural importance, they ultimately reflect the shortcomings of man, and susceptibility to regression, ignorance, and violence.

■ ■ ■

In Richard Hugo's war poetry, thematic and contextual variation is a hallmark of how war informs otherwise ordinary scenes. As exemplified in the preceding sections, Hugo's reflections on World War II use interpretations of distance and traumatic memory to show that any poem has the potential to be a war poem for those irreparably changed by combat experience. Hugo's 1975 poem "The Hilltop" from *What Thou Lovest Well, Remains American* exemplifies how the war creeps into nonwar poems. The speaker in "The Hilltop" seemingly innocuously describes his ideal bar as a "run down" (line 1) place where regulars tell the "Same jokes" (line 4), and there is a hopeless "anticipation of the girl / sure to walk in someday fresh from '39, / not one day older, holding out her arms" (lines 7–9). While the dive bar scenery mirrors many of Hugo's poems, the suggestion that a girl will arrive for him from 1939 (thirty-six years earlier) is a subtle expression of longing for someone untouched by World War II, or for oneself to be taken back by nostalgia to the prewar days.

Hugo cultivates empathy through testimonial war poetry and poems in the form of letters. This goal is advanced by helping civilians connect with and make sense of the war through more relatable imagery of landscapes and skyscapes. For his own benefit, Hugo confronts fear, guilt, and traumatic memory by revisiting the sites where he experienced war trauma. Though he channels that guilt through exercises of ekphrasis, the confirmation that one's trauma has persisted decades after war pushes Hugo to find creative ways to try to make sense of what he has experienced and how he sees the world. Where Hugo succeeds in each of these bridges between the internal and external is in establishing links between two oppositional modes, showing the interconnectedness of the individual and the whole, present and past, light and dark, earth and sky, home and abroad, and be-tween soldier and civilian, the enemy, and one's allegiances. Understand-ing the relationship between binary choices is how Hugo saw war: "When someone is trying to kill you, you try to stay alive. The side you happen to be on makes little difference, and even if it did, you had little or no control over it to start with. Idealism is a luxury most poor people can't afford. I wish this weren't true" (*Real West* 96). In a post-1945 world, these all-or-nothing views were consequences of "dealing with the threat of global annihilation that war now brings," out of which "the lyric self necessarily confronts its participation and stake in the collective destiny" (Templeton 51). Stripped of notions of heroism or bravery, Hugo's poems of war service are largely poems of duty. For Hugo, volunteering for this service was "for the cheap-est kind of romantic personal reasons. I felt weak and inadequate, and fool-ishly thought facing and surviving danger would give me spiritual depth and a courageous dimension I lacked and desperately wanted" (*Real West* 98–99). Among similar reflections from those who survived World War II, Hugo's war poems are "diachronic self-examinations that contrast youthful errors with mature criticism" and serve as "testimonies of that wrestling with conscience that ultimately transformed memory culture" (Jarausch 369). While World War II may have created more unanswered questions and unfulfilled desires than it resolved for Hugo, he nonetheless recog-nized that he had become collateral damage of the war, just like the millions of deaths, casualties, and civilians who had been impacted by its scope.

Resigned to the knowledge that he will forever carry the war within him, Hugo reflects on the psychological longevity and cost of war in one of his final poems, "Here, but Unable to Answer." An elegy for his stepfather, "Here, but Unable to Answer" pleads:

Forgive the bad nerves I brought home,
these hands still trembling with sky, that deafening
dream exploding me awake. Books will call
that war the last one worth the toll.

(lines 24–27)

This phrasing of a "dream exploding me awake" is nearly identical to his earlier comments on his postwar trauma that "bad dreams exploded me awake" (*Real West* 70). Perhaps Hugo perceives these nightmares and symptoms of trauma as a karmic retribution for the night bombing missions where the bombs he dropped would have exploded civilians awake, if not killing them instantly. Yet, despite the human cost, and Hugo's frayed nerves, shaking hands, and nightmares, he believes history will decide it was "worth the toll." Hugo stops short of revealing whether he agrees, though he affirms worth by drawing an example of how his wartime skill set could metaphorically bring him closer to his stepfather. Hugo draws a parallel between his stepfather's ability to navigate by looking at the stars and the lengths he would go to tear "the clouds apart right / beneath the north star long enough" for his stepfather to correct his course (lines 9–10). Even while asleep or in overcast skies, Hugo suggests he is on course by concluding, "When I dream, the compass lights stay on" (line 34). Hugo is determined to navigate through the traumatic memory of war and is staying the course even when he is asleep, because even in that moment of potential calm he is visited by nightmares.

Few of Hugo's poems directly or obliquely related to war chronicle battle, which hinders discussion of his contribution to war poetry and the literature of World War II. Since Hugo did not seriously write poetry until after the war, his reflections on the war are almost entirely through the spectrum of survivor's guilt, reflection, and the places, people, and culture in war's wake. Many may expect a bombardier like Hugo to write more explicitly about his flying missions and the thrills of air combat, but aside from a few exceptions such as a poem about crash landing ("Where We Crashed") and a bombing mission over Austria ("Mission to Linz"), the majority of Hugo's war poems are from the perspective of a middle-aged man negotiating his memory of war with the person he has become. By wrestling with the actions of his past Hugo attempted to achieve psychological peace, a common pursuit for many who survived the war.[13]

Reflecting on one's past is the undercurrent of Hugo's war poems, a contrast to the immediacy of many First World War poems. There is undeniable value in transmitting the sensory and psychological barrage of combat, as proven in the sustained recognition of Owen, Sassoon, Graves, Blunden, Brooke, Thomas, Jones, and many others. Yet, just as Sassoon's postwar poetry is not as vaunted as his terrified dispatches from the Western Front, poets like Richard Hugo took time to process the trauma of World War II. Hugo waited nearly twenty-five years to confront the war in his poetry and, subsequently, has been largely overlooked in canonical consideration. As Paul Fussell argued, the World War II generation was "Faced with events so unprecedented and so inaccessible to normal models of humane understanding, literature spent a lot of time standing silent and aghast" (Norris, "War Poetry in the USA" 43). Despite Hugo's quiet postwar and prepublication period of going to the University of Washington, getting married, and staying involved in the world of aviation by working for Boeing, the war poems that would eventually surface warrant attention and a place for Hugo in the canon of World War II poets. For all the recognition Hugo receives as a regionalist, it must be acknowledged that he processed the Pacific Northwest with the same eyes that sought to make meaning of the windswept fields of 1940s Italy.

4

HOWARD NEMEROV

RECLAIMING NARRATIVES AND
INTERROGATING MEMORIES
OF "THE GOOD WAR"

> *Speculati nuntiate* (Having watched, bring word)
> —Motto of Nemerov's 236 Squadron RAF

> There is a knowledge in the look of things
> —HOWARD NEMEROV, "A Spell before Winter"

Howard Nemerov published his first poetry collection, *The Image and the Law,* in 1947, and his 1950 follow-up, *A Guide to the Ruins,* contains one of his few anthologized war poems, "Redeployment." An exploration of post-traumatic stress disorder, "Redeployment" is a poem that, as argued by James M. Kiehl, shows readers that "war, far more than its victim, is horribly insane" (252). "Redeployment" is a valuable signpost for Nemerov's poetry, marking early in his career that war was a pervasive topic he would have to confront throughout the remainder of his life, culminating in the 1987 collection *War Stories: Poems about Long Ago and Now.* Nemerov's consistent returns to the topic of war until his death in 1991 at age seventy-one were a dark testament to the persistence of traumatic memory and the desire to protect others from experiencing war by bringing word of what he saw.

While it may seem counterintuitive to argue that the poetic contributions of a United States poet laureate, Pulitzer Prize winner, and National Book Award winner have not been fully recognized, Howard Nemerov's war poems offer more value than is typically attributed to them. Leon Stokesbury's anthology *Articles of War* acknowledges that "most of the best American poems about World War II were written ex post facto, after the war, and in many cases as long as one or two generations after the war" (xxi). Despite Stokesbury's acknowledgment, "the publication of this anthology . . . has not led to the sort of critical interest [in World War II poetry] that one might have expected" (Lee 301). Nemerov's war poetry does receive recognition in a few of the major war poetry anthologies, such as Desmond Graham's *Poetry of the Second World War* and Harvey Shapiro's *Poets of World War II*, and even though "his war poetry is extensive enough and of sufficient quality to merit critical inquiry," it "has been followed by little critical attention" (Lee 300). William Ward Mills's 1972 dissertation, "A Critical Introduction to the Poetry of Howard Nemerov," which focuses on the philosophical, contemplative, and satirical elements of Nemerov's work, offers a glimpse at Nemerov's reputation as a poet in the 1970s (3). Confoundingly, twenty-seven years after World War II, the study makes no mention of Nemerov's war poems, or that he was involved in World War II at all. A 1978 review of Nemerov's *Collected Poems* by G. S. Fraser states that Nemerov's "war service does not bulk large in his poetry" ("The Part of the Natural Man" 1124). Similarly, and nearly twenty years later, journalist Victor Selwyn in his 1995 anthology *The Voice of War: Poems of the Second World War* proclaimed that, "Unlike [First World War poets], so many leading poets did not return to continue writing and counter the myth that the Second World War produced little of note" (xxii). Such omissions of major elements of Nemerov's life and work reinforce the myth that poets of World War II were a "Silent Generation." Nemerov's retrospective war poems are rarely poems of combat, a trait that makes them difficult to categorize if one is expecting the type of chaotic scenes of combat popularized in the Greek epics and First World War trench lyrics.

Atypical treatment of subject matter was not the only aspect of Nemerov's poetry that critics have struggled to describe. Attempts to categorize Nemerov's poetic style often revert to describing him as a formal poet with modernist tendencies, having evolved from self-described "imitative" beginnings ("Howard Nemerov"). One such example is noted by fellow World War II poet Randall Jarrell in a 1955 review of *The Salt Garden,* who writes that while "Yeats has spoiled some of [Nemerov's] poems," Yeats's influence had ultimately "helped [Nemerov's] poetry" (Duncan 84). Similarly, critics have equated Nemerov's poem "Grand Central, With Soldiers, in Early

Morning" with Ezra Pound's "In a Station of the Metro." R. S. Edgecombe quips that Nemerov's poem "owes something to Pound's Metro poem, except that here the imagism is pointed and moralized," with Nemerov using the ephemeral nature of people in transit to exemplify a society's blind spot for its "underlying militarism" (41). In a 1979 review, F. Moramarco describes Nemerov's *Collected Poems* as "a cacophony of contrary and conflicting voices" (121). While Nemerov's poetry exuded modernist characteristics such as experimentations with "point of view, time, [and] space," it also showed a transition toward postmodernism in its expressions of "disillusionment" and "irony" (Guerin et al. 300). Yet, a few decades to digest a larger catalogue of Nemerov's poetry would help give shape to his legacy, as seen in a 2003 *Poetry* review of Nemerov's *Selected Poems* by poet-critics Adam Kirsch and Kevin Young. After a discourse on Nemerov as an allegorical poet chiefly concerned with nature and time, Kirsch and Young consider titles such as "nature poet" and "war poet" for Nemerov (167). While they do not conclusively settle on a category for Nemerov, they are left wanting a "sense of outrage" in Nemerov's poetry, a feature that is largely absent except for the poems of *War Stories* (168). Exemplified in these reviews is the intersection of expectation and reality, in which some expect war poetry to sound a particular way and to take a stance of either patriotic support or revolutionary resistance. While Nemerov objects to war and those who have not learned from the mistakes of the past, the lasting influence of First World War poets is apparent in the expectation that war poetry be synonymous with overt protest poetry. Soldiers of World War II did not fail to produce poetry of significance, but rather, they did not produce a body of work that fulfilled the predetermined expectations that critics and the public had for their generation of war poets.

A native of New York City, Howard Nemerov was born in 1920 to David and Gertrude Nemerov, a Russian-Jewish couple who owned Russeks Fifth Avenue department store. Howard was the oldest of three artistic children; his two younger sisters were renowned photographer Diane Arbus and visual artist Renee Nemerov Sparkia Brown (Lane). Prior to the United States entering World War II in 1941, Nemerov graduated from Harvard University while Theodore Spencer and F. O. Matthiessen were among the faculty. Nemerov's affluent upbringing and Ivy League education pose a challenge to Kenneth Baker's emphasis that First World War poets were largely in a social and educational class of their own in comparison to war poets who came before and after them (Baker xxiv). Unsuccessful in the flight-training program to become a pilot in the U.S. Army Air Force, having "washed out. Couldn't fly well enough" (Nemerov, Letter to Parents, Nov. 28 1941), Nemerov turned to the Royal Canadian Air Force in 1943. Upon deployment with the RAF Coastal Command, Nemerov was stationed in England, where "he flew anti-submarine and anti-shipping patrols" over "the North Atlantic and the North Sea" (Vaughan 82). The U.S. Army Air Force commissioned Nemerov in 1944, and he cumulatively flew fifty-seven missions over the final two years of the war (United States Army). According to the archived RAF pilot's flying logbook that belonged to Nemerov, he piloted nine different planes during his service, but most frequently manned a Bristol Beaufighter, Oxford I and II, and Wellington on his runs (Royal Canadian Air Force). A pilot's secluded vantage point of experiencing war from the air had an immeasurable influence on Nemerov's poetry, which he wrote over a roughly forty-year period after the war's end. Yet, his war poems did not come in a concentrated burst during or immediately after the war but were dotted throughout his collections. Only late in his life did Nemerov devote an entire collection to the topic of war, with the 1987 publication of *War Stories: Poems about Long Ago and Now*. As emphasized by Ross Labrie, Nemerov's work demonstrates that "he did not grasp the significance of the war until it was well behind him" (71). Published just four years before he died of esophageal cancer in 1991, *War Stories* punctuates Nemerov's earlier war poems with an unhindered directness in his social commentary (Kumin 63).

As arguably the most outspoken critic of war among the five poets highlighted in this study, Howard Nemerov used his poetry to reinforce a duty to peace championed in Wilfred Owen's sentiment, "All a poet can do today is warn" ("Preface"). To achieve this objective, Nemerov—like Owen and Sassoon before him—attempted to reclaim war narratives from the mythmaking and popularized glorification of war that had arisen in Western depictions. Nemerov bridged the divide between experience and interpretation through his perspective as a pilot. In other words, he mirrored his experience of literal distance from elevated altitudes by using figurative distances such as elapsed time and emotional separation. In addition to exploring forms of distance in Nemerov's poetry, this chapter will examine Nemerov's use of skyscapes and postwar memory to try to convey how war is an event continually experienced by its combatants. Lastly, this chapter will analyze Nemerov's poems reimagining the war and examine how returning to the subject of war subsequently means reliving the trauma he experienced.

In contrast to the intensity and immediacy of the trench poetry of First World War British soldiers, Howard Nemerov's poems are tempered and delayed contemplations that suggest the permanence of war memory in the postwar consciousness. Well documented is the historical commonality of how soldiers "were frequently reticent" to discuss the war upon returning home, and "often waited until late in life to do so" (Rodney Watson, "Memories" 18). This repression of experience, and the narrative gap it left, is one contributing factor to the mythologizing of World War II as the "good war," a title implying moral duty, a pivot from the First World War's reputation as the "Great War" due to its grandiosity (Terkel vi). The moral implication that World War II was the "good war" comes from the consensus that the war was necessary to defeat fascism in Europe and defend the millions persecuted by the Nazi regime, while subsequent challenges to the "good war" myth deploy the phrase sarcastically, as a knowing veil over the brutality and human suffering. When reflecting on the Allied perspective of World War II, the nicknames the "good war" and the "Greatest Generation" for those who served in World War II are part of a war mythology that has gradually been accepted as fact rather than moral posturing. Christina S. Jarvis further explains this phenomenon as "Perhaps the greatest legacy of America's postwar victory culture and preservation of wartime masculine ideals" because "it fostered the idea of 'the good war' and firmly positioned World War II as the nation's most commonly agreed upon moral reference point" (188). Michael C. C. Adams challenges the historical memory of World War II, arguing that although there are truths to these positive assessments of the 1940s and American military might, the complexity of the era is distorted through acts of nostalgia, deliberate journalistic misrepresentation, and revisionist history. Adams explains, "Myths are ways we try to shape a usable past to help in directing present actions and setting our future course. . . . In World War II, only positive aspects of the war received mainstream attention, setting a pattern for interpreting the war's meaning" (131). Therefore, the delay of World War II soldier poets to direct the narrative of their experience allowed for a heightened role of other forms of media to fill that void. Nemerov's poetry is often emotionally distant, syntactically indirect, ironic, and uses ethereal imagery. Qualities such as

indirectness and emotional ambiguity are a departure from the most resonant poems of the First World War. Though Howard Nemerov's reputation
is not defined by his war poetry, he wrote poems tinted by war throughout
his career. These poems reflect on the disparity between his view of the
war and public and political perception, routinely engaging with the "good
war" myth, humanity's connection to war, and postwar traumatic memory.

The Reclamation of War Narratives

Rarely seen in twentieth-century war poetry is politically motivated commentary overtly directed at enemy nations and people. Rather, many prominent First World War writers expressed neutrality toward oppositional
countries, in particular contrast with the contention they felt toward authority figures from their homeland who initiated and sustained the war.
More commonly expressed than hatred toward enemy nations and soldiers
was the combatant's sense of obligation toward one's compatriots, and the
desire to finish the conflict so that all could return home. While Siegfried
Sassoon, Wilfred Owen, Edward Thomas, and other Allied soldiers wrote
of this compartmentalization of duty and emotion, writers serving for the
Central powers also shared thoughts over the futility of the prolonged conflict. In First World War veteran Erich Maria Remarque's *All Quiet on the
Western Front,* a tattered German regiment voices their neutrality toward
their opponents in a reflective conversation:

> "Right, but just think for a minute—we are almost all ordinary people
> aren't we? And in France the majority are workers, too, or tradesmen or
> clerks. Why on earth should a French locksmith or a French shoemaker
> want to attack us? No it's just the governments." . . .
> "So why is there a war at all?" (145)

This disconnection between soldier and cause competes with the posthumous narratives that shape our understanding of the world wars. The story
of the First World War is often told from the perspective of the Allies as
an immense sacrifice of life to prevent the aggressive expansionism of the
Central powers (National Archives, "Why Did Britain Go to War?"). Yet, arguments amplified and popularized by trench poetry focus on the growing
feelings of futility as the First World War was prolonged with minute gains

in relation to the staggering human cost. The view that it was futile to prolong the First World War, supported by enormous losses in stalemates and the subsequent return to war a generation later, is challenged by Vincent Trott, who suggests this reputation was only developed in retrospect because a boom of war books "played an integral role in shaping the memory of the First World War throughout the 1920s" (49).

An opposite trajectory exists for the legacy of World War II, for which the narrative orbits predominantly around the necessity of defeating Nazi Germany and ending the Holocaust. Though the British sought to suppress German aggression and expansion in Europe after the invasion of Poland, and the United States entered the war in retaliation against Japan for the attack on Pearl Harbor, civilians of Allied nations entered war with competing feelings of necessity and skepticism. With the memory of the First World War still fresh in the collective consciousness, the Allies had varied levels of public support, with many not wanting to reengage in a costly ground war on European soil. As Tom Burns explains, "public opinion in the US began to polarize between the old isolationism and a new interventionism—two irreconcilable positions" (104). For example, in 1930s Britain, the Peace Pledge Union, pacifists, and Labour Party were among the outspoken groups in opposition to plunging Britain back into war ("British Pacifism in World War 2"), and a wave of isolationist movements argued that the United States was better off staying out of another European conflict ("Angry Days"). Despite public awareness of the persecution of European Jews, the scope of the Holocaust was not widely comprehended until after the war. As a result, the war was retroactively justified for any remaining skeptics, even though many troops were not aware of Nazi atrocities until the liberation of the concentration camps in 1945. For Nemerov, the quotidian frustrations of armed service during World War II were brought on by the government and were sustained by the retrospective mythmaking that occurred.

Recurrent in war poems are the many possible consequences of combat service, such as resentment toward those responsible for initiating and sustaining the traumatic conditions of war. Howard Nemerov wrote poems that critiqued governments and authority figures in positions of power and influence for their decision-making and shaping the narrative of war in a way he felt was not representative of his experience. Nemerov's poetry, like Siegfried Sassoon's before him, attempts to make whole the disparate interpretations of soldiers' war experiences. Though both Sassoon and Nemerov wrote in contrast to the war narratives pushed by authorities and the media, the war poetry of Sassoon is popular, routinely recognized, and extensively anthologized. Conversely, Howard Nemerov's war poetry has received far less canonical recognition, despite his attempts to reclaim memory of the narratives of war to more accurately reflect the experience of the average soldier, distinct from those portrayed by authorities and the press. Nemerov's life and poetic career ran parallel with an ebb and flow of social acceptability for criticizing one's government and military actions. He began writing in a period of elevated patriotism during and after World War II and continued writing through the Vietnam War, when American sentiment toward intervention was starkly divided. The difficulty in gauging this sociohistorical context is highlighted by analyzing Nemerov's prolonged warnings against war as a former combatant, particularly in light of Sassoon's criticisms of government and war during and after the First World War.

Howard Nemerov was among the many World War II combatants who voiced similar qualms to his First World War poetic predecessors. Having witnessed immense loss from his service in World War II, Nemerov felt such loss was rendered inconsequential by subsequent American wars. Nemerov's war poems are frequently in the spirit of Siegfried Sassoon's 1917 letter of protest. Sassoon's "A Soldier's Declaration" is an objection to the government-sanctioned narratives used to sustain the First World War. In it, Sassoon writes, "the war is being deliberately prolonged by those who have the power to end it" because what began as a war of "defence and liberation" has become a war of "agression [*sic*] and conquest" ("Finished with the War"). As a serving member of elevated rank, Sassoon takes the initiative to speak to the deterioration of morale caused by immense losses and an offensive rather than defensive war strategy as stark departures from the expectations, however naïve, about how the war should transpire. The lack of perceptible progress at the Western Front cast much of the First World War as a meaningless act of sacrifice. Similarly, included in Nemerov's early war writings is a poem from his first collection *The Image and The Law* (1947), "For W___, Who Commanded Well," an elegy to a fellow serviceman that confuses the personal narratives of war and those from the press. The first stanza is an attempt to come to grips with the thought of a dead friend: "You try to fix your mind upon his death / Which seemed it might, somehow, be relevant / To something you once thought" (lines 1–3). This act of compartmentalization is Nemerov's attempt to equate death with something meaningful, as if something must be learned from the loss. Yet, having experienced World War II and retaining an awareness of the immense death toll it produced, one would understandably struggle with becoming callous from an overexposure to death. After using the second stanza to question death, "the most possible of dreams," Nemerov uses the third stanza to return to realities of death (line 5). From Nemerov's perspective, while remaining neutral about the morality of war, "the press commends / A rational greed" (lines 9–10). A more pertinent conclusion for Nemerov is that "money is being made . . . / And death is paying for itself" (lines 12–13). In other words, the emotional weight of loss has been overshadowed by the economic benefits reaped by the victors of war, and it is because of this economic advancement that "It does not seem that anything was lost" (line 14). Here lies the buried frustration of Nemerov's early reflections on the war. So soon after being fortunate enough to return home alive, he feels the media has forgotten about the cost of war in favor of highlighting the prosperity that has taken its place. The position that Nemerov has taken here has not gone unchallenged, as shown by poetry critic and scholar Helen Vendler, in a review of Harvey Shapiro's *Poets of World War II* anthology, in which she felt the poems possessed "a relative absence of guilt" (Samet 171). Elizabeth D. Samet elaborates, saying "This poetry tends to simmer with an anger more often directed at American institutions than at the enemy" in which speakers are cast as "victims of the state" and not as "the perpetrators of shocking violence" (171). Similarly, in discussing the "myth of the trauma hero," Roy Scranton writes that this myth "makes the American veteran a sympathetic victim, rather than a perpetrator of violence" (3), and that the contradictions in how veterans are perceived "led to a corresponding neglect of those literary responses" (Samet 22). Yet, as evidenced particularly in the poetry of Nemerov, Hugo, and Jarrell, both perspectives can coexist. Feeling guilt for one's wartime actions and feeling resentment toward the political establishment are not mutually exclusive responses to wartime violence.

"For W___, Who Commanded Well" is akin to Sassoon's "Song-Books of the War," a poem in which Sassoon idealistically predicts that a world at peace will override a culture's collective memory of catastrophic loss and horror:

In fifty years, when peace outshines
Remembrance of the battle lines,
Adventurous lads will sigh and cast
Proud looks upon the plundered past.

(lines 1–4)

Just as Sassoon is afraid that future generations will feel a longing nostalgia for the First World War, the underlying concern Nemerov exposes in "For W___, Who Commanded Well" is the absence of reckoning with what is sacrificed at war, and how quickly millions of lives have been supplanted in the press by issues of lesser existential importance. "Song-Books of the War" concludes in resignation that the whitewashed narrative of the war has prevailed in the minds of a later generation, as the boys "dream of lads who fought in France / And lived in time to share the fun" (lines 23–24). The envy and nostalgia these boys feel for an event they are not old enough to have experienced drives their ignorance over the cautions of those who lived through it. To elevate and glorify war and the idea of serving in the masculine tests of armed conflict is a common response for those who came of age in a time when the mythologizing of the Great War saturated English culture. Christopher Isherwood remarked, "Like most of my generation, I was obsessed with the idea of 'War.' 'War,' in this purely neurotic sense, meant The Test. The test of your courage, of your maturity, of your sexual prowess" (74–75). While Sassoon and Isherwood warn of viewing war as if it is role-play or a test of masculinity, Nemerov warns of viewing war in economic terms of gains of losses. Most damaging to Nemerov as he contemplates the death of a commander is that so soon after the conclusion of World War II he feels that the individual losses of soldiers and civilians were perceived as inconsequential by-products offset by the margin of economic progress.

To minimize the human impact of war is unacceptable for Nemerov, who personifies war as monstrous and insatiable in the 1958 poem "The Old Soldiers' Home." Though "The Old Soldiers' Home" was published more than a decade after "For W___, Who Commanded Well," a common thread between the two poems is the triumphant message making of wartime narratives and press propaganda in contrast with the harsh realities of armed service. In "The Old Soldiers' Home," led into war by "Trumpet and drum, the old soldier" inquires as to what has become of the regiment, company, and squad (line 1). Recognizing that "Some must be living, though cracked or bent," he acknowledges that even the survivors of war do not leave unscathed (line 4). Despite the survivors, the old soldier is preoccupied because he

> . . . can't get it out of my head
> How trumpet and drum paraded before
> The marching young men, how they led
> Us, green and dumb, where the war
>   Opened his mouth to be fed.
>
>   (lines 5–9)

This imagery of soldiers marched off to war—reminiscent of opening lines by Sassoon, "The boys came back. Bands played and flags were flying" ("Fight to a Finish" line 1)—contrasts the innocence of youthful exuberance with the seemingly inevitable and unceremonious deaths they will face. Sassoon's references to soldiers as "young men . . . green and dumb" or "The boys" are literal implications of youth, immaturity, and naivety. As the First World War progressed, the enlistment and conscription ages were lowered to eighteen under the Military Service Act of 1916, and it was not uncommon for underage boys to lie or find other ways to join the war as a need for more troops intensified ("The Military Service Act, 1916"). While World War II belligerents also had minimum age requirements for drafting and enlistment that varied by country, parental consent could enable those a year below the limit to enlist (Rosen 77–91).[1] Furthermore, desperate countries ordered increasingly younger soldiers into battle as their prospects of victory waned, such as Hitler ordering the Hitler Jugend to fight when the Allies invaded Germany toward the end of the war (Singer 14). References to age, both young and old in Nemerov's "The Old Soldiers' Home," therefore carry much broader implications on the far-reaching scope of war.

In addition to focusing on age, Nemerov emphasizes acts of movement through the use of enjambment—"paraded before / The marching men," "they led / Us," "the war / Opened his mouth"—as if each line break is a step in the processional. Tragically, these movements lead to war death, a notion that is repeated as a refrain at the end of each stanza, as if no amount of death is enough to satiate the bloodlust of war. "There was a hill" the second stanza begins, "The military and manly thing / Was to take the hill, and we near did" (lines 10–12). This stanza posits war as a challenge of manliness, echoing the idea that war is a test of maturity and masculinity. Though the second stanza narrates a retreat, the retracted position still leaves the troops "Bleeding and chill, where the war / Opened his mouth to be fed" (lines 17–18). Whether soldiers are deployed or in retreat, the war demands to be fed and will feast upon the lives of its combatants. The third, and final, stanza shows the same degree of vulnerability, as the old soldier recuperates in a war hospital, sarcastically saying, "God bless the State!" (line 19). This ironic salute feels more like a warning, like Sassoon's old veteran in "Song-Books of the War" whose warnings are ignored by the eager young generation. Even as the old soldier repeats "roll call" (line 22), "The order of battle, the old parade" (line 23), he knows the "Trumpet and drum" loom over him and may signal his own death soon (line 25). Resigned to his fate, the old soldier rests "chill and dumb, where the war / Opens his mouth to be fed" (lines 26–27). Anticipating death, the old soldier narrates the slightly changed refrain, where death from war is no longer past tense—"the war / Opened his mouth" (lines 8–9, 17–18)—but is here in the present: "the war / Opens his mouth" (lines 26–27). Nemerov uses three nine-line stanzas with a refrain to end each, an echo of the recurrent, predictability of death in the consciousness and experience of a soldier.

Unavoidably, "The Old Soldiers' Home" contains multiple nods to Ernest Hemingway. Specifically, Nemerov draws upon the title of Hemingway's 1925 short story "Soldier's Home," which deals with the lasting ramifications of war service on the individual readjusting to civilian life, and a subtle allusion to the 1940 novel *For Whom the Bell Tolls* by using the sounds of war, parades, and clocks to signify facing death. While poems such as "The Old Soldiers' Home" and "For W___, Who Commanded Well" are subdued disagreements highlighting the disconnection between the media narratives of war and the deadly reality of combat, it was not until later in life that Nemerov wrote with more direct condemnation of the trumpets and drums of war. As a counterbalance to traditional war poetry such as Alfred, Lord Tennyson's "The Charge of the Light Brigade"—a poem that lionizes the saber-wielding British soldiers during the Crimean War, asking, "When can their glory fade?" (line 50), and instructing readers to

"Honour the Light Brigade" (line 54)—Nemerov warns of such sacrificial action by focusing on the human cost.

After decades of writing poetry collections that included occasional war poems about his experience and the aftereffects of that experience, Howard Nemerov found renewed focus on the topic of war as he was nearing the end of his life. In response to the election and rhetoric of Ronald Reagan, the myth of World War II as "the good war," and notions of World War II as the "Greatest Generation," Nemerov published *War Stories: Poems about Long Ago and Now* in 1987 (Oostdijk, *Among the Nightmare Fighters* 222). Echoing the concerns of Sassoon, Nemerov also found it troublesome that those who did not serve in World War II were shaping its narrative, particularly media and authority figures. A number of Nemerov's *War Poems* challenge this precise disagreement, such as "Authorities," which pinpoints "Commanders, and behind them heads of state" (line 1). These figures "Are said to care for and spend sleepless nights / About the children they commit to war" (lines 2–3); Nemerov, and by extension, readers, "can't help wondering, though, whether they do" (line 4). This is a simple question: is there substance behind the rhetoric that authority figures use to justify sending young men into battle? Nemerov does not believe so and asserts that their rhetoric is a smokescreen because they are "safely in their place / Of power" (lines 5–6). In other words, they do not *need* to care because they are unlikely to be held accountable or directly feel the consequence of their decisions. From their safely distanced position, they can accept criticism and condemnation without fear that their lives will be in jeopardy the way that those sent to wars are, and therefore public condemnation is relatively innocuous. Nemerov takes a subdued approach to his criticism of authorities and the press, in contrast to Sassoon's murder-fantasy poem "Fight to the Finish," in which he envisions soldiers exacting revenge on the media ("the Yellow-Pressmen") and politicians ("Junkers" in Parliament) (lines 10, 12). While one would interpret "Junkers" as a throwaway, or something to be discarded, by capitalizing "Junkers" Sassoon is offering a second layer of implication.[2] "Junkers" is twofold in its intended offense, first in that it calls out Parliament for their position of social and political privilege (and their elevated power over the average soldier), and second because it equates Parliament with the Germans, as if to say they are no better than the enemy and the propaganda directed against Prussian militarism. Sassoon's poem imagines violent revenge, while Nemerov's poem uses guilt and conscience to condemn the powerful.

Nemerov seeks to understand the callous perspective of politicians by writing what he perceives one would say if they were in such a position of privilege. Underneath the guise of sleepless nights spent worrying about the "children they commit to war," Nemerov devotes the second half of the poem to imagining the internal monologues of the authorities, who think to themselves:

"Poor bastards, little shits,

They never learned their history in schools
And now they never will, and cannot know
They are the hinges on which the oily valves
Of history will balance before they close

Upon our reputations now, our fame
In aftertimes, when children will be schooled
Again in truths belatedly belied,
To shoulder our burden and their hopeless charge."

(lines 8–16)

First, Nemerov points to a recurring theme in *War Poems*, the shortsightedness of those who do not learn from history. From the perspective of the speaker in "Authorities," it is the new generation of soldiers—the "Poor bastards" and "little shits" (line 8) who "never learned their history in schools"—who have not learned from history, while the authorities should know better (line 9). The ignorance of how war consumes lives harkens back to "The Old Soldiers' Home" in which war "Opens his mouth to be fed" (line 27), and individuals are seen as nothing more than "the hinges on which the oily valves / Of history will balance before they close" ("Authorities" lines 11–12). Soldiers are the instrument upon which force is exerted, the tool within a greater mechanism over which they have no say. While the authorities are preoccupied with their "reputations" and "fame" (line 13), they are aware that war participants "shoulder our burden and their hopeless charge" (line 16). Nemerov gives dual function to the word "charge" to call to mind the movement of battle and the responsibility of authorities to own the ramifications of their decisions. Though Nemerov is imagining the perspective of authority figures, he is writing from the vantage point of his late sixties and a lifetime bookended by war. Nemerov was born a few years after the First World War, served in the Second, and witnessed the return to conflicts in Korea and Vietnam. Toward the end of his life the threat of nuclear war amid Cold War tensions with Russia had spiked, and (a few years after the publication of *War Poems,* but during the last year of Nemerov's life) the Gulf War began. Nemerov witnessed the continual return of war, and he was concerned that the lessons of the past become elusive in the face of new conflicts.

The anger, frustration, and narrative course-correction offered in these poems by Nemerov catalogue the rift between soldiers and the authorities and press. He believed that when those who have not experienced war directly write its prevailing narrative, members of the armed services are reduced to the type of caricatures one would find on propaganda posters, such as anonymous patriots and vigilant heroes, without acknowledgment of variation or dissenting thought. Though there are soldiers who fit this character sketch, much of the lasting poetry, fiction, and nonfiction war writings delineate between the individual participants and the collective forces at play. Stark examples of the relationships between opposing sides take center stage in various world war poems across generations. For example, in the poem "IFF," an abbreviation used on aircrafts meaning "Identification Friend or Foe," Nemerov writes, "Hate Hitler? No, I spared him hardly a thought" (line 1); rather, it was the fellow soldiers who were "bastards in your daily life" that commanded more immediate disdain (line 8). Nemerov delineates between "cultural memory" and "collective memory," to use the terminology of Jan Assman, by which propaganda is a form of "cultural memory" in which "texts, icons" and other forms of communication (117) are based on a "mythical, absolute past" (van Hout 33). In contrast, the inner workings of Nemerov's squadron are an example of "collective memory," knowledge shared by a smaller group of people and framed by "autobiographical memory" (Assman 117).

British poets of the First World War expressed similar sentiments to Nemerov. Edward Thomas's most overtly war-focused poem "[This is no case of petty right or wrong]," expressed how he did not hate "Germans, nor grow hot / With love of Englishmen" (lines 3–4). Each individual soldier has their own sense of purpose and motivation for service, and these declarations by Nemerov and Thomas speak to motivations that extend beyond retribution for German aggression. Despite this nuanced view of enemy belligerents, the depravity of the Holocaust often overshadows questions over whether the Allied "all-out bombing campaign" of Germany was "strategically or morally justifiable" (Sebald 13). Instead, the widespread bombing damage was viewed by some Germans as punishment or retribution "with which there could be no dispute" (Sebald 14). Historian John Bodnar suggests that the romanticized myth of World War II as a triumph of good over evil requires one to "disregard the darker legacy of the conflict," such as "Allied bombing raids, which killed hundreds of thousands of civilians in Germany and Japan" (208). In addition to Thomas's discrepancy between patriotic fervor and the cooler emotions between combatants, British First World War soldier David Jones, who is best known for his epic poem *In Parenthesis*, dedicates the poem to

MY FRIENDS . . .
AND TO THE ENEMY
FRONT-FIGHTERS WHO SHARED OUR
PAINS AGAINST WHOM WE FOUND
OURSELVES BY MISADVENTURE.

Similar to Jones's feelings of being compatriots with the soldiers of the opposing army, different sides of the same coin, Wilfred Owen's speaker in "Strange Meeting" is reunited in hell with the enemy soldier he had killed. While Owen's speaker addresses that "Strange friend," the enemy soldier confesses, "Whatever hope is yours, / Was my life also" (lines 14, 16–17). Each soldier is victim to circumstance, recognizing that borders are the primary, imperceptible barrier between similarly situated individuals.

Though not all soldiers possessed these feelings of mutual respect between opposite sides, what is shared between Sassoon, Owen, Thomas, Jones, and Nemerov, among others, is that each identifies war service as an altogether unique circumstance that cannot be encapsulated by conventional narratives of good and evil, right and wrong, or victorious and defeated. Instead, from the perspective of these poets, war positions its participants in a gray area from which none emerge unaffected. It is for this reason that a rejection of the press and authority-directed narratives is recurrent in twentieth-century war poems. What distinguishes these narratives most from the conventional storytelling of war is that these poems disarm the rhetoric used by governments to influence public opinion about foreign conflict. While war films, newspaper articles, songs, and even other examples of war poetry often serve to reinforce ideals, encourage action, and motivate the necessary sacrifices in order to conduct battle, poems of the world wars reclaim the narratives and memory of war for the soldiers who experienced it firsthand. First World War trench poetry and the delayed response of World War II poems force us to see the world differently, most powerfully by showing soldiers, civilians, and all those touched by war as vulnerable, flawed, and unique human beings aware of what is lost and carried forward in the aftermath of war. The difficulty of recognizing this nuance stems from what Samet describes of the legacy of World War II in American self-definition, that "there is no more important part of the myth of World War II . . . than the figure of the American soldier as an agent for good in the world" (271). This is not a uniquely American problem of repurposing the past, though, as other nations such as Russia have continued to speak about World War II as the "Great Patriotic War," and use the defense against, and defeat of, Nazi Germany to frame political rhetoric in the decades that followed. By framing World War II through the "sacred, messianic myth of victory and 'liberation,'" Russia has continually evoked this narrative to justify violations of territorial sovereignty as being defensive in nature, exacerbating a "memory war" that contests fact with fiction (Domańska). Warning of such acts of disinformation, Nemerov broke his silence to challenge the mythmakers and rhetoricians who would bend historical narratives in opportunistic directions.

"The War in the Air": Skyscapes and Postwar Memory

Rapid technological advancements in the world wars have had an immeasurable impact on how theaters of combat are perceived. Developments such as poison gas, flamethrowers, and evolutions of the machine gun in the First World War, and improved tanks, ships, and planes equipped with weapons of mass destruction such as the atomic bomb in World War II greatly influenced the conflicts themselves, and how each is remembered.

A. Torrey McLean encapsulates the cost of failing to evolve military strategy to technological advancement during wartime by arguing that "millions died needlessly because military and civilian leaders were slow to adapt their old-fashioned strategies and tactics to the new weapons of 1914." The style of combat in major battles of the First World War was a mix of shelling enemies from distance and facing increasingly deadly weaponry when trying to advance from the trenches through no-man's land, resulting in staggering death tolls. World War II, by contrast, placed greater emphasis on two types of bombing: *precision* and *area*. The targets of precision bombing included war production and supply centers such as "airfields, defense industries (e.g., steel and chemicals), the communication network, petroleum installations" and other sites crucial to the war effort (Garrett 21). Area bombing, or "indiscriminate bombing," was intended to suppress morale by targeting population centers and infrastructure (Garrett 21). These changes contributed to the discrepancy of civilian deaths within the death toll of the First World War being roughly 14 percent, while the percentage of civilian deaths in World War II rose to roughly 67 percent (Sadowski 134). This shift prompted new moral concerns about the conduct of countries at war and the immense destruction capable from long-range acts of engagement. The gradual, though not complete, distancing between warring nations and their targets during World War II altered the emotional investment of combatants by often anonymizing their targets. As explained by Eric Hobsbawm, the rise of barbarism in war was "the strange democratization of war" in which "civilians and civilian life became the proper, and sometimes the main, targets of strategy," and victims were rendered invisible by their murderers as "adversaries are naturally demonized in order to make them properly hateful" (49–50). Furthermore, from the view of World War II soldier and poet R. N. Currey, there is a damaging disconnection for "a civilization in which a man, too squeamish to empty a slop pail or skin a rabbit, can press a button that exposes the entrails of cities" (43). In other words, human culpability struggles to keep pace with rapid technological advancement. Any illusions of nobility in battle disappear when a pilot can press a button that releases an atomic bomb that can instantly destroy tens of thousands of lives from miles above the earth. Even if a soldier has psychologically dehumanized adversaries in order to cope with the act of killing, modern warfare is not comparable to the way close-range combat forces one to recognize the humanity of an enemy combatant.[3]

Howard Nemerov's war poetry shows how firsthand experience engages with public perception of war, how the delayed response to traumatic experience manifests itself in daily life, and the ways these issues influence emotional engagement between the soldier-turned-civilian and the war they carry inside them. The persistence of postwar memory in Howard Nemerov's poetry often finds a transmission channel through the skyscapes in which Nemerov experienced the war. Nemerov was aware of and attracted to the danger of flying, explaining to his parents during Canadian RAF pilot training that "it is fascinating to develop a technic [sic] which will enable you to tell, with nothing but sky around you, just where you wd [sic] be if you came down" (Letter to Parents, undated). Poems such as "An Old Warplane" and "The War in the Air" use the sky, airplanes, and pilot's perspective to convey the war experience in more easily imaginable and digestible forms. Furthermore, poems such as "The War in the Air," "Ultima Ratio Reagan," "Redeployment," and "30th Anniversary Report of the Class of '41" confront the emotional distance that exists between an event and its memory as time passes. In particular, these poems confront postwar memory by urging humanity to learn from war, describe living with PTSD, and explore the difficulty of trying to say something of consequence after war.

Nemerov used the distanced perspective of air combat to reflect on the ground war. His poem "An Old Warplane" uses the physical details of a warplane and sensory observation of flying as a conduit for transmitting war experience. The speaker is a pilot relaying what he can see from his position, describing the heavily used plane that has "rust flaking the paint / And oil stains streaked" (lines 2–3) and "Burnt patches on the cannon ports" (line 13). In contrast to the landscapes of the earth, the skyscapes and details Nemerov includes in "An Old Warplane" are told using narrow sight lines of the immediate shell of the plane and what, if anything, can be seen through the clouds. As Blunden in "Concert Party: Busseboom" and Simpson in "Carentan O Carentan" experience, Nemerov recalls the same distant rumbling of war despite the earth being miles below:

> For only a moment, as she passed
> Close to the shore, we heard again

The empty thunder of the war
By engines drummed on the stretched sky.

(lines 9–12)

In Nemerov's case, he is not on the ground hearing the reverberating cannons and guns; he is flying over land and sea, and even from this distant
position he feels the weight of his actions. As a pilot delivering death from
above, Nemerov believes "all our future rusts inside / The bright invention
of the war" (lines 27–28). The warplane is emblematic, a harbinger of that
which is yet to come, a future that Nemerov believes will decay like the destruction brought with each technological advancement of war. Nemerov's
use of such weaponry is similar to the realization many of his First World
War predecessors had upon exposure to machine guns and poison gas:
"memory is seen at last / As obsolete and simplified, / Inadequately armed"
(lines 29–31). The knowledge of the destruction of war and depravity of
man that was laid out for the world thirty years before is "obsolete" now,
and this inability or unwillingness to learn from the past becomes a recurring theme in Nemerov's reflective war poetry. Notably, this desire to connect with a civilian readership is important not just to share what the war
was like by those who experienced it in terms that noncombatants could
understand, but to be a reminder to the world of the consequences of war.

Like "An Old Warplane," Nemerov's poem "The War in the Air" conveys
a skeptical combatant's view of the war. Specifically, "The War in the Air"
challenges the conventional war narratives of *winners* and *losers,* and the
heroism of those who survived, by using the backdrop of the air war to
sarcastically dispel those misconceptions. Since combat deaths of those in
the air forces often mean corpses go unrecovered, unreturned, or unburied,
Nemerov facetiously mentions how the absence of a body or the lack of a
specific death narrative leads to sanitized depictions:

For a saving grace, we didn't see our dead,
Who rarely bothered coming home to die
But simply stayed away out there
In the clean war, the war in the air.

(lines 1–4)

Saved from the brutal sight of dead airmen who have perished in any number of terrible ways, Nemerov is highlighting the way war can be depicted in a more positive light if governments and citizens are spared the unnerving proof of death. Therefore, the unreturned dead, upon "hitting the earth, the incompressible sea" (line 6), stay "up there in the relative wind" (line 7) with "no graves but only epitaphs" (line 9). This romanticized version of the death of airmen redirects public sentiment to focus on "the good war, the war we won / As if there was no death" (lines 13–14), while the absence of those who did not return forever suspends them "In the air, in the empty air" (lines 15–16). Unnamed and largely forgotten in Nemerov's view, the dead airmen of the war are rendered as footnotes in the public's simplified story of the war. For Nemerov, the skyscape is like an invisibility cloak where the dead are relegated. They inhabit a void in the war narrative, and since people do not have to confront the physical evidence of these deaths, the illusion that there is a "clean war" persists (line 4).

Poems such as "The War in the Air" also demonstrate how emotional distancing is a key characteristic of Nemerov's poetry. Nemerov's poems explore numerous cross-sections, such as firsthand war experience with public perception of war, how the delayed response to traumatic experience manifests itself in daily life, and how these issues influence emotional engagement between the soldier-turned-civilian and the war they carry inside them. "The War in the Air" also exemplifies the divide between his experience in World War II and the generally accepted rhetoric of war commentary. Writing of service in both the Canadian Royal Air Force and the U.S. Air Force, Nemerov begins "The War in the Air" with a silver lining about the effect of pilots' deaths on other members of the air force. Resigned to the knowledge that encountering death in wartime is inevitable, the speaker is cognizant of the relative anonymity with which airmen die. Yet, the subtlety of referring to air combat in World War II as "the clean war" (line 4) alludes to the distance of engagement for pilots, not having to literally be embedded in the earth like the soldiers in foxholes or the trenches of their First World War predecessors, or to figuratively describe the messiness of killing at close range. One could argue that to be absolved of the close visual trauma of combat is a mental and emotional respite, but Nemerov's mention of "the clean war" decades after the conclusion of World War II is proof that the war, regardless of how far removed a pilot is from face-to-face action, stays with its combatants all the same. Pilots who die in service are often relegated to the ether of memory, and Nemerov continues: "Seldom the ghosts come back bearing their tales" (line 5) of crashing to earth or sea, but rather, Nemerov believes they remain "in the relative wind" (line 7).[4]

Nemerov then alludes to the motto of the Royal Air Force, "Per ardua ad astra," as an elegiac nod to those who were lost. This motto is translated roughly as "Through struggles to the stars" or "Through adversity to the stars" (Royal Air Force Museum). In the context of Nemerov's poem the motto is both a dedication to service and an allusion to the death of airmen who did not return, who remain in the stars, an allusion to a heavenward departure from earth. "Per ardua, said the partisans of Mars, / Per aspera, to the stars" ("The War in the Air" lines 11–12), Nemerov writes, the Latin phrases reminding us that it is through adversity ("Per ardua") and through hardship ("Per aspera") that the airmen succeeded or sacrificed (Edgecombe 238). The poem's turn occurs in the final stanza, where Nemerov sarcastically engages the mythology of World War II as "the good war," declaring, "That was the good war, the war we won" (line 13). Nemerov's reaction is particularly potent because the poem was written at a time of heightened public discourse over the controversial legacy of the Vietnam War and rising tensions in the Cold War. The retrospective shaping of American intervention in World War II as a moral act helped to "transform the meaning of killing and dying into virtuous acts," and this pervasive vision of the American military as only a force for good has been used for subsequent generations of military recruitment, national support, and justification for military intervention (Bodnar 2–3). In referring to World War II as "the war we won," Nemerov points out the fallacy of wars being deemed good, bad, great, or otherwise based on the outcome of winners and losers, highlighting the callousness of reducing millions of dead not as *the lost,* but losers. Nemerov continues to challenge the mythmaking conventions that whitewash World War II "As if there was no death, for goodness's sake" (line 14). Nemerov is countering the reduction of war to such simplistic terms by using the terminology of the media and public to position them to accept guilt, to recognize that it was "With the help of the losers we left out there / In the air, in the empty air" that the Allied Forces were victorious in World War II (lines 15–16). By repurposing the language used by those who retrospectively shape the narrative of war, Nemerov forces readers to recognize that there are no true *winners* in war, and that to suggest so is to ignore those who died for country and cause.

Another charge against the rhetoric of war-making from Nemerov's collection *War Stories* is the poem "Ultima Ratio Reagan." In the wake of the Vietnam War, and as the Cold War was heating up, "Ultima Ratio Reagan" is a play on words referencing then president Ronald Reagan and Stephen Spender's poem "Ultima Ratio Regum," which is translated as "the ultimate, or the final argument of kings." Outraged by the cycle of war, seemingly without any regard for previous generations and conflicts, Nemerov's "Ultima Ratio Reagan" begins, "The reason we do not learn from history is / Because we are not the people who learned last time" (lines 1–2). Dispelling the inflated sense of wisdom of the current generation, the presumption that the current state knows more than those who preceded them, Nemerov is implying that if the current generation had direct experience with the wars of the past, they would not be so quick to reengage militarily. Though Reagan had enlisted in the army, he never served overseas, a detail that makes Nemerov more skeptical of Reagan's affiliation with war glory without the combat experience that may give him pause before sending others to war. Nemerov reinforces a generational divide over the appetite for war by writing, "Because we are not the same people as them / That fed our sons and honor to Vietnam / And dropped the burning money on the trees" (lines 3–5). This challenge to the methods and economic motives of war further muddies the morality of American intervention, as suggested by the youth, honor, and money lost to the conflict. As explained by Subarno Chattarji, "Ultima Ratio Reagan" is a poem that highlights the "arrogance of each generation that believes in its ideals as absolute entities . . . a contributory factor in the destruction of Vietnam which, paradoxically, America was trying to 'save'" (lines 63–64). This "arrogance" that Chattarji identifies is most noticeable as Nemerov writes, "We know that we know better than they knew" (line 6). Here, Nemerov facetiously criticizes the American political mindset that because there are moments of military victory acting on behalf of a greater good, other countries do not know what is best for them and America is incapable of wrongdoing. This misappropriation and cultural blindness is perpetuated in ongoing global interventions, a certainty that Nemerov is resigned to at the conclusion of the poem: "And history will not blame us if once again / The light at the end of the tunnel is the train" (lines 7–8). America's reversion to the economic and cultural boom generated by World War II, in the form of patriotism, industrial output, and societal development, is a methodology that encourages cultural amnesia for the human cost of war. In these final lines of "Ultima Ratio Reagan," Nemerov warns that the world will not look kindly upon America or extend sympathy if, in time, America endures the repercussions of sustaining a perpetual state of war. The matter of public perception is the primary difference between "Ultima Ratio Reagan" and "The War in the Air." The legacy of each twentieth-century American generation was shaped by its own war, the trauma and loss they endured, and the subsequent narratives that emerged. In Nemerov's view, this forced a more discerning public to question American involvement in Vietnam while the legacy of World War II as "the good war" remained largely unchallenged by the general populace.

Any discussion of a war's legacy is bound to drum up conflicting opinions based on perspective, experience, and the varying strands of repercussion. Howard Nemerov's attempts to internalize and externalize the impact of war were a work in progress throughout his life. In discussing post-traumatic stress disorder, Cathy Caruth explains, "there is a response, sometimes delayed, to an overwhelming event or events, which takes the form of repeated, intrusive hallucinations, dreams, thoughts or behaviors stemming from the event" and that the structure of the experience contributes to its reception in the individual (*Trauma* 4). In other words, "the event is not assimilated or experienced fully at the time, but only belatedly, in its repeated possession of the one who experiences it" (4). Belated returns to a traumatic event are exemplified in Nemerov's poems "Redeployment" and "30th Anniversary Report of the Class of '41."

Meshing his experience as a soldier and civilian, Nemerov explores the idea of emotional detachment from family and community life in "30th Anniversary Report of the Class of '41." Most notably indicative of a sense of detachment in this poem is the fact that getting married, having children, working, having an affair and dealing with the fallout, having relatives die, and watching family members grow old—events that mark the speaker's life—are all presented as an aside to the poem's main point. If you reconstruct the poem as a streamlined narrative, removing the aforementioned segments from lines 1–12, and leave the first thought and final stanza, what remains is, "We who survived the war . . . // Are done with it.

What is there to discuss? / There's nothing left for us to say of us" (lines 1, 13–14). One can imagine a university reunion marking thirty years since graduation, and not wanting to be defined by war service or continually relive the trauma of war amid a lifetime of love, loss, death, betrayal, and countless other happenings. Similar to the stunted aspirations of poets at the start of World War II who stood in the long shadow of First World War poets, Nemerov feels the narrative of World War II has been exhausted. In the vein of Keith Douglas's nod to Isaac Rosenberg in "Desert Flowers"— "Rosenberg I only repeat what you were saying"—Nemerov is trying to be mindful not to rehash the past so he can try to live his life out from behind the shadow of war ("Desert Flowers" line 2). Yet, Nemerov publishes "30th Anniversary Report of the Class of '41" in the early 1970s, sparking a creative outburst of writing poetry about war. Nemerov's struggle to suppress war's presence in his life became increasingly difficult as a civilian who lived through America's reentry into war. Ultimately, Nemerov felt he had no choice but to confront the lasting memories of his own war experience. Despite posing the question, "What is there to discuss?," the speaker learns that war will not leave his periphery. Precisely because of having to deal with his own traumatic memories, Nemerov is pushed to write poems that warn of the consequences of war, which is the case in "Redeployment."

Nemerov's 1950 poem "Redeployment," published in his collection *Guide to the Ruins,* reinforces the presence of war's lingering effects in its opening lines: "They say the war is over. But water still / Comes bloody from the taps" (lines 1–2). This imagery distinguishes the literal and figurative difference between a war's conclusion for the narratives of history and the ongoing processing of trauma for the individual participants. Nemerov deceptively deploys precise terminology to describe the way soldiers are always carrying with them the legacy of war:

The war may be over. I know a man
Who keeps a pleasant souvenir, he keeps
A soldier's dead blue eyeballs that he found
Somewhere—hard as chalk, blue as slate.
He clicks them in his pocket while he talks.

(lines 6–10)

Like a nervous tic, the soldier clicks these hardened eyes against one another in his pocket, a hallucinatory moment suggesting that unseen objects take on haunting qualities. This imagery continues the trend of World War II poets using forms of sight to convey trauma, with seeing being synonymous with witnessing. Prefaced by "The war may be over," the poem positions reality and illusion side by side so that the reader can understand the dissociative properties of traumatic memory, and how, despite the war being over, the memories and sensory observations are not easily forgotten. The final stanza shows this attempt of a soldier to take one step at a time to return to a normal functioning life:

> The end of the war. I took it quietly
> Enough. I tried to wash the dirt out of
> My hair and from under my fingernails,
> I dressed in clean white clothes and went to bed.
> I heard the dust falling between the walls.
>
> (lines 16–20)

For this speaker, quietly washing hands, putting on clean clothes, and going to bed—mundane acts, as well as metaphorical acts of purifying oneself—are not enough to keep the mind quiet. Senses are heightened and haunting, as he hears dust "falling between the walls," a remark that magnifies the speaker's postwar silence. In other words, by not saying much about their experience, soldiers endure a heightened sensitivity to their memory. Conveying jarring images within the syllabic meter of ten-syllable lines results in enjambments that pivot between interpretations, such as "I took it quietly / Enough" and "wash the dirt out of / My hair." Formal considerations such as meter and syllable count are accentuated by the percussive stress of "clean white clothes," while the assonance of "falling . . . walls" exemplifies aural attentiveness. Additionally, the call-and-response construction of the poem—with three of four stanzas beginning with, "They say the war is over" (line 1), "The war may be over" (line 6), and "The end of the war" (line 16), each followed by traumatic visions—allows the speaker to demonstrate the reality that is being told to him versus the manifestations of his PTSD. A key to this being a PTSD poem, beyond the text telling us what the speaker deals with despite the war being over, is the title itself. For the speaker to suggest each day is an act of "Redeployment," quotidian events become reminders of the war and disruptions that renew memory of a war the speaker must relive.[5] For Nemerov, war interjects traumatic imagery into turning on a faucet, a cat vomiting, reaching into one's pockets, cockroaches scuttling in the house, washing, getting dressed, and trying to sleep. To recall Cathy Caruth's words, Nemerov is displaying traumatic memory through descriptions of "intrusive hallucinations."

In each of these four poems by Howard Nemerov—"The War in the Air," "Ultima Ratio Reagan," "30th Anniversary Report of the Class of '41," and "Redeployment"—there are varying levels of emotional engagement that his two selves, soldier and civilian, intentionally and begrudgingly have with war. Nemerov's poetry is continuously influenced by his war experience, whether he is decrying the misleading mythology of war rhetoric in "The War in the Air" or exposing the shortsighted, reckless, and ignorant willingness to engage in perpetual war in "Ultima Ratio Reagan." Nemerov also catalogues a veteran plagued by traumatic thoughts in "Redeployment," and expresses defeat from trying to move on from war in "30th Anniversary Report of the Class of '41." Nemerov's moments of heightened emotional engagements with war are intended to honor the sacrificial dead pilots in his sarcasm-riddled homage to "the losers" ("The War in the Air"), warn current and future generations about PTSD by detailing how one relives the horror and loss experienced in World War II ("Redeployment"), and call out the ignorance of world leaders acting without a sense of history or consequence ("Ultima Ratio Reagan").

Though Nemerov experienced a large literal distance between himself and other combatants as a pilot, the figurative distance between himself and the war was indistinguishable in his work. As noted with other soldiers serving in the air force, such as Randall Jarrell, the distance of war experienced from the air or from airbases forces the individual to fill in the gaps of experience that are not processed with the same acuity as ground combat. Since pilots and instructors contribute to the war effort from a physically distanced perspective compared to ground troops, up-close traumatic images are supplanted by seeing explosions and damaged targets from above, and photographs and video documentation of the war have the potential to become extensions of one's memory and guilt. In other words, if a pilot or instructor who facilitates the bombing of foreign targets encounters or imagines the visual documentation of that damage, this delayed experience of causing death and destruction can result in a delayed onset of trauma. Despite the literal distance that exists between skyscapes in which members of the air force operate and targets below, postwar memory can render the figurative distance between a veteran and traumatic experience imperceptible.

Reliving War Trauma in Dreams and Waking Life

In 1961, Howard Nemerov wrote to Reed Whittemore that poetry is about "trying to say the silence" (Letter to Reed Whittemore). Perhaps in part due to this quieter exploration of experience and memory, in contrast to earlier renditions of war poetry that transmitted the gore of battle, conventional belief has maintained that "The poems of the Second World War have had less impact" on readers (Stallworthy, *Survivors' Songs* 195). While Jon Stallworthy argued this lesser impact was partially because "Word has lost ground to the Image"—referring to the rapidly increasing popularity of film—the contemplative language of self-examination in World War II poetry is received with a diminished impact compared to the image-driven war poetry of the past (195). In other words, poems that convey the sensory barrage of First World War mudscapes in which soldiers writhed in agony, if they were not obliterated altogether, are more visceral representations of battle compared to the poems examining the post-traumatic stress of veterans struggling to reacclimate to civilian life. Yet, the cultural value of listening and understanding the traumatic experience of veterans is a wholly underrecognized facet of the way modern societies think of, act in, and remember times of war. Nemerov's poems "Returning to Europe," "Armistice," and "Redeployment" reimagine and relive war through the veteran's dreamscapes and daily experiences transformed by traumatic reverberations.

According to David K. Vaughan, Nemerov was among a cohort of World War II soldiers who wrote from a "narrower, more personal perspective instead of broader philosophical frameworks" (11). While Nemerov's later poetry would suggest a shift toward broader philosophical commentary on the intersection of war and society, his earlier war poems tend to confine themselves to the inner workings of the mind. One such example is a 1955 dreamscape poem titled "Returning to Europe" from his collection

The Salt Garden. Explaining a recurring dream, the poem's speaker details how "in my dream I am always lost / In ruined streets, in roofless houses / Under a sky splintered with rafters" (lines 2–4). Contrary to Nemerov's perspective as a pilot looking down at the earth below, most often from behind the controls of a Bristol Beaufighter X, which the 236 Squadron RAF was using in the final two years of the war, "Returning to Europe" is a dream in which the speaker is looking up from a destroyed home ("No. 236 Squadron (RAF): Second World War"). Unsurprisingly, airmen rarely see the destruction they have caused on the ground, and therefore the imagination of what one's bombs have wrought has startling consequences. Such a divide between cause and effect has been stated to have varying degrees of consequence and guilt. In his 1989 book *Modernity and the Holocaust,* Zygmunt Bauman writes, "As long as one does not see the practical effects of one's actions, or as long as one cannot unambiguously relate what one saw to such innocent and minuscule acts of one's own as pushing a button or switching a pointer, a moral conflict is unlikely to appear, or likely to appear in muted form" (194). Yet, recent reports show how the operators of unmanned drones "experience mental health problems, like depression, anxiety and post-traumatic stress at the same rate as pilots of manned aircraft who are deployed to Iraq or Afghanistan" (Dao), proof that the human cost of war extends far beyond numbers of battlefront combat casualties to the "moral injury" incurred by drone operators (Press).[6] Literal distance between airmen and their bombing targets does not preclude them from feeling guilt over the destruction they brought. In "Returning to Europe," while the speaker laments that the dream "tells me nothing" (line 5), one time when it recurred, "This dream forgot to wake me . . . / And told me this one thing" (lines 10–11). The speaker continues: "There is / A room in one of those ruined houses / I must not enter" (lines 11–13) because "Any door / Might be the one" (lines 13–14). Nemerov initially suspends revealing what is feared to be found behind these doors, clarifying that soldiers "are not / The one I fear to find" (lines 18–19), before ultimately revealing the speaker is afraid to find "the self, / The image of the lost war" (lines 19–20). The fear of confronting oneself is a stark example of unresolved guilt. The speaker is haunted by these dreams and the core of their imagery: sifting through the rooms of a bombed-out house fearful that he will find himself. This image can fray two ways: either one is afraid to come to terms with dropping the bombs that would have created such a scene or to acknowledge that the targets are people that could easily be him. This vision of himself the speaker is afraid to find is "Secret and pale with long denial, / Who will embrace me brotherly / And put his greedy mouth on mine" (lines 21–23). This dreamed act of physical intimacy embodies the fear the speaker feels over having to face, and feel, the repercussions of his wartime actions.

Nemerov's poem "Armistice," which directly follows "Returning to Europe" in *The Salt Garden,* also touches on the veteran experience. By invoking imagery of past wars, remembrance imagery, and support environments for veterans, "Armistice" outlines an interaction and emotional response. The poem begins, "His name is Legion, and . . . / he offers me / The paper opiate of this poppy" (lines 1–3). Here, Nemerov is personifying the American Legion (or equivalents such as the Royal Canadian Legion or the British Legion), a nonprofit organization providing services and a sense of community to veterans ("History"). The paper symbol of First World War remembrance, the poppy, is described here as having the same addictive depressant qualities as the opium poppy. In the second stanza of this three-quatrain poem, it is unclear whether the speaker, Legion, or poppy is controlling the narrative. "Remember who died for you" (line 5) the stanza begins, "They sleep / In Flanders, in the poppy beds" (lines 5–6). Recalling the familiar refrain of commemoration of First World War sacrifice and the imagery of red poppies dotting Belgian fields, as a poet who served in the Canadian RAF Nemerov would no doubt be familiar with "In Flanders Fields," the poem by Canadian First World War soldier and surgeon John McCrae that inspired the poppy campaigns. So the speaker thinks of "The real, narcotic and forbidden / Beds of huddled buddies dead," a pair of lines that aurally replicate the percussive thudding of artillery through repetition of *b* and *d* sounds in "forbidden," "Beds," "huddled," "buddies," and "dead" (lines 7–8). These repeated consonant pairings of *b* and *d* sounds make the reader anticipate the word *bodies,* though it does not appear in the poem. Instead, we are left to visualize this image of war death, whether a mass grave, military cemetery, or battlefield site. Furthermore, "buddies" works as a homonym alluding to imagery of the death of soldier friends, and the budding life of the flowering poppies. While wondering if the man at the Legion is drunk in the final stanza, perhaps intoxicated "on poppy seed?" (line 9), the speaker shares in the pain of loss and remembrance of the moment by weeping "my green and paper blood" (line 12). "Armistice" participates in the act of remembrance while perpetuating an absence of self, mention of World War II, or the speaker's own service (if we are to assume a link between the speaker and Nemerov, or that the speaker is likely a veteran because he is visiting a Legion post). Nemerov's intentional absence of self and World War II from the poem has led some to state the poem is about veterans celebrating the anniversary of the end of the First World War (Vaughan 84). Yet, the power in the poem comes from its ambiguity: veterans wrestling with the importance of remembering and honoring their own war dead, while also juggling all of the subsequent wars that have erupted and smoldered out since. Mary A. Favret believes that "The idea of a last war is always the idea of a world war," and Nemerov's malleable allusions to indeterminate world wars reinforce Favret's notion that "each last war dreams (again) of being finally the only world war. Counting (first, second, third) marks the repeated failure of this dream" (43). Nemerov's tragic simultaneity of cyclical mourning is a rebuke of a culture driven by war. How can a culture adequately mourn and learn from one war if it has not yet completed that process for the preceding war?

In Nemerov's 1950 collection *Guide to the Ruins,* dedicated to Reed Whittemore, the poem "Redeployment" is one of the purest examples of a PTSD poem to emerge from World War II. As a poem of postwar civilian life, "Redeployment" demonstrates its title's implication that one is being metaphorically redeployed each day by experiencing trauma-induced hallucinations and unsettling sensory events. "They say the war is over," the poem begins, "But water still / Comes bloody from the taps" (lines 1–2). For the speaker, a surrender and a peace treaty bear little influence on the state of the war because morbid visions dominate his waking life. Like recursive war memories, even the speaker's pet cat "vomits worms which crawl / Swiftly away" (lines 3–4) and are "flecked with the cat's blood" (line 5), a mirrored act of regurgitation, of trying to expel something damaging from within. The second stanza repeats the speaker's skepticism as he says warily, "The war may be over" (line 6), as if mulling over the fact in contrast to his inability to shake the aftereffects of war. The speaker's recollection of a man who "keeps / A soldier's dead blue eyeballs" (lines 7–8) and "clicks them in his pocket while he talks" (line 10) exemplifies contrasts in "Redeployment" that demonstrate Nemerov's use of "the binary oppositions of inside and outside, invisible and visible, dirt and cleanliness, and war and peace" (Oostdijk, "Debunking"). Attempts at cleaning or purifying oneself transform into bloody reminders of war participation. These binaries reinforce the way Nemerov dispels concepts such as the "clean war" in the air, or World War II as "the good war." The third stanza adds a furthers unsettling image set, this time of cockroaches "drunk on DDT" ("Redeployment" line 12), an insecticide used by the Allies to limit the spread of diseases such as typhus (Berry-Caban). These cockroaches "can be drowned" ("Redeployment" line 13) if you hold them under water for "quite some time" (line 14). Like the regurgitated worms and the hard-clicking eyeballs, the resilience of cockroaches is a third example in the poem of tactile representations of disturbing images haunting the speaker. Exemplifying "Affect Theory," Nemerov's "Redeployment" uses "psychoanalytic models" such as his emotional discomfort in tandem with a "politically oriented critique" of the traumatic repercussions of war (Hogan 6). In the fourth and final stanza, the speaker returns to the rhetorical structure of responding to how external voices have declared "The end of the war" (16), by powerlessly relenting: "I took it quietly / Enough" (lines 16–17). As if feeling pressure to be quiet about the struggle of carrying war memory back into civilian life, the speaker appears beholden still to a sense of duty. He does his best to sterilize himself from the past by washing "the dirt out of / My hair and from under my fingernails" (lines 17–18) and putting on "clean white clothes" before going to bed (line 19). The speaker in "Redeployment" physically cleans himself in an attempt to psychologically purify himself of war trauma. In a compelling conclusion, the poem's speaker goes to bed, and either in a state of dreaming or insomnia hears "the dust falling between the walls" (line 20). Each of these examples in which the speaker experiences the unseen through sensory hyperawareness, does not feel the war is over, is pushed toward disturbing thoughts, and keeps these hallucinations and triggers private, is typical of an individual coping with post-traumatic stress. Among the four major symptom types of PTSD (reexperiencing, avoidance, arousal, and negative changes in beliefs and feelings), Nemerov's "Redeployment" exhibits each of them ("How Is PTSD Measured?"). While "Redeployment" initially reads as if it could be a surrealist dreamscape, the immense importance of such a poem is to give concrete examples of what it is like to experience PTSD in the postwar life of a veteran.

For surviving war veterans, who commonly carry a reputation of not speaking about their service—a notion that emerged during the First World War in W. H. R. Rivers's "The Repression of War Experience" (Rivers)—the notion of silence, sacrifice, anxiety, and emotional scarring is a prominent portion of the legacy that has been crafted on their behalf. It is for these reasons that Howard Nemerov's poetry of war-induced PTSD is an invaluable representation of the lasting and often unseen consequences of war for those directly involved. Nemerov's poems prove that war poetry is not merely that which chronicles how the individual enacts change upon conflict, but how conflict enacts change upon the individual.

■ ■ ■

The opening couplet of Nemerov's 1975 poem "A Memory of the War" from the collection *The Western Approaches* perhaps best encapsulates the nature of World War II soldiers and their turn to poetry: "Most what I know of war is what I learned / When mine was over and they shipped me home" (lines 1–2). Nemerov's initial naivety is compounded in the lines that follow, in which he describes his role as a pilot as a "chauffeur for the RAF" (line 3) who "didn't know the first damn thing about / The American way of doing anything" (lines 4–5). Placed on guard duty one night for a ship crossing west over the Atlantic, he is given a gun and told to keep watch and shoot anyone trying to escape (lines 13–15). "So that is what I did," the speaker concludes, "and how I learned / About the War: I sat there till relieved" (lines 16–17). Remarkably consistent in many World War II soldier poems is this brand of a subdued conclusion, an understated point said as if simultaneous with a shrug or a genuflection. Like Hugo's bombardier who does his job so he can go home ("Letter to Simic from Boulder"), the soldier speaking in "A Memory of the War" uses this isolated incident of simply waiting out their time following orders as a description of soldierdom itself.

Even when experimenting with form, such as a variation of a sestina that reorders the end words and omits the envoy tercet in the 1967 poem "Sarajevo," repeating "In the summer, when the Archduke dies," the subject matter Nemerov is exploring is still the cyclical nature of time and the recurrence of war (line 1). Twenty years later, in "The Afterlife" (1987), Nemerov again echoes the idea of waiting for a respite from war when he writes, "The many of us that came through the war / Unwounded and set free in Forty-Five / Already understood the afterlife" (lines 1–3). Armed service during a war is presented as a rite of passage in which you line up "for uniforms and shots / And scream incomprehensible commands / Until you learn obedience again" (lines 15–17). Like the war poems of Randall

Jarrell that speak to the routines, anonymity, and dehumanization that soldiers undergo as a means of adapting to the armed forces, Nemerov is using form to mimic content, and stanza construction to maintain order and procedure. The uniformity and rigidity of army life "will feel strange at first," Nemerov writes, "But so it goes" he laments to end the poem (line 18).[7] From the veteran's perspective, the time that has passed since one's war experience, and what those memories mean to the individual, paint a complex picture of postwar life. Dividing one's life into before and after war echoes Nemerov's comments in a lecture titled "What Was Modern Poetry?" from his essay collection *Figures of Thought*. Nemerov references both Louis Simpson and Randall Jarrell in explaining how a poem can be understood differently as a stand-alone work compared to when it is contextualized within the poet's body of writing. Of Jarrell, Nemerov comments that his poems "fit with one another, lead on from one another, reinforce one another's meanings" (196) and that they exemplify the "Great Change" of "growing up, . . . the sudden after-realization of what growing up has entailed" (197). Each of these poets is unified through a shared experience of World War II, a "Great Change" that has demarcated their lives into before and after.

Despite being encouraged by the inclinations of First World War soldier poets to warn forthcoming generations about the cost and consequences of war on humanity, culture, and psyche, Howard Nemerov is a nontraditional war poet. His war poems avoid reenacting battle and flying missions, opting instead to speak about the immediate and prolonged consequences of being at war. Through retrospective examinations of the war, Nemerov sought to reclaim war narratives from those who opted to oversimplify the motives, actions, cost, and repercussions of war. Participating in the war from a greater distance than the likes of infantryman Louis Simpson and tank commander Keith Douglas, Nemerov channeled his postwar memory through the imagery of skyscapes and the metaphorical landscape of the "clean war" from which their dead did not return ("The War in the Air" line 4). As Nemerov explains in his essay "On Metaphor," "If you really want to see something, look at something else. If you want to say what something is, inspect something it isn't . . . if you want to see the invisible world, look at the visible one" (621). The lasting consequences of combat, such as PTSD, are apparent in Nemerov's poems of both dreams and waking life in which visions, hallucinations, and nightmares disrupt and derail his ability to move beyond the war. Such explorations of distance and traumatic memory in Nemerov's war poems are characteristic of World War II soldier poetry. With a body of work that spans over forty years, Nemerov's continual attempt to exorcise his memory of the war shows how an individual processes traumatic experience, how the distance between a pilot and their bombing targets is mirrored in the delayed processing of surfacing postwar trauma, and how the actions of one generation leave their mark on all that follow.

5

RANDALL JARRELL

THE VICARIOUS TRAUMA
OF PROCESSING WAR
AT A DISTANCE

> Ich hatte einst ein schönes Vaterland / . . . Es war ein Traum.
> (I once had a beautiful fatherland / . . . It was a dream.)
> —HEINRICH HEINE, "In der Fremde" ("Abroad")

> He has been dead for months—that is to say for minutes, for a
> century; if because of his death his armies have conquered the world,
> and have brought to its peoples food, justice, and art, it has been a
> good bargain for all of them but him. Underneath his picture there
> is written, about his life, his death, or his war: *Es war ein Traum.*
> It is the dream from which no one wakes.
> —RANDALL JARRELL, "1914"

Like the upbringing of fellow World War II poets Louis Simpson, Keith
Douglas, and Richard Hugo, Randall Jarrell's childhood was one of separated parents and multiple places. Randall Jarrell was born in 1914 in Nash-
ville, Tennessee, a city his family would leave for California when he was
a child, and to which he would return with his mother after his parents'
divorce. Jarrell attended Vanderbilt University, where his poetry and criticism developed under the tutelage of the New Critics (self-identified Southern Agrarians or Fugitives) Robert Penn Warren, Allen Tate,[1] and John
Crowe Ransom (a First World War artillery officer himself), a cohort of
poets and critics who, along with Cleanth Brooks and others, developed

New Criticism. Over time, Jarrell would distance himself from his early influences such as the New Critics, high Modernists, and major poets such as W. H. Auden (Oostdijk, *Among the Nightmare Fighters* 110). After a few years spent teaching at Kenyon College and the University of Texas, Austin, Jarrell joined the U.S. Army Air Force in 1942, the same year that his second collection of poetry, *Blood for a Stranger*, was published (Pritchard, "About Randall Jarrell"). After the war, Jarrell served as consultant in poetry to the Library of Congress (a title that would become poet laureate), received a Guggenheim Fellowship, and served as chancellor of the Academy of American Poets. Toward the end of an eighteen-year career at the University of North Carolina, Greensboro, Jarrell attempted suicide. After his discharge from the hospital, Jarrell was struck by a car and killed on 14 October 1965, an event that authorities deemed an accident, though those close to Jarrell have disputed whether it was an accident or a suicide. Each of his roles and awards gave him an influential platform to shape the reception and development of midcentury American poetry. This chapter will illuminate the ways—despite such reputable accolades and classification as one of the few notable soldier poets of World War II—that the range, insight, and perspectives in Jarrell's war poetry have not been fully realized.

Jarrell was an avid reader, and he channeled this passion in his pursuit of education, becoming a poet and a writing and literature professor, a reviewer, and literary critic. Though Jarrell was too old to become a pilot when he enlisted in the U.S. Army Air Force, his service as a celestial navigation tower operator and flight instructor markedly changed him and his poetry. Around the spring of 1943, Jarrell noted a change in his poetry after enlisting in the U.S. Army Air Corps, from a "political economy" to an "army" style (Pritchard, *Randall Jarrell* 100). This new style pushed Jarrell toward impersonality and "cultivated anonymity of viewpoint" (111), while also "expressing enlisted men's frustration at being stuck in the military, curtailing their sense of privacy and their sense of freedom" (Oostdijk, *Among the Nightmare Fighters* 79). Though Jarrell's war experience was entirely stateside, never seeing armed combat himself, he was keenly aware of the traditions of combat poetry, writing to Robert Lowell that "a good deal of [Wilfred] Owen is the best anybody did with the First World War" (Pritchard, *Randall Jarrell* 112). "Along with Karl Shapiro," in the opinion of Stephanie Burt, "Jarrell became the prominent highbrow soldier-poet of

America's war" (10). While select war poems by Jarrell have received substantial critical acclaim over time, most notably "The Death of the Ball Turret Gunner," "Losses," and "Eighth Air Force," Jarrell fatalistically believed his armed service would elicit "some good, dreary poems about the army" that would not "be liked by anybody until the '20s [AD 2020]—when they return" to war (*Randall Jarrell's Letters* 81). In addition to Jarrell's army poems, he wrote a broader body of work that addresses the war experience and the plight of civilians that receives significantly less attention. Jarrell expands the focus of war poetry beyond the perspective of soldiers, and it is this "recognition between reader and speaker, speaker and listener, actor and observer" for which his poetry should be applauded (Burt 29).

In a 1941 issue of *The Listener,* Stephen Spender explains his thinking on the relationship between war and art, claiming that "The war of 1914–18 provided a great stimulus to the arts, especially to painting and poetry. . . . The present war has had comparatively little effect on either" because the First World War was a largely stationary war for soldiers at the front, while World War II "has no stage setting easily visualized by the imagination of the whole world" (Swift 36). Despite Jarrell's harsh criticism of Spender's *Collected Poems,* describing him as "open, awkward, emotional, conscientiously well-intentioned and simple-minded" (Jarrell, "Page 043"), Jarrell would likely be inclined to agree with the latter portion of Spender's analysis. Jarrell was situated at a safe distance from the main theaters of World War II and did not have a "stage setting" of war he could easily visualize. Writing from stateside experience strengthens the argument of Jarrell's accomplishment as a poetic contributor to the emotional and human cost of war, given the quality of his work and lack of firsthand combat experience. Despite the persistent suggestion that "Works of literature are fewer and less enlightening about the second world war than the first [*sic*]," as A. J. P. Taylor wrote in *English History 1914–1945,* what poetry of World War II teaches us is that compassion and empathy for man is necessary to avoid calamitous destruction and loss of life (647). With many of the same nations returning to war less than twenty-five years after "the war to end all wars," the horrific suffering of the First World War and the pity it produced were not persuasive enough to prevent war in the name of murderous expansionism. Jarrell's poetry pursues the noble cause of peace in the face of an industrialized war effort.

Since World War II was equal parts combat and humanitarian crisis, it is understandable that the major works of poetry associated with it come from the perspective of the civilian experience. Among the many examples of civilian experience in World War II is the poetry of T. S. Eliot, who wrote in a letter to Neville Braybrooke that "There is some reference to the Blitz, of course, in Little Gidding," the final section of *Four Quartets,* inspired by his time as a fire warden in London during the Blitz ("In Eliot's Own Words"). Boris Pasternak was also a fire warden when the Luftwaffe began bombing Moscow (Ivinskaya 72–73). The German bombing of Warsaw and outbreak of war inspired Auden's "September 1, 1939." H.D.'s "The Walls Do Not Fall" section in *Trilogy* takes inspiration from living in London during the Blitz ("The Walls Do Not Fall by H.D."). Denise Levertov wrote of the Blitz as a civilian nurse in Britain. Czesław Miłosz and Zbigniew Herbert wrote of life in Poland during the Nazi invasion and occupation. Among the many examples of noncombatant poetry written as observers of World War II, these testimonial witnesses have provided immeasurable insight into life during the war. So what, then, does Randall Jarrell have to offer as a noncombatant member of the armed services writing from America during the war?[2] While Jarrell's war poetry has been applauded for his depictions of soldiers as empty vessels to be used at the pleasure of the State, his poems expressing compassion for the victims of war are less commonly recognized. These two facets of Jarrell's war poetry are the World War II equivalent of Owen's call to acknowledge "the pity war distilled," the notion that war has no true winners ("Strange Meeting" line 25).

While one could suggest that Jarrell's noncombatant status explains why Jarrell himself never appears in his war poems, the "assorted faceless types in uniform" and civilians who inhabit his poems are intentionally ambiguous to allow readers to imagine themselves and their loved ones as if they are the subjects (Fussell, *Wartime* 67). Despite the belief of James Dickey that this anonymity prevents readers from emotionally investing in the poems, Jarrell creates the possibility for empathic outreach (67). Jarrell uses his literal distance from World War II battles to focus on the victims of war, give voice to silenced populations, and bridge the emotional distance between soldiers and civilian victims. Furthermore, as a noncombatant soldier, Jarrell possesses a nuanced connection to soldiers and civilians. He writes about multiple facets of guilt, over soldiers' behavior at war and over shepherding some into situations where they may die. Since Jarrell must imagine what combat is like, his imagination also extends to the civilians impacted by the war, particularly the Jewish population facing Nazi persecution. Stationed in Arizona and Illinois, Jarrell had to imagine what the war was like while being a cog in the machinery of the State he often spoke against, and he used dreams and the traumatic experiences of others to voice discontent.

Many of Jarrell's war poems are acts of "vicarious trauma" that describe the consequences of war by magnifying the traumatic experience of soldiers and civilians (Kaplan 91). Turning his focus to the millions of victims of war places Jarrell in rare company for soldiers writing on World War II. Jarrell was an early voice drawing attention to the plight of Jews and Holocaust victims, and his output challenged the conventional belief posited by the *Times Literary Supplement:* "It is probably true that war has inspired little poetry of lasting value except in retrospect, that the imagination can only grasp its deeper meaning when the torrent of sensational violence has swept by" (Swift 13). In the March 1944 issue of *Horizon,* Stephen Spender again wrote of the nature and difficulty of writing war poetry: "War poetry and poetry of violence is particularly difficult to write because the images the poet uses mean either too much to the reader, or too little. . . . A bomb means either the bomb which fell next door, in which case the reader ceases to think the poem, and thinks his own experience, or else it means the thousand tons rained last night on Berlin, which are beyond our comprehension" ("Lessons of Poetry" 209). Spender makes a valuable point about the ability of readers to either be able to relate the war to their own lives or, if they cannot directly relate to war, feel completely distanced by an inability to imagine it. Yet, Spender's dichotomy limits the way readers can think about war poetry by creating a false choice that readers can either relate the war to their own lives or they cannot. Jarrell's war poetry challenges Spender's conventional approach, suggesting instead that readers empathize with those whose lives we should hope never to be able to relate to: soldiers and civilian casualties of war. Jarrell encourages readers to cultivate a sense of shared humanity with the subjects of his poems by highlighting forms of powerlessness felt by both soldiers and civilians during war. Jarrell crystallized this idea in a critique of Marianne Moore's poem "Keeping Their World Large": "most of the people in a war never fight for even a minute—though they bear for years and die forever. They do not fight, but only starve, only suffer, only die: the sum of all this passive misery is that great activity, War" (Hutchinson 137).

Distance and War Mechanization: Jarrell and the Machinery of the State

Randall Jarrell's relegation to a stateside training role was a circumstance that would indelibly shape his writing. As a celestial navigator and flight instructor in the U.S. Army Air Force, Jarrell resisted Auden's suggestion that a war poet "can only deal with events of which he has first-hand knowledge" (Oostdijk, *Among the Nightmare Fighters* 110). Jarrell used his distance from World War II combat as an asset and took a creative approach to his subjects, including drawing his attention to soldiers away from battle (either seeing the war from above or from training grounds in the United States), to women and children civilians, and to Holocaust victims, oftentimes speaking on behalf of "those who cannot testify for themselves" (Gubar 23). By presenting thoughts from the perspective of both participant and outsider—balancing the closeness to troops, machinery, and strategy with the distance from battle—Jarrell's poems speak to war mechanization and distance by focusing on the machinery of the State, for both allies and enemies.

Jarrell views soldiers as cogs in the machinery of the military-industrial complex, and though this term was not introduced until 1947 by Winfield W. Riefler, and popularized by President Eisenhower who used it in a 1961 speech, the fear that soldiers were feeding into a machinery beyond their control had been apparent since the skepticism of First World War combatants (Ledbetter). Paring down the inherent value of the individual soldier in "The Sick Nought," Jarrell writes:

> But you are something there are millions of.
> How can I care about you much, or pick you out
> From all the others other people loved
> And sent away to die for them? You are a ticket
> Someone bought and lost on, a stray animal.

> (lines 8–12)

One cannot help but read into feelings of powerlessness incited by Jarrell in this poem, yet the fact that this insignificance occurs in a crowd alters interpretation. The uncared-for soldier is one of millions and therefore or-

dinary, just as in the poem "Losses" the replacement soldiers arrive to replace the dead in their missions and are described merely as "operational"
(line 17). According to Robert Kuntz, "It is this inhuman mechanization,
this use of men as 'replacements,' interchangeable parts of a greater body,
that concerns Jarrell" (146). This deconstruction of identity and self-worth
in contrast to the larger goals of the State mirrors the efforts of the military to have soldiers trade personal desire for collective purpose. Jarrell
further explains this development as a transaction, arguing that "lives"
are "the one commodity" ("The Sick Nought" line 22).[3] Jarrell fights for
relevance, identity, and purpose in his poems, just as the soldier in "Mail
Call" "simply wishes for his name," literally as a sign that he is thought of
and cared for because someone has mailed him a letter or a package, and
figuratively to show that he is still an individual and can be distinguished
from his role, rank, and duty (line 11). Jarrell expertly writes out lists of actions in orderly procedure, showing the mechanization of the wartime experience as seen from the distance of a stateside soldier in "A Lullaby," the
intimacy of children taken to a concentration camp in "Protocols," and the
technological manipulation of distance by telescopic sights in "Siegfried."

Just as Jarrell's "The Death of the Ball Turret Gunner" shows the transition from birth to death and armed service to sacrifice—the soldier cast
as a pawn acted upon by the State—"A Lullaby" describes a mundane existence of a soldier controlled by the authorities. "A Lullaby" begins with
what the soldier gives up by committing to service: "For wars his life and
half a world away / The soldier sells his family and days" (lines 1–2). In Jarrell's view, being a soldier means absolving oneself of family and one's own
life, a literal fear that one will die and forever be separated from family and,
figuratively speaking, that one's life and relationship to others is inexorably
changed by war service. As Jarrell's poems demonstrate, war service means
being distanced from normal life and an awareness that one may be exposed to traumatic experiences. Jarrell then invokes jail-like descriptions
for the living conditions of soldiers, saying that while "He learns to fight for
freedom and the State; / He sleeps with seven men within six feet" (lines 3–
4). This close-distance description of the cramped barracks and structure of
the military depicts the soldiers as incarcerated. Lorrie Goldensohn argues
that Jarrell shows "a sense of the army and the state fusing to produce an
inherently totalitarian institution. Within it, individual identity and moral
agency are torn away by mass crowding within narrow space, demeaning

labor, institutional clothing, and control by a command hierarchy indistinguishable from prison" (*Dismantling Glory* 200). Jarrell exemplifies demeaning labor and institutional clothing in the second stanza, writing of the anonymous soldier "He picks up matches and he cleans out plates; / Is lied to like a child, cursed like a beast. / They crop his head, his dog tags ring like sheep" ("A Lullaby" lines 5–7). Jarrell's soldier is humbled by grunt labor, is not being trusted or respected, and is ultimately stripped of individualism and described as a submissive sheep blindly following direction. In "War Is a Force That Gives Us Meaning," Chris Hedges describes this systematic deconstruction of identity exerted by the military on soldiers: "In comradeship, the kind that comes to us in patriotic fervor, there is a suppression of self-awareness, self-knowledge, self-possession. Comrades lose their identities in war time for the collective rush of a common cause, a common purpose." The machinations of the State maintain order, and the military forces the soldier into the position of selfless, identity-less servant, a trade-off made, as Hedges suggests, on behalf of "a common cause, a common purpose." The final stanza of "A Lullaby" emphasizes the insignificance of a single soldier by saying he is either "Recalled in dreams or letters, else forgot" (line 9). Dead soldiers have been relegated to memory as "life is smothered like a grave," another image of a tightly enclosed space (line 10). The concluding image of the poem suggests the slow, but persistent momentum that is beyond challenge for the soldier, their "dull torment mottles like a fly's / The lying amber of the histories" (lines 11–12). In Jarrell's mind, the sacrifice of soldiering means to be overcome with torment and forever frozen in that time. Jarrell's assembly-line descriptions of the path from enlistment to death paint the duty of soldiers as a submissive act, becoming marionettes whose strings are controlled by the State. Yet, this critique of how war shapes the populace is not reserved for those who are enlisted, as Jarrell's poem "Protocols" draws attention to the plight of noncombatants impacted by the power structures of World War II.

Though consistently critical of the State and military of which he was a part, Randall Jarrell was not averse to defining World War II as a conflict that needed to be fought. Jarrell's strongest arguments against the Axis powers come in the form of empathic poems spotlighting civilians victimized by war. "Protocols" is an example of the compassion he held for others by giving voice to child victims of the Holocaust, and, appearing in a 1945 issue of *Poetry,* it may be the first American poem published on the topic of the Holocaust (Flanzbaum 260). "Protocols" vacillates between the voices of two children taken by train from Odessa to the Auschwitz-Birkenau concentration and extermination camp. There is no judgment, only recollection, as the children's observations exude innocence and foreshadow the unknowable horror they are about to encounter. The two voices are denoted as one in plain text, the other italicized. Here is the three-quintet poem in its entirety:

We went there on the train. *They had big barges that they towed,*
We stood up, there were so many I was squashed.
There was a smoke-stack, then they made me wash.
It was a factory, I think. *My mother held me up*
And I could see the ship that made the smoke.

When I was tired my mother carried me.
She said, "Don't be afraid." But I was only tired.
Where we went there is no more Odessa.
They had water in a pipe—like rain, but hot;
The water there is deeper than the world

And I was tired and fell in my sleep
And the water drank me. That is what I think.
And I said to my mother, "Now I'm washed and dried,"
My mother hugged me, and it smelled like hay
And that is how you die. And that is how you die.

The use of slant rhymes– "squashed"/"wash," "towed"/"smoke," and "dried"/ "die"—ricochet off one another to create tension and an echoing of voices. Like the systematic directives relayed by the average soldier in "A Lullaby," the retold memory of the children depicts the systematic operation of the Final Solution in plain, simple speech. "We went there on the train" ("Protocols" line 1) one child says at the outset of the poem, to which the other child adds, "there were so many I was squashed," referring to the overcrowded trains shipping Jews to concentration camps (line 2). Upon arrival at the camps, the first child notices a smokestack—"It was a factory, I think"—the awful irony being that the child is right to associate the image of a smokestack with a factory, unaware that they are bound for death (line 4). The first speaker recalls, "they made me wash," unaware that being taken to the showers meant being led to a gas chamber (line 3) . This lie was sustained until the last moments of life, a systemic deception like the "Arbeit macht frei" (work sets you free) signage placed at the entrance of the Auschwitz concentration camp. The double meaning of this act of cleansing, literal and ethnic, makes the pending betrayal all the more appalling. This deception makes the contrapuntal construction of "Protocols," two melodies played simultaneously, a harrowing sleight of hand. The children in "Protocols" recall the efforts made by their parents to free them from fear, as one child is held up by their mother so they "could see the ship that made the smoke" (line 5) while the other is told, "Don't be afraid" (line 7).

To understand the power of this historical moment is to recognize the ease with which image association rapidly paints a scene of dread. In the first stanza, by learning that the speakers are on a "train," "squashed" with people, and their destination is a factory-like area with a "smoke-stack," like a game of word association, many would leap to visions of the Holocaust. Yet Jarrell does not say it himself, nor does he mention the war, the year, or any biographical detail other than, "Where we went there is no more Odessa," a reference that could be absorbed as a definitive detail to confirm the poem's subject (line 8). Jarrell embodies the voices of children he never met to bring the darkest acts of the war to his readers, and in doing so eliminates the buffer between safe citizens and victims. Jarrell intentionally discomforts the reader by describing Jews forced into overcrowded train cars, imagery clearly understood by readers to mean that the poem's speakers are being taken to a concentration camp. Just as soon as these puzzle pieces begin to reveal the true nature of the children's testimonials, the poem concludes with naivety, tenderness, and admission. The children go into the showers with their families and feel consumed by the water: "The water there is deeper than the world . . . the water drank me" (lines 10, 12). The first child follows orders, says, "Now I'm washed and dried," and is hugged by their mother (line 13). In the harrowing final line, both voices say, "And that is how you die," a haunting echo that simultaneously brings mass suffering down to the level of the individual while the repetition of the line ensures we do not forget that this is a story that happened over and over (line 15).

To mechanize the murder of civilian populations in wartime, the Nazi regime instituted protocols to structure their attempt to eradicate the Jewish people. The contrast created by having a poem titled "Protocols," a word defined by *The Oxford English Dictionary* as "the official procedure or system of rules governing affairs of state or diplomatic occasions," and having this systematic procedure shown through the eyes of innocent children, highlights the inhumanity of the process being described. Eva Hoffman's description of second-generation children, "the direct descendants of survivors," is an applicable parallel when thinking about the transference of traumatic experience (xi). Though the children in "Protocols" are victims themselves and not the descendants of victims, readers experience a form of secondary or vicarious trauma through this Holocaust narrative. Hoffman continues, listing the repercussions of traumatic experience: "the internal impact of gratuitous violence and the transmission of traumatic experience across generations; the emotional intricacies of dealing with victims of persecution and the moral quandaries implicit in dialogues with perpetrators; the difficulty of witnessing the pain of others and thinking about tragic pasts; and the relationship of private memory to a broader understanding of history" (xii). Though Jarrell refrains from explicit pathos, he utilizes readers' knowledge of the Holocaust to generate an emotional reaction to the intricacies of traumatic visions and implied violence. Lorrie Goldensohn describes how Jarrell brings us close to this horrible reality, suggesting that "parts of the reader-writer contract ask that we, altogether too safe outside the text, not be made voyeurs of pain and that we not turn too expeditiously away from the children to examine ourselves" (*Dismantling Glory* 216). Though any document on the Holocaust will be emotionally impactful, Goldensohn is arguing that the importance of Jarrell's "Protocols" is that it strikes a balance between drawing our attention to the suffering of others and showing caution not to veer so hard in the direction of the grotesque and thereby push readers away from viewing the speaking children as if they could be their own. These considerations echo Adam Smith's ideas of the sympathy of the spectator in *The Theory of Moral Sentiments,* that "The compassion of the spectator must arise altogether from the consideration of what he himself would feel if he was reduced to the same unhappy situation" (11). "Protocols" is emotionally resonant, particularly when considering the 1945 publication date and how awareness of the depravity of the Holocaust was spreading.

Though Randall Jarrell's poems "A Lullaby" and "Protocols" address different topics, both speak to the structure of the military-industrial complex. While it would seem backwards to describe war as orderly when all impulses point to it being a chaotic agent of change, the mechanization of weaponry, strategy, and the systematic control of soldiers and civilians that occurred during World War II is undeniable. In these poems, Jarrell shortens the distance between the realities of World War II and the reader by invoking comprehensible details of the regimented lives of soldiers and the observations of children forced to a concentration camp. In doing so, Jarrell compartmentalizes World War II into details that noncombatant readers can understand, and that will allow them to emotionally connect to the suffering of others. A further act of bringing the reader closer to war experience is through the technology of war, which Jarrell does by writing of sight and telescopic scopes in the poem "Siegfried."

Jarrell's use of telescopic sights, sextants, astrocompasses, and other technological devices greatly influenced the way he visualized the air war and conceived of the images of war ("Celestial Navigation"). Returning to the central image from his most anthologized poem, the ball turret, Randall Jarrell's poem "Siegfried" uses tools and weapons to further explore the abbreviation of sight through telescopic lenses. "Siegfried" begins with the literal and metaphorical description: "In the turret's great glass dome, the apparition, death, / Framed in the glass of the gunsight . . . / Flares softly" (lines 1–3). Ghostly, this vision of death is represented through the perspective of the gunsight used to aim at a target. It is not the gunner who is described in this image, even though he would be the one pulling the trigger, but it is the machinery itself that embodies death. Again, the strength of the concept is reinforced by using the technology to emphasize the role of sight, seeing, and things coming into view with greater clarity. The use of gunsights and telescopic lenses is a clear parallel to knowledge and awareness; both are revelations that bring the speaker a step closer to killing. Inside the mind of the gunner, the act of war "is a dream: and he, the watcher, guiltily / Watches the him, the actor, who is innocent" (lines 10–11). In contrast to Douglas's extrospective "How to Kill," Jarrell's gunner homes in on his target with the guilt of knowing he is about to end a life. For Jarrell's gunner, the use of gunsights and scopes brings reality closer, and as John Whittier-Ferguson explains, "Siegfried's present is burdened by his too-intimate knowledge of death: in the form of past trauma—a 'first world' where the young man realizes how proximate death is—and the certainty of another, mortal encounter in the time to come" (121). Though both Douglas and Jarrell are stepping inside the moments preceding firing a kill shot, Douglas's speaker is programmatic and uses technology as an emotional barrier, while Jarrell's "Siegfried" feels guilty making the decision to end a life. There may be many explanations for this discrepancy, but most notable is the fact that Douglas was on active duty, died in service, and had been exposed to death and killing in a way that Jarrell had not. While Douglas was killed in the invasion of Normandy, Jarrell lived with the emotional weight of war after it had ended. "Siegfried" concludes, "it is different, different—you have understood / Your world at last: you have tasted your own blood" (lines 66–67), which is "an allusion to the mythological Siegfried, who tastes the dragon's blood" and acquires a greater understanding of who he is (Ferguson, *Jarrell, Bishop, Lowell, & Co* 138). Jarrell's "Siegfried" comes into a greater understanding of his place in the world and the way war breeds war by having tasted his own blood. Both soldiers behind the scope in Jarrell's "Siegfried" and Douglas's "How to Kill" are coming into knowledge through experience of war, and both learn the unsettling reality that they are ordered to kill someone they know as little about as a civilian they would pass on the street. While Jarrell's 1945 poem "Siegfried" is described as having "Audenesque" features (Oostdijk, *Among the Nightmare Fighters* 65), and Jarrell was an avid reader who critically engaged with Auden's work, "Siegfried" preempts Auden's 1949 poem "Memorial for the City," which contains echoes of Jarrell. Jarrell's "Siegfried" expresses resignation over the events of war—*"It happens as it does because it does"* (line 12)—and four years later Auden would also write helplessly of the destruction of war and the Holocaust: "That is the way things happen; for ever and ever" ("Memorial for the City" line 16).[4] Regardless of who influenced whom and how they received one another's work, Jarrell, Auden, and Douglas similarly express the inevitable feelings of powerlessness that arise from intimate knowledge of war.

The physical distance between Jarrell and the war he prepared his pilots for heightens the significance of telescope and sight imagery in his poems, for he was always observing from a distance. Douglas, on the other hand, used the imagery of telescopes and lenses to bring the war to the people through concrete objects and occurrences. Even though Jarrell was more outspoken in his view of military life and war than Douglas, both knew their experience could not be entirely conveyed, and so to tell it as it happened would need to suffice. By manipulating the way notions of distance are conveyed, war poetry traditions are disrupted because readers are made complicit in actions to which they were previously ignorant. This shift toward exposing readers to the battlefield experience and the degrees of inner turmoil of soldiers was particularly notable in First World War poetry because of the sensory intensity of trench warfare and the enormous death tolls from artillery fire. With the further change in World War II combat, where greater damage could be done from greater distance and civilians became military targets, the importance of maintaining a sense of intimacy in war poetry is heightened because such irrevocable and divisive behavior leaves less room for blind patriotism. Jarrell's attempts to refocus public attention on these broader concerns echoes Sassoon's "The Ultimate Atrocity," an overt warning that simultaneously addresses the physical distance from which modern warfare is conducted, how this causes soldiers to be devoid of a direct sense of responsibility for human loss, and how the mechanization of war rapidly devolves concern for humanity:

> . . . but if from that machine should fall
> The first bacterial bomb, this world might find
> That all the aspirations of the dead
> Had been betrayed and blotted out, and all
> Their deeds denied who hope for Humankind.
>
> (lines 10–14)

Sassoon is close with his prediction of the future of warfare as World War II concluded, not with a bacterial bomb but with the dropping of the atomic bombs in Hiroshima and Nagasaki, an act that one could argue denies the deeds of those "who hope for Humankind" and betrays "the aspirations of the dead." Similarly, Jarrell's war poetry uses such technological advancements as a warning, reminds noncombatants of the true cost of war with empathy and varying levels of distance, and shows that war also comes at a moral price.

Jarrell's Distance from Battle: Processing Air War Losses from the Ground

As a celestial navigation tower operator and instructor in the U.S. Army Air Force, Jarrell experienced war by training others and seeing home front preparations for foreign missions (Pritchard, *Randall Jarrell* 106). Kenneth Baker used the decentralized locus of World War II to explain its perceived lackluster poetry in comparison to the First World War: "The geographical spread and fluidity of the various campaigns did not bring about the intensity of experience felt by those soldiers who had been confined to the mud of Flanders" (xxiv). What Baker misses in this contrast between poetry of the world wars is the strength through diversity that is achieved by disparate experiences of World War II. Such variation helps the poetry of Randall Jarrell stand out as a unique perspective of an enlisted noncombatant. Jarrell was stationed primarily in Arizona, and the physical distance separating him from the war divided his war poems into two primary (though not exclusive) categories: quotidian life on an U.S. Army Air Force base where service members are viewed as cogs in a wheel, and imaginative explorations of what the war was like for those experiencing it. To apportion some of Jarrell's most popular war poems in the first category of daily life in the armed services, one could include "Losses," "Mail Call," and "A Lullaby," while the second category of portraits of those drawn into the war could include "The Death of the Ball Turret Gunner," "Protocols," "A Camp in the Prussian Forest," "Come to the Stone. . . . ," and "The Dead Wingman." Jarrell's air force poems reflect his distanced perspective and are largely written with the ground a more prominent focal point, as opposed to the sky. Jarrell was not flying himself, yet many of his war poems touch on the act of taking off and landing, crashing, or dreaming of what happens in the air.

Written from a child's perspective, Jarrell's "Come to the Stone. . . ." follows the takeoff and landing of airplanes in a field. The innocence of a child trying to understand war is seen in lines such as, "In the sky the planes are angry, like the wind, / The people are punishing the people—why?" (lines 9–10). This child's perspective extends to envisioning the war from the air, looking down at the terror below and seeing that "ants had littered with their crumbs and dead," an image that could be literal ants scattering or people reduced to ant size from the perspective of warplanes (line 5). Similarly, Jarrell's "The Dead Wingman" recounts a pilot's perspective of earth as he searches for another plane in the fleet that had been shot down. Beginning with panic—"Seen on the sea, no sign; no sign, no sign / In the black firs and terraces of hills" (lines 1–2)—the view of earth from the sky is again described in children's imagery: "the surf streams by: a port of toys / Is starred with its fires and faces" (lines 6–7). As suggested by Suzanne Ferguson, "One of Jarrell's strongest intuitions about the enlisted men is that they revert to a childlike innocence in times of stress" (*The Poetry of Randall Jarrell* 47). Though Jarrell is abstract about where these emotions are being directed, the pilot feels a range of emotions including "hatred and misery and longing" ("The Dead Wingman" line 10) as he looks "Over the blackening ocean for a corpse" (line 11). "The Dead Wingman" encompasses the skyscape, seascape, and landscape, concluding with the acknowledgment that the missing pilot has died, emblematic of how war is taking its toll on mankind:

> Gliding above the cities' shells, a stubborn eye
> Among the embers of the nations, achingly
> Tracing the circles of that worn, unchanging No—
> The lives' long war, lost war—the pilot sleeps.

> (lines 19–22)

These enjambed lines cast the pilot as a panoptic figure seeing destruction who, through the metaphor of sleep, succumbs to the death they have perpetuated. End words like "eye" and "No" reverberate with their homophones "I" and "know," suggesting an enlightenment, that in war one learns death is inescapable. For a poet and airplane navigation instructor, it is essential for Jarrell to possess "a stubborn eye," yet in "The Dead Wingman" the scouring of surroundings tells the speaker the unfortunate answer that the wingman is dead, and the world around them is smoldering. Furthermore, it is hard to ignore the echo of Wilfred Owen's poem "Miners," with the use of the word "ember," when commenting on the legacy of war. For Jarrell, "the embers of the nations" remain after war, while Owen writes "The years will stretch their hands, well-cheered / By our life's ember" ("Miners" lines 27–28) as he equates a mining disaster with the war dead, both of whom will go unremembered, and both of whom involve "poor lads / Lost in the ground" (lines 33–34). William H. Pritchard speculates in his biography of Jarrell that because of this model of war poetry set by Owen, "it is reasonable to assume that he thought about Wilfred Owen's example as he attempted to do something comparably good with the Second World War" (line 112). Among other shared concepts and imagery between Jarrell's "The Dead Wingman" and Owen's "Miners" are the equation of death and sleep, time and memory, forests, fires, different uses of air, and the war dead returned to the earth. While Jarrell is writing from a drastically different body of experience compared to what Owen had suffered, he is using Owen as a guide for capturing the war through landscape.

Jarrell's "Losses" is a poem about a plane crashing in training as opposed to combat. Though both scenarios would be classified as death during war service, Jarrell notes the difference being that those in training "died on the wrong page of the almanac" (line 6). This loss is used as a spark for examining the purpose of war, particularly when the chief outcome is death and destruction. Later, when these pilots are deployed overseas, their actions are categorized as duty and execution without regard for consequence. As if a bombing run is a simple transaction, "They said, 'Here are the maps'; we burned the cities" (line 28). Crucial to "Losses" are the reassurances made by (and perhaps to) the speaker that war "was not dying— no, not ever dying" (line 29). Bombed cities, personified, ask the speaker in response, "Why are you dying? / We are satisfied, if you are; but why did I die?" (lines 31–32). Enough death and destruction occurred that the cities are willing to relent if the bombers are, but both sides are left to wonder about the cost of war, whether the amount of death was justified. Questions of justification, responsibility, and guilt are pervasive in Jarrell's war poems, and as the next section exemplifies, these themes were channeled through sympathy for both military and civilian victims of war.

Sympathy as a Dislocation of Guilt

Tasked with the responsibility of transmitting their experience, war poets face the recurring issue of describing the indescribable. As Paul Fussell noted, "writers about the war had to appeal to the sympathy of readers by invoking the familiar and suggesting its resemblance to what many of them suspected was an unprecedented and (in their terms) an all-but-incommunicable reality" (*The Great War and Modern Memory* 174). The Second World War differed from the First in a multitude of ways, and these variances contributed to the experiences captured in the poetry of soldiers. While quoting W. H. Auden's poem "Spain," John Palatella established a link showing how poets like Randall Jarrell entered World War II with "The conscious acceptance of guilt in the necessary murder" of others (1).

Though Auden's comments were on the Spanish Civil War in 1937, the sentiment that soldiers willingly kill to advance a cause remains relevant for all combatants. In maintaining a healthy skepticism about war in place of diplomatic resolution, servicemen like Randall Jarrell faced the difficulty of negotiating the need to prevent the Axis powers from world domination and having to engage in the killing of others to do so. World War II poets like Jarrell advance a tradition of realism as a mode of lyrical expression that yields empathy, transformed by their own experiences over the guilt of committing violence on behalf of a cause and the guilt of survival.

Jarrell's war poems are at their most poignant when channeling the experiences of others. Echoing Wilfred Owen's "Preface" that "My subject is War, and the pity of War" (line 6), Jarrell explained to Amy Breyer while stationed at an army base in Tucson, "My two subjects are bombing Hamburg and bombing crews. I feel sympathetic and sorry for both of them" (*Randall Jarrell's Letters* 116). "If you'll notice," Jarrell would later write to Robert Lowell, "I've never written a poem about myself in the army or war" because one is not "the primary subject" of the war (*Randall Jarrell's Letters* 151). Whether World War II poets documented the actions they witnessed or wrote as an act of "proxy-witnessing" on behalf of the voiceless, guilt manifests itself in a multitude of ways (Gubar 23). By focusing on both the bombers and their targets, Jarrell is demonstrating how a traumatic experience, in the words of Cathy Caruth, is a "double telling, the oscillation between a crisis of death and the correlative crisis of life" (*Unclaimed Experience* 7). As First World War poets forced their readers to acknowledge the terrible sights of the trenches and generate sympathy for soldiers, Jarrell displays the dehumanization of both soldiers and civilians in World War II.

In his most anthologized poem, "The Death of the Ball Turret Gunner," Jarrell identifies the vulnerability of individuals to die for "the State" by using the imagery of an airplane gunner who has been shot to death and is washed out of the turret like a stillborn child from a womb. The five-line poem callously describes a young airman who, miles above the earth, is "loosed from its dream of life" (line 3). An archived draft reveals the initial title of the poem as "The Life and Death of the Ball Turret Gunner," though "Life and" are crossed out ("Item 001a Front"). This draft title further accentuates the life cycle motif and imagery used in the poem by completing the birth-life-death narrative of the gunner who is seemingly born into the womb-like ball turret he is soon aborted from. What has made this an emblematic poem of World War II, amid a generation of work that is largely overlooked, is what is implied. Much like the focus on wasted youth that is highlighted by Owen and Sassoon, Jarrell opens the poem by taking on the voice of the deceased gunner, writing, "From my mother's sleep I fell into the State," which simultaneously suggests the transition from birth to enlistment was immediate, as if the speaker is still just a child now under protection of the government (line 1). Furthermore, this line implies an absence of choice or self-determination, as if it is a role that servicemen are born into, a duty they are required to fulfill. To be woken from "its dream of life" to "black flak and the nightmare fighters" is a shift from life to death and from dream to nightmare, a literal and figurative awakening to the reality of death (lines 3–4). Archived draft copies of the poem show varied phrasing that Jarrell considered, such as opening the poem with the phrase, "Escaped from my mother," in place of, "From my mother's sleep" ("Item 001a Front"). The final version serves the poem more effectively because it removes the sense of choice or free will, as if the gunner is too young to know the consequences of enlistment. Jarrell also struggled with the third line of the poem, weighing alternative ways to convey the moment of the gunner's death. Earlier edits try to capture the altitude as "30,000 ft from the earth," twice the number of syllables as the final version, showing Jarrell's ultimate desire for concision in such a short poem ("Item 001a Front"). The gunner's death also saw numerous edits, all circling around some combination of the words "gasped," "dream," "warmth," and "air," with the third line undergoing drafts such as "I gasped a dream of warmth and air" and "I gasped for my life, and made a dream of breath" ("Item 001a Front"). Jarrell settles for a much more subdued implication of death, "Six miles from earth, loosed from its dream of life" ("The Death of the Ball Turret Gunner" line 3). The final line is grim, memorable, and attests to the feeling by soldiers across generations that their lives are inconsequential in the overall scope of war and societal progression because, as the speaker relays unceremoniously, "When I died they washed me out of the turret with a hose" (line 5). This was an awful fate that was met by some of Jarrell's fellow airmen, the type of stories that are withheld from family, just like the "gallant lies" that Sassoon's "The Hero" says are told to mothers to retain an unblemished memory of their dead sons (line 8).[5] Each of the five lines in "The Death of the Ball Turret Gunner" is end-stopped, emphasizing each as a declaration. The staccato rhythm of phrases like "wet fur froze" (line 2) and "woke to black flak" (line 4) burst like the aural percussion of artillery fire. The dehumanization of the gunner is heightened with the poem's only end rhymes, "froze" and "hose," describing one's "fur" freezing in the high-elevation temperatures of flight before being mangled by flak and fire, requiring one's corpse to be hosed "out of the turret." Randall Jarrell boiled down his opinions on soldiering and the tragedy of armed conflict in a letter to Robert Lowell when he wrote, "The main feeling you have about most people in the army—and in the war, too—is that you're sorry for them; everything else comes after" (*Randall Jarrell's Letters* 151–52).

Jarrell's guilt for guiding these soldiers as their navigation instructor, for fairly or unfairly feeling like the shepherd leading them to slaughter, is made clear through the direct language of his war poems. Jarrell routinely comments on the conflicted nature of his role away from the war's front lines and his own survival, such as in the poem "Eighth Air Force," in which he finds "no fault in this just man" (line 20), yet he does so as he refers to his fellow armed service members as "murderers" (line 6). Jarrell writes from the precarious position of being both critical of the actions of airmen and an active participant in training them. For Jarrell, the violence committed is imagined from a great distance, and he therefore conceives of himself as speaking with a "middle voice" between perpetrator and victim, a method that requires "modulations of proximity and distance, empathy and irony" (LaCapra 30). Such a gray area between participant and witness, soldier and civilian, and perpetrator and victim, is a by-product of "secondary witnesses to traumatic events" whose response "must involve empathic unsettlement" (LaCapra 47). Jarrell is tiptoeing the line between recognizing a soldier's duty and feeling complicit in murder. Zygmunt Bauman describes this circumstance as one determined by the victors of war, using Robert Servatius's legal defense of Nazi SS leader Adolf Eichmann as an example: "Eichmann committed acts for which one is decorated if one wins, and goes to the gallows if one loses" (18). Despite Servatius's attempt at moral equivocation, a drastic distinction must be recognized between soldiers killing soldiers and systematic genocide. The presence of empathy for victims is the difference between Jarrell's view of military killing as an unfortunate duty carried out by soldiers and Eichmann's stance that the Nazi genocide committed against European Jews was only deemed immoral because Germany lost the war. This moral fluctuation encapsulates

Bauman's idea of "social production of distance" (192), which Eva Hoffman summarizes as "a process that permits a radical detachment and denial of empathy, or even a minimal recognition of the other as human" (114). While Eichmann's defense attempted to justify mass murder as acceptable if the Nazis were victorious, it is devoid of empathy for the millions they murdered. Conversely, though Jarrell accepts that war entails killing, he maintains empathy for the victims and compassion for the persecuted. Writing from the perspective of a noncombatant member of the armed services, Jarrell is witness to "the gulf—moral, political, affective—between the victim and the perpetrator" that is created "by the perpetrator's utter failure to recognize the humanity of the victim," reinforced by the injustice of the dead, and sealed by a lack of remorse (E. Hoffman 111).

Describing the veil between lived traumatic experience and the narratives used to convey it, Eva Hoffman believes "the politics of trauma are themselves a kind of displacement, wherein the actualities of suffering are placed at a safe distance and relegated to the sphere of abstract compassion and morality" (276). Similarly, as Mary A. Favret reasons on the relationship between war distance and expression, "the experience of war at a distance prompts a move toward abstraction" (10). There is no dispute that Randall Jarrell's war poems and empathic poems of war victimhood are written from a safe distance, yet it is precisely the compassion and complicated feelings of morality that make Jarrell's poems unique. As demonstrated in the following section, Jarrell's war poems invoke dreams, nightmares, and visions in response to the vicarious trauma of his distanced war experience and gradual knowledge of the Holocaust.

Dreams, Nightmares, and Visions: Jarrell's Vicarious Trauma

Dreams are one of the most prominent motifs used in Randall Jarrell's poetry. Whether subconscious manifestations of the mind, aspirations, or imagination filling in gaps of lived experience, varying uses of dreams are all crucial to Jarrell's work. As a reader and admirer of Sigmund Freud, Jarrell includes the subconscious in his writing in the form of dreams, nightmares, and visions.[6] Spurred by noncombatant war experience, Jarrell's array of imagined visions is an inevitable by-product of an individual who spends years working for the armed services without entering battle. The pervasiveness of dreams in the psyche of Jarrell is so ingrained that others associate Jarrell with dreamscapes. For example, in Robert Lowell's poem titled "Randall Jarrell," Jarrell visits him in a dream: "The dream went like a rake of sliced bamboo, . . . Tonight it's Randall, his spark still fire though humble" (lines 1, 10). Jarrell harbored guilt both for training others who might meet their death in combat, as if he were sending them to slaughter, and for needless suffering of civilians caught in the crosshairs of fascist quests for domination and Allied retaliation. Imagined spaces of air combat and civilian casualty dominate Jarrell's overt war poems, through which he exhibits vicarious trauma to generate concern for "The defacement of the individual" (Hutchinson 129). The literal distance of Jarrell's home front service from the spaces of World War II battle means that—rather than Louis Simpson and Keith Douglas's poetic landscapes of the ground war, or Richard Hugo and Howard Nemerov's skyscapes of the air war—Jarrell writes about the war through dreamscapes and visions in which he can explore themes of guilt and vicarious trauma.

Jarrell's use of binary oppositions, such as dreaming and waking, is one way of creating a discrepancy between imagination and reality, death and life, a tightrope walk that gives license to the unimaginable truths of World War II. Helen Vendler categorized "the lyric poetry written in America immediately after World War II" as the "'Freudian lyric'" (31), another name for the Confessional mode that carries the implication that a poem is "a symbolic study of a speaker's psychology" (White 135). Jarrell counted on Freud's guidance for exploring the psychology of his poems' speakers, remarking in a 1961 interview that he would "rather be wrong with Freud than right with most other people" (Glick 10). A sampling of Jarrell's war poems referencing dreams or waking includes the idea that war is "the dream from which no one wakes" ("1914" line 203); an aircraft shot down falling through "miles to warmth, to air, to waking" ("A Pilot from the Carrier" line 9); "the thousand necessary deaths" who sleep in "slow, dreaming sparks" ("Pilots, Man Your Planes" lines 6, 8); a pilot who dreams of searching for his wingman ("The Dead Wingman"); "sleep" compared to "the drowned" amid "the last dreaming light" ("Second Air Force" lines 28, 29, 30); a soldier who compares the stars to the bars of a jail cell when they wake up and feel freed by "sleep" ("New Georgia" lines 1–2, 10); a child who struggles to distinguish dreams from reality because they think that when they wake up, "dreams / Are in the room with you, like the cinema" ("The Truth" lines 4–5); life itself characterized as a port of embarkation for soldiers who are disconnected from the dead civilians who preceded them, and a speaker who wonders who will believe the dying wishes of "The slow lives sank from being like a dream?" ("Port of Embarkation" line 12); a traumatized soldier jarring themselves awake into "A kind of ache / Of knowing troubles," aware they are "dreaming" ("A Field Hospital" lines 2–3, 15), yet unaware that waking from nightmares will not protect one's mind from PTSD; wondering about "The dream I woke to, that holds you sleep-ers still— / What is it now, The War?" ("The Survivor among Graves" lines 10–11); thinking to oneself that "I am a grave dreaming / That it is a living man" ("Terms" lines 62–63); a poem titled "The Dream of Waking" in which morning is a sign of life and a respite from its homophone mourning, im-plying death (line 21); an early poem unpublished during Jarrell's lifetime in which the speaker and his wife discuss the dreams that had him whim-pering in his sleep ("The Dream"). Unsurprisingly, Jarrell shared plans in a 1958 letter to Peter Taylor for "a book showing dreams and poems have same structure, roots, etc" (Burt 93). The recurring dream motif in Jarrell's poetry shows a steady fascination with these binary concepts of life and death, and reality and imagination, and is perhaps most representative of his views on war in the poem "The Learners."

Jarrell's 1945 collection *Little Friend, Little Friend,* a title drawn from "how bombers call in fighters over the radio" (*Randall Jarrell's Letters* 124), contains the poem "The Learners," which begins with an illumination of the "old crews" in the barracks by the lights of the planes coming in through the night (line 2). With faces "shapeless at waking" (3), the anonymized soldiers are looking for "old, lost faces" (4), but their vision is obfuscated by "The dream of the old wars" (5). These vestiges of the past, memories of the deceased are a reminder of war's continual cost of human life. As a ten-line poem comprised of just two sentences—the first eight and a half lines are the first sentence—the barrage of clauses that turn and complicate the trajectory of the poem builds tension until the completion of the first sen-tence. Jarrell eventually steers the poem toward the question, "when you remember / Will you care then—dead in someone else's dream— / That you lived, that you died?" (lines 7–9). Characteristic of Jarrell's war poetry, "The Learners" depersonalizes, distances the self, and turns the attention to oth-ers by invoking second person. Addressing the poem to "you," whether this is intended to be the reader or the anonymous soldiers, conversationally engages readers as if they should have something at stake in the poem. The direct question as to whether one will care that they lived and died is the underlying question of war's consequence. Jarrell searches for meaning in life, war, and death: "Waking at twilight to the haunting brain / That is your world now, ghosts, have you learned anything?" (lines 9–10). By applying the classification of "ghosts" to the "you" in the poem, Jarrell wonders if they have learned anything from their past, their service, their death. The questions this conclusion raises are many, including: Who are the ghosts— are they the war dead who learn lessons in death or the survivors who roam the earth haunted by what they have lost? Are the titular learners those who have experienced war or withstood it? What is it the learners are supposed to learn? While Jarrell leaves these questions unanswered, he undeniably leaves readers wondering what is the value of human life if we must ask ourselves if we learned anything from war. Such attempts to return to basic comprehension result from "the experience of World War II," which "baffled realist narrative and description" (Hutchinson 55).

Given Jarrell's preoccupation with dreams, the omission of dreams from "A Camp in the Prussian Forest" has the deliberate effect of the poem being a vision of reality. Since it is not written from firsthand experience, our attention is again drawn to the suffering of others to understand events that are seemingly beyond comprehension. Both of these traits bolster the importance of recognizing the Holocaust as a real, depraved, and horrific persecution. Jarrell's use of form further accentuates the matter-of-fact presentation of disturbing content, with nine quatrains in AABB, CCDD (etc.) rhyme scheme until the final stanza concludes with an ABAB rhyme, giving a sense of cohesion from aural cues. The orderliness of the poem is mirrored by movements in the poem, such as the speaker who walks "beside the prisoners to the road" (line 1) while beside them "Load on puffed load, / Their corpses, stacked like sodden wood" (lines 2–3). Like the industrialized and systematic operations of mass murder described in Jarrell's "Protocols," "A Camp in the Prussian Forest" uses such organization to accentuate the deliberateness of Nazi depravity, exemplified by the break from routine: "No one comes today / In the old way / To knock to fillings from their teeth" (lines 5–7). As the poem continues, Jarrell uses directness and simile to describe the dehumanization of Holocaust victims: "One year / They sent a million here: // Here men were drunk like water, burnt like wood" (lines 15–17). Repeating "here" at the end of one stanza and beginning of another emphasizes locality, the tactile landscape that houses mass murder. Furthermore, comparing the consumption of human life to drinking water and burning wood exemplifies Vernon Scannell's commentary on Jarrell's war poems, that they "often show man being reduced to animal or object" (*Not Without Glory* 194). Literal acts of reduction are also recounted: "The fat of good / And evil, the breast's star of hope / Were rendered into soap" ("A Camp in the Prussian Forest" lines 18–20). These specific details, such as how human fat from those murdered at concentration camps was used to make soap, aid the speaker and, by extension, Jarrell and his readers to process the horror of the Holocaust ("Human Fat"). Literally reducing humans to physical properties erases the nuance of human complexity, an act of destruction that treats "good / And evil" inconsequentially. By imagining minute details, down to the needles on the forest floor "chalked with ash," one can begin to visualize the tactile elements of an otherwise inconceivable horror (line 29). Jarrell uses visions derived from the firsthand accounts of others instead of using dreams or imagination, thereby serving as a witness to their testimonies.

This exercise in vicarious trauma, being a witness to the psychological damage prompted by the discovery of a concentration camp, can be interpreted as a way for Jarrell to process the guilt of being a survivor, safely distanced from the sites of the Holocaust. According to Dori Laub, the role of the listener is to "become the enabler of the testimony" by simultaneously being "a witness to the trauma witness and a witness to himself" (Felman and Laub 58). Jarrell's Holocaust poems routinely give voice to victims and trauma witnesses as a way of making civilians listen to the testimony of others. The importance of such testimony is heightened in light of the reality that the majority of Holocaust documentation and photographs from before the liberation of the concentration camps "comes from Nazi sources" (Hartman 22). In Jarrell's own words, the speaker of "A Camp in the Prussian Forest" is an American soldier "after the capture of one of the German death camps" (*The Complete Poems* 10). Jarrell understood that the goal of the Holocaust and the death camps was to "kill all Jews, thereby eliminating witnesses," and he responded by writing poems intended to bring attention to victimized populations (Felman and Laub 81). Dori Laub also outlines three levels of witnessing, all of which are essential for understanding World War II, the Holocaust, and the processing of traumatic memory: "witness to oneself within the experience," "witness to the testimonies of others," and "witness to the process of witnessing itself" (Felman and Laub 75). While most of Jarrell's war poems from the home front are from a speaker who is "witness to oneself within the experience," experiencing one facet of the war away from the combat itself, Jarrell's Holocaust poems veer toward being a "witness to the testimonies of others" or "witness to the process of witnessing itself," as is the case in "A Camp in the Prussian Forest." As a critic of the army's systematic depersonalization of soldiers, Jarrell emphasizes testimony from alternative voices because, in the words of Geoffrey H. Hartman, "the greatest danger to public memory is *official history*" (101).

Allied advancement in World War II was counterweighted with the jarring knowledge that a Germany in defeat meant accelerated murder for their captives.[7] Additionally, as historian Laurence Rees reminds us about the nature of World War II testimony, "the survivors of camps like Auschwitz, Sobibor and Treblinka did not represent the normal experience of those who were sent there. The normal experience was to be murdered" (427). While there are many invaluable first-person testimonies of Holocaust survival, the grim reality of a significant absence of testimony by those who were murdered is a sign of the need to recognize them. Even prior to learning of the Holocaust, Jarrell turned to poetry to manage existential problems, as he explained in a letter to Amy Breyer de Blasio after enlisting: "For to write what you can about the world makes it almost bearable" (Pritchard, *Randall Jarrell* 97).

■ ■ ■

Randall Jarrell's war poetry forces readers to contemplate difficult realities of war, such as guilt and justification for killing in the name of country, ideals, and duty. Echoing Pontius Pilate's words "I find no fault in this man" (Authorized King James Bible, Luke 23:4), Jarrell's "Eighth Air Force" concludes with the line, "I find no fault in this just man," a pivot after blaming suffering on humankind (line 20). Such a statement exemplifies the tragic underpinning of Jarrell's war poetry, that the suffering of Holocaust victims, the waste of youth, and the dehumanization of soldiers are manmade problems. The repetition of conflict and sacrifice is accentuated by the subtle equation of the crucifixion of Jesus to the sacrifice of life during war, Pilate being a homonym with pilot, as if the two are interchangeable. From Jarrell's perspective, the common denominator is that both Pilate and pilots are responsible for the death of others, since Pontius Pilate ad-judicated Jesus Christ's trial and crucifixion, and Jarrell classifies pilots as "murderers" (6). Contrary to Janis P. Stout's suggestion that "Eighth Air Force" utilizes the First World War trope of soldier as Christ (142), Jarrell is identifying the victims of war as Christ-like, sacrificial symbols. While one may suggest such harsh reduction of the role of soldiers to that of murder-ers is a result of Jarrell's feelings about the army, that "the atmosphere was entirely one of lying, meaningless brutality and officiousness, stupidity not beyond belief but conception" (Hutchinson 53), it could also be a conse-quence of popular culture and media not capturing the war for its unparal-leled brutality. For example, postwar films and reporting were notoriously soft toward the realities of World War II, such as the film adaptation of *The Diary of Anne Frank*, which "largely omitted the Holocaust from the narra-tive" (Power 72), or the film *Judgment at Nuremberg*, which was edited for TV because the American Gas Association "objected to the mention of gas chambers" (Power 73), and Frank Capra's series of propaganda films *Why We Fight*, which "made no mention of the Nazi program for exterminating the Jews" (Samet 11). Jarrell's condemnation of wartime violence positions him similarly to Siegfried Sassoon, who called out the "drunken-boasting" of British soldiers over killing German prisoners ("Atrocities" line 1). Both Jarrell and Sassoon challenge the double standard over the morality of one's own side as being distinct from the evil of the opposition, which Sas-soon criticized by writing in a letter accompanying the draft of "Atrocities": "But of course these things aren't atrocities when we do them" (Alberge). By challenging wartime oversimplifications such as the binary view of good versus evil, Jarrell's war poetry always returns to questions of humanity, how "men with our faces" ("Jews at Haifa" life 14) are "capable of such de-meaning acts" (Oostdijk, *Among the Nightmare Fighters* 114).

Though Randall Jarrell wrote one of the only regularly recognized and anthologized poems of World War II, "The Death of the Ball Turret Gun-ner," the depth and quality of his war poems have yet to be adequately rec-ognized. Jarrell's perspective as a stateside, noncombatant soldier places his work in a unique category of war poetry, which can be classed as neither purely civilian poetry nor conventional combat poetry. Recognizing the distance between Jarrell and the war itself is essential to understanding how he processed the war, related to his fellow soldiers, and expressed un-ending guilt over the civilian victims of war. In addition to this physical distance, the emotional connection Jarrell felt to the victims of war and the vicarious trauma he inherited from Holocaust victims are central to his work. In tandem, distance and trauma push Jarrell to imagine, sympathize, and envision the lives of others. Though Jarrell uses the language of dreams to conceptualize the war from a safe distance, his poems remind us that nightmares are a form of dreams. Therefore, when Jarrell writes of war and alludes to Heinrich Heine in "1914," "Es war ein Traum" (it was a dream), the implication is *it was a nightmare.*

Jarrell's poetry of witness and vicarious trauma has not yet been sufficiently acknowledged. A 1940 issue of the *Times Literary Supplement* called for poetry to respond to the war, arguing, "The monstrous threat to belief and freedom which we are fighting should urge new psalmists to fresh songs of deliverance" (Swift 12). Jarrell's poetry provides no such deliverance from evil but rather brings it clearer into focus. Returning to Carolyn Forché's descriptions of poetry of witness, Jarrell is showing a "responsibility for the other as present in the testamentary utterance" of the poem, an awakening of awareness in the experience of others (*Poetry of Witness* 20). Jarrell's contribution to the canon of war literature is through verse that recognizes the value of individual lives against the backdrop of humanitarian crisis.

CONCLUSION

Soldier poetry of World War II by Louis Simpson, Keith Douglas, Richard Hugo, Howard Nemerov, and Randall Jarrell offers a complex view of how distance and traumatic memory underpinned their service. When writing about the poets of the so-called "Silent Generation," Louis Simpson felt it essential that a poem "evolve a definite action of narrative, idea or metaphor," which he prompted by asking, "Does it move?" ("Poets of the Silent Generation" 112). In this question one might hear an echo of Richard Hugo quoting Galileo speaking of the earth in relation to the sun: *"eppur si muove"—and yet it does move* ("Galileo's Chair" line 33). The poets of World War II advanced new narratives about the world as they saw it, their role as combatants, and the lessons of wars that go unlearned. As opposed to an oversimplified view of World War II as if it were a singular narrative, the war would be more accurately visualized like the circulatory system: millions of individual vessels linked to a centralized system. World War II narratives are the consequence of that centralized system in crisis. This study has shown a range of critical response (and dismissal) of World War II soldier poets in scholarship, anthologies, and cultural commentary, while highlighting new ways to view this generation of poets in a unified way. While thematic parallels exist between the poetry of both world wars, World War II poetry is a stylistic departure from the First World War and "the gold standard of war literature" that has routinely valued "fidelity and accuracy" above all else (Krimmer 89). Distinguishing itself in the canon of war literature, World War II soldier poetry possesses a heightened emphasis on internal conflicts compared to battle itself. Loyd E. Lee believes "there is a need to consolidate [World War II poetry], through either analyses of individual poets or, particularly in the case of the American war poetry, more comprehensive studies" (301). The aim of this study has been to address such a need by arguing that the World War II poets warrant greater cultural recognition for their insight into conflict and consequence, with particular regard for their innovative expressions of distance and traumatic memory.

The conclusion of this study will address three issues. First, decades of dismissals and ignorance of World War II soldier poets have impacted their reputation and led to a largely unrevised legacy that they were a "Silent Generation," which has only begun to be challenged in more recent scholarship. Second, a consequence of the unifying characteristics of World War II soldier poetry—distance and traumatic memory—has been disproportionate recognition by editors, literary critics, and tastemakers. Lastly, readers and broader communities can be enriched by these perspectives of armed service and testimonies of the traumatic lifelong repercussions of war.

The underrepresentation and lackluster reputation of World War II soldier poets in anthologies and literary criticism have projected their generation as an underwhelming collective who produced little work of literary, cultural, and historical importance. In contrast to the effusive praise and cultural absorption of the First World War trench poets, only a fraction of World War II poetry has received positive critical reception. Within those few examples of acknowledged poems, such as Jarrell's "The Death of the Ball Turret Gunner" or Douglas's "Desert Flowers," one can identify connective tissue to the exalted qualities of earlier combat poetry. Both poems invoke the gore of battle and chronicle the suffering of men at war, as if ticking the traits of the previous generation's canonized war poems (let alone referencing them by name, as Douglas does with Rosenberg) is one's path to critical acceptance. One key distinction between soldier poets of World War II and their predecessors is their disparate experiences of war compared to the unifying experience of a centralized location in trench warfare. World War II service members wrote of war from land, air, sea, and home front, spanning theaters of Europe, the Pacific, North Africa, America, Britain, and beyond. Rather than viewing diversity of experience as an asset that mirrors the range and reach of World War II, some critics have pointed to such variation as having a dislocating, decentralized effect on this generation of poetry. For example, Margot Norris believes the formal and thematic diversity of World War II poetry "defies classification and frustrates any sense of coherence" ("War Poetry in the USA" 43). What, though, could be more dislocating and decentralizing than war? For poets such as Louis Simpson, who was born and raised in Jamaica, then a British colony, familiarity with dislocation and countries exerting international power and control over others was an inextricable component of his world-view, or, as Paul Giles suggests, "an emblem of the ontological limitations that circumscribe a poet's imaginative world" (392). Simpson explains of growing up in Jamaica that, "You learned English history and literature, and that you owed everything to England, and owed her your loyalty in return. But you were not English—to be English you had have been born in England. So there was a sense of inferiority built into the colonial psyche" (*The King My Father's Wreck* 33). Furthermore, the vast range of theaters, roles of service, and events makes the processing and reimagining of distance an incomparable facet of the World War II experience. From the blistering heat of El Alamein to the freezing Battle of Stalingrad, the D-Day landings on the beaches of Normandy to the dropping of atomic bombs on Hiroshima and Nagasaki, World War II unmoored society from conventional interpretations of distance.

The stylistic diversity of World War II soldier poetry has delineated the poets selected for this study in different schools of contemporary poetry. With the exception of Keith Douglas, whose war death has forever linked his legacy to World War II, the remaining cohort in this study are more commonly categorized as a deep image poet (Simpson), a regionalist (Hugo), a nature poet or poet of irony (Nemerov), and a shrewd literary critic and poet (Jarrell). While these are justified characterizations, what unites these five markedly different poets of markedly different war experience is the distance and traumatic memory in their war poems. Whether writing during the war or in reflection decades later, each of these five poets turned to these themes to process an experience that exists beyond words. As opposed to the commonly anthologized poems of the First World War, which capture the sensory intensity of trench warfare, World War II poetry is linked by varied explorations of distance and traumatic memory. This retrospective work emerged after the distance of time and space were afforded for adequate reflection, and traumatic experience was confronted. Distance and traumatic memory are, therefore, shared themes of World War II poetry and factors contributing to its neglect. One could apply Orwell's opinion of 1930s writers like Auden and Spender to the relationship World War II poets have with the trench poets: "although technically these writers owe something to their predecessors, their 'tendency' is entirely different" (Childs, *The Twentieth Century in Poetry* 114). The fact that poetry of World War II was not a simple re-creation of First World War trench poetry, though many strands of influence exist, has prevented critics from acknowledging the potential range of how a war poem can look and sound, the emotional register it can explore, and the narrative it can tell.

The objective of this book is not to put soldier poetry on a pedestal above that of the civilian experience, with particular mindfulness not to drift into "military worship," which can lead to the "abdication of civic involvement" and preclude some from distinguishing that while "Military operational experience is unique . . . it is not all-knowing" (Karlin and Friend). Rather, this research offers a revised legacy of World War II poetry to more accurately reflect the contributions made by service members both during the war and through the decades that followed. Continually referring to these poets as part of a "Silent Generation" actively ignores a body of work that spanned roughly a half century. Furthermore, recognizing the contributions these poets have made to the canon of war literature expands our understanding of what constitutes war literature.

While many factors contribute to the high expectations placed upon World War II soldier poets, variables such as historical context, artistic variation, and personal circumstance have contributed to their under-recognized catalogue, particularly in contrast to First World War soldier poetry. The world was thrust back into war roughly ten years after the height of the war books boom at the end of the 1920s, and expectations were cast on World War II poets to fulfill a demand for war writings, including by Robert Graves, who gave a radio talk "on the question of 'Why has [World War II] produced no war poets?'" (Swift 13). The moral difference between the two world wars complicated expectations of war poetry and antiwar sentiment because, even though World War II did produce antiwar poems, the war required nuance from its poets to process the obvious necessity of the war to defeat the fascist and imperialist Axis powers and end the Holocaust. In contrast, during the First World War and interwar period, many soldiers who wrote poetry, fiction, and memoir created antiwar narratives. Notable examples include poems by Siegfried Sassoon and Wilfred Owen, the immensely successful 1929 novels *All Quiet on the Western Front* by Erich Maria Remarque and *A Farewell to Arms* by Ernest Hemingway, and the postwar memoirs *Good-Bye to All That* by Robert Graves and *Undertones of War* by Edmund Blunden, and Sassoon's fictionalized

George Sherston memoirs. Categorized as antiwar writings, these works are among the loudest sustained voices in the canon of First World War literature (and war literature in general), despite a glut of wildly popular war literature that glamorized notions of duty, courage, and patriotism. Arguably the most prominent voice of such patriotic verse was Rupert Brooke, whose *Collected Poems* had sold 300,000 copies by 1930, proving the public appetite for both patriotic and antiwar literature, though the literary legacy of the First World War has veered toward the latter (Trott 56). Ultimately, such a vast body of work that reflected on the First World War by those who participated in it established a narrative that emphasized the horror, futility, and brutality of war, and was influential in shaping public opinion from the 1920s to the outbreak of World War II.

The deployment of patriotic rhetoric, particularly in American political messaging, military recruitment, and popular culture, has maintained an outsized influence in shaping public opinion. Yet, in times when a wedge has been cleaved between blind nationalistic support for the military and the objectives of foreign intervention, such as the antiwar and anti-interventionist sentiment that stemmed from the protracted wars in Iraq and Afghanistan, there develops a greater willingness to acknowledge dissenting voices. It is perhaps in these moments of global (and particularly American) self-reflection that voices challenging the conventional patriotic messaging can become more palatable. Revisiting historical narratives and challenging the concept of American exceptionalism has enabled more critical voices to find daylight. By acknowledging that the legacy of World War II is more complex than a collision of binary opposites, the reputation of World War II poetry is gradually evolving, particularly for poets who often confronted their own behavior and questioned the morality of war.

All examinations of the historical context of World War II must include the Holocaust. While an all-encompassing narrative of the Holocaust will never be possible due to millions of silenced victims, the importance of reminding each subsequent generation of the darkest period in humanity and the depths of human depravity is incalculable. Yet, Theodor Adorno's now-famous argument that "To write poetry after Auschwitz is barbaric" has generated debate over whether repeating cultural acts (such as writing poetry) born out of the same culture in which the Holocaust occurred is a failure to reform a culture capable of committing genocide (34). Parallel arguments suggest that the Holocaust is an altogether incommunicable

event, and therefore any attempt would be inadequate. Yet, Holocaust testimony is not literally unspeakable, as demonstrated by many accounts of
oral history, memoir, film, and other forms of expression. The hurdle, then,
is "a moral prohibition" (Richardson 2) or "taboo" toward the acceptability
of such attempts at sharing testimony (Trezise 43). As Anna Richardson
deftly identifies, this concept is nuanced because "silence can also be seen
as memorialization," as is so often seen by moments of silence in the wake
of tragedy (4). There continues to be debate over the role of Holocaust literature, such as the appropriateness of Holocaust fiction, and fears that
"Terrible things, by continuing to be shown, begin to appear matter-of-
fact, a natural rather than man-made catastrophe. Zygmunt Bauman has
labeled this the 'production of moral indifference'" (Hartman 100). History has shown, through acts of genocide against Bosnians in Srebrenica,
the Tutsi in Rwanda, Cambodians by the hand of the Khmer Rouge, the
Rohingya in Myanmar, and the detention of Uighurs in Chinese concentration camps, that "there is an 'after' Auschwitz, without any sign that we
are 'beyond' Auschwitz" (Hartman 7).[1] Samantha Power, former U.S. am-
bassador to the United Nations under President Obama, urges that knowledge, influence, will, and accountability are the building blocks upon which
countries should base their response to genocide (Power 504–10). For not
only is it a duty to act in moments of moral obligation, but it is "a duty
to listen" (Hartman 133). While Geoffrey H. Hartman believes that listening and watching oral testimony is a duty that helps to restore "the survivor's humanity," the same applies to the narratives of combatants (156).
Whether one reads Jarrell's "Protocols" to envision the perspective of a
child victim of the Holocaust or Nemerov's "Redeployment" as a portrait of
a veteran living with PTSD, the poems of World War II soldiers urge readers
to acknowledge the often-unseen consequences of war and conflict, and by
seeing, validate the existence and experience of others. One is reminded
of how Hannah Arendt understood that "under conditions of terror, most
people will comply but *some people will not*" and that "no more is required,
and no more can reasonably be asked, for this planet to remain a place
fit for human habitation" (233). When faced with acts of dehumanization,
mass violence, and atrocity, it is through objection and resistance that people assert their humanity.

In addition to the historical context of war literature in the first half
of the twentieth century, war narratives have been continually uncovered

since World War II, and a deeper cultural knowledge of the events and experiences of the 1939–45 conflict has emerged. The postwar outpouring of information and the arts was a stark contrast to during the war, when forums for publicly disseminated information were often limited to newspapers, radio broadcasts, and cinemas showing newsreel. Furthermore, going to the movies became a premier mode of entertainment. Film presented a growing competition to war literature and, judging by unofficial estimates, more than 450 war films were made worldwide in the 1940s (joe_538). In Britain alone, "79% of teenagers and 43% of young adults reported that they went to the cinema at least once a week" in 1943 (Glancy 8). Much like the war books boom in the late 1920s and early 1930s that followed the First World War, the persistent release of films about World War II simultaneously speaks to the magnetism of World War II's scale, extremity, and influence, as well as its continual effectiveness in telling allegorical stories about national identity and individual choice.

During World War II, despite film's growing popularity, particularly among younger audiences, still imagery retained a firm place in advertising and journalism. Restrictions on publicly shared information led to a misrepresentation of the realities of war, such as selective photography used in war reporting, and propaganda posters eliciting war support through subjects of labor, morale, and economics. The U.S. Office of War Information, the War Department's Bureau of Public Relations, and Hollywood's War Activities Committee were influential bodies that shaped the war narrative for the public (Jarvis 97), and the U.S. government "prohibited publication of any photographs of American dead . . . for the first twenty-one months of American involvement in World War II" (Roeder 8). A sanitized view of the war reinforced the image of strength projected in propaganda posters and war movies, amid fears that representations of death, wounding, or combat stress (later known as PTSD) projected weakness.

Efforts to conceal the sanguinary in favor of the saccharine created an implicit cultural silence, but the World War II poetry that eventually emerged was often beyond the margins of what was deemed culturally palatable, such as some of Jarrell's "antiwar poems" that were rejected on "ideological grounds" by New Republic during the war (Randall Jarrell's Letters 104). Each passing generation further affirms that the consequences of war extend far beyond losing a public relations battle, and World War II soldier poets were not shy in representing unsavory aspects of war. Douglas's descriptions of a defiled corpse (*"Vergissmeinnicht"*), Simpson's brothel-based narrative ("A Bower of Roses"), Hugo's overt guilt for bombing foreign targets ("Galleria Umberto I"), Jarrell's unceremonious cleaning of a liquefied corpse from a ball turret ("The Death of the Ball Turret Gunner"), and Nemerov's disdain for his fellow squadron members ("IFF") are all examples that evolve World War II's legacy from a moral obligation, "the good war," into that of a complicated global conflict.[2] After all, World War II produced bombing raids so powerful their shock waves have been measured in responses in the ionosphere (Scott and Major). World War II impacted the literal and figurative atmosphere, and its survivors and witnesses are indelible sources for examining the depth of such imprints.

The personal circumstances of many World War II combatants have also contributed to their insufficient recognition. While Louis Simpson's postwar mental breakdown forced him to focus on poetry instead of the sustained concentration required for prose, his development as a poet did not occur until after the war had ended. Keith Douglas wrote and published war poems during World War II, but his poetic trajectory was cut short when he was killed in Normandy. Many critics have used Douglas's death to align him with Wilfred Owen, though Douglas's poetry argued for processing the war through an extrospective lens. Not until the 1951 publication of his *Collected Poems* and later advocacy by Ted Hughes did Douglas's poetry garner recognition. The gap in time between Richard Hugo's war service and his first book publication in 1961 has kept him almost entirely out of the conversation of World War II poetry. The "Silent Generation" legacy had been cemented long before Hugo's *Good Luck in Cracked Italian* was published in 1969, his collection with the greatest concentration of war poems. Similarly, Howard Nemerov's delayed processing of his war experience meant his poems of PTSD and challenging conventional World War II narratives were delayed reactions. Living with PTSD and feeling an obligation to speak out about his experience against the backdrop of subsequent wars elicited Nemerov's retrospective war poems. The recognition of Randall Jarrell as a war poet is limited to a select number of anthologized poems, while the depth of his war poetry guided by dreams and vicarious trauma is frequently overlooked. Jarrell's death in 1965 could have precluded him from creating a larger body of war poetry, as Simpson, Hugo, and Nemerov all wrote war poems for decades afterward. With a clearer understanding of PTSD, including the delayed processing of memory, gaps in memory, and the physical and mental disruptions it can cause, it is time that literary criticism accommodates such realities when evaluating the contributions and legacy of a generation. Therefore, ironically, the distinguishing themes of World War II soldier poetry, its diverse interpretations of distance and traumatic memory, are factors that have directly contributed to its critical mischaracterization. While many traumatized soldiers wrestle to suppress memories of their war experience, those who have expressed themselves deserve to be heard.

Each of the preceding chapters exemplifies why these five poets are invaluable contributors to our understanding of World War II, and how their interpretations of distance and expressions of traumatic memory unite them. The drastic differences between World War II and any war fought before it are reflected in the diversity of its poetry. These poets give firsthand perspectives of the European ground war, the North Africa campaign, bombing campaigns in the Mediterranean, shipping patrols and attack runs along the coasts of Britain and Europe, and of aviation training from an American army base. Those who survived the war initially turned inward before revealing their disparate experiences. These poets probed traumatic memory, revisited the sites of their war experience, and tried to make sense of what they had experienced by finding commonalities with other historical events. By listening to these historical testimonies, readers can better understand how soldiers experienced World War II, and the psychological repercussions they were forced to confront. While one could argue that World War II soldier poets should be included in the canon of war literature purely for posterity's sake, the quality of these poets is validated by their success beyond the realm of just war poetry, including being selected as U.S. poet laureates, and as recipients of the Pulitzer Prize, National Book Award, and many other accolades. Therefore, it would be counterintuitive to suggest that the soldier poets of World War II are simply not good enough to be included in canonical discussions. A gradual increase in recognition has evolved in recent decades, which can perhaps be partially attributed to the fact that, for many, World War II is framed chiefly through the perspective of civilians subjected to the conflict. As a result, civilian World War II poetry could justifiably be seen as a first port of call for understanding the war, despite self-reflective questions explored by such writers inquiring, "Must war poetry originate exclusively in the experience of combatants?" (Galvin 1–2).

Eighty years have passed since the end of World War II, and the world has been inundated with World War II narratives in the form of literature, film, television, museums, testimony, and more. What could a spotlight on this generation of poets add to an already crowded corpus? World War II soldier poetry gives firsthand dispatches from the most influential historical event in modern history while offering creative cultural enrichment, the inherent value of testimony, and unique historical documentation. If future generations hope to learn from the past, make diplomatic decisions with an understanding of the lifelong ramifications of armed conflict on both the individual and society, and better understand the world we live in as the sum of previous generations, it is incumbent upon us to listen to those who preceded us. With this responsibility in mind, as each day the distance grows between us and the millions who served in World War II and the estimated 50–75 million who died, we should recall Louis Simpson's retrospective warning:

He supposed this is what life taught you,
that words you thought were a joke,
and applied to someone else,
were real, and applied to you.

("A Bower of Roses" lines 74–77)

The soldier poets of World War II were not a "Silent Generation," and it is the responsibility of subsequent generations to acknowledge their contributions by speaking up when confronted with the warnings of the past.

NOTES

1. This photograph's title alludes to Alfred Lord Tennyson's war poem "The Charge of the Light Brigade": "Into the jaws of Death, / Into the mouth of hell / Rode the six hundred" (lines 24–26).

2. Historian Stephen Ambrose's books have been immensely influential in shaping public perception of World War II, serving as inspiration for the television series *Band of Brothers* and as reference points in the making of the film *Saving Private Ryan*. Ambrose reinforces a popular narrative about American servicemen: "They knew they were fighting for decency and democracy and they were proud of it and motivated by it. They just didn't talk or write about it" (*Citizen Soldiers*, "Introduction and Acknowledgments").

3. Such generational comparisons present a paradox of critical and nostalgic bias: if one considers First World War poetry the gold standard, war poetry that did not resemble it would be seen to pale in comparison, and poetry that did resemble it would be dismissed as derivative.

4. A range of texts from recent decades have begun uncovering varying facets of World War II literature, such as Sarah Wasson's *Urban Gothic of the Second World War*, which examines poet Roy Fuller and others, John Pikoulis's biography *Alun Lewis: A Life*, and Helen Goethals's research on Edward Thomas, Timothy Corsellis, and others.

5. Keith Douglas used the word "extrospective" to describe outward-looking poetry in which writers detached themselves from their observations, akin to reportage (Graham, *Keith Douglas* 214).

6. Waterman analyzes Keith Douglas, Alun Lewis, Randall Jarrell, Charles Causley, and Louis Simpson.

7. Axelrod analyzes soldiers Randall Jarrell and Karl Shapiro, civilians Gwendolyn Brooks and Elizabeth Bishop, and conscientious objector Robert Lowell.

8. To further understand the aims of Douglas's extrospective poetry, one may look to Roland Barthes's "The Death of the Author," which employs distance in the form of impersonality when stating, "writing is the destruction of every voice, of every point of origin" (*Image-Music-Text* 142).

9. Porter and Peace's investigation into the consistency of traumatic memory over time has provided clinical perspectives for analyzing World War II poems of sustained trauma and

its lifelong repercussions, relevant to each of the selected poets, but particularly Louis Simpson and his postwar struggles with PTSD.

10. Eva Hoffman's "second generation" perspective of Holocaust memory and testimony in *After Such Knowledge: Memory, History, and the Legacy of the Holocaust* contributes to understanding Jarrell's poems of witnessing.

11. Forms of World War II trauma differ immensely whether one has experienced combat, is a Holocaust victim, has been displaced, has suffered a loss, vicariously experienced trauma on behalf of others, or countless other potential sources. The trauma theory invoked in this study aims to align appropriate analysis with related traumatic experience.

12. Arguments that World War II poetry did not possess the quality, accomplishment, or importance compared to other generations are difficult to defend when Howard Nemerov and Randall Jarrell served as U.S. poet laureates, or when Louis Simpson won a Pulitzer Prize.

13. A few weeks into his 1944 deployment to Burma, Alun Lewis died by gunshot, allegedly self-inflicted.

14. Sidney Keyes died in combat at twenty years old, approximately three weeks into his 1943 deployment in Tunisia (G. Hill 398).

15. James Dickey's reputation as a war poet is muddled due to fabrications surrounding his war service and that "he lied about his military record" (Dickey xxii).

16. Of related concern regarding representation, the Commonwealth War Graves Commission concluded an investigation in 2021 that found that the Imperial War Graves Commission had unequally commemorated "45,000–54,000 casualties (predominantly Indian, East African, West African, Egyptian, and Somali personnel)" and that a further 116,000–350,000 casualties were "not commemorated by name or possibly not commemorated at all" (Commonwealth War Graves Commission 6).

17. While not poets, other African American war veterans also contributed to the Black Arts Movement, including academic and critic Harold Cruse, fiction writer John O. Killens, and editor and critic Hoyt W. Fuller (Barksdale viii).

18. Written from the perspective of a Black mother whose sons have been sent off to war, this poem is a prayer for peace abroad and peace at home from racial strife. The speaker laments: "Better let em die in the desert drinkin sand [. . .] / Than they come back an see they sufferin for vain" (Dodson, "Black Mother Praying in the Summer 1943" lines 60, 62).

19. The NAACP published *The Crisis*, a periodical founded by W. E. B. Du Bois in 1910, to discuss "civil rights, history, politics and culture" and "to educate and challenge its readers about issues that continue to plague African Americans and other communities of color" (*The Crisis*).

20. *Phylon*, also founded by W. E. B. Du Bois, was a journal on race and culture that began in 1940 (*Phylon*).

21. Pearl S. Buck wrote in the December 1941 issue of *The Crisis*: "The colored American, thanks to an education in democracy, now really wants to see his country a democracy. When he defends the United States of America he does not want to do so segregated and limited. This contradicts his idea of a democracy. He has grown up a good deal since the World War. And he has not forgotten that war. He is willing to fight and die again, but not for something he does not possess anyway" (376).

22. Despite initial resistance toward recognizing Miller for his actions, he was awarded the Navy Cross in 1942 and was posthumously given a Purple Heart after dying in service in the Pacific in 1943 ("Miller, Doris").

23. This relative similarity of ground combat between Simpson, Douglas, and their First World War predecessors lends itself to more frequent connections, comparisons, and analysis between the two generations in these chapters.

24. Hamish Henderson's poem "4 September 1939" also laments the return to war after "twenty years for building and learning" (line 1).

1. LOUIS SIMPSON

1. The Welsh World War II poet Alun Lewis also wrote a poem titled "The Sentry" equating the night with death (Lewis).

2. Whitman, too, witnessed the aftermath of battle while working as a nurse during the American Civil War (Roberts 787).

3. Sassoon's "Glory of Women" begins with a similar critique:

You love us when we're heroes, home on leave,
Or wounded in a mentionable place.
You worship decorations; you believe
That chivalry redeems the war's disgrace.

(lines 1–4)

4. Timothy Snyder emphasizes the link between war and the cultivation of land, such as in Hitler's desire for *Lebensraum* (living space) so that Germany could have a "land empire that would even the scales between London and Berlin" in terms of industrial and agricultural production, shifting away from dependence on British naval supply lines (12).

5. Pastoral imagery is subverted when Simpson intertwines flora with dead soldiers, writing "green grows the grass on the infantry." This subversion is like Blunden's "Vlamertinghe: Passing the Chateau, July 1917," in that the deaths are so many that they do not stand out from one another; they are dull in contrast to the vibrancy of the natural world. "Vlamertinghe: Passing the Chateau, July 1917" uses the notion of death as dullness when in contrast to the "daisies" (line 9), "roses" (line 10), and "poppies by the million" that once adorned the Belgian battlefield (line 11), Blunden sees the deaths of millions, writing frankly, "if you ask me, mate, the choice of colour / Is scarcely right; this red should have been duller" (lines 13–14).

6. In doing so, Blunden's "Vlamertinghe: Passing the Chateau, July 1917" makes multiple allusions to Keats's "Ode to a Grecian Urn"—"'And all her silken flanks with garlands drest'" ("Vlamertinghe" line 1; "Ode on a Grecian Urn" line 34) and "brute guns lowing at the skies" ("Vlamertinghe" line 8) like Keats's "that heifer lowing at the skies" ("Ode" line 33)—to foreground the reader's interpretation with the notion of sacrifice.

7. In addition to the poets of the First World War, Walt Whitman's poem "O Captain! My Captain" directly influences Simpson in "Carentan O Carentan." Whitman's poem has the

unanswered call of "O Captain! My Captain! rise up and hear the bells" ("O Captain! My Captain!" line 9) only for the speaker to realize the captain has "fallen cold and dead" (line 16).

8. The war dead for both the Allied and Central powers accumulated in trenches, fields, woods, rivers, and other landscapes, and would not always be buried, due to location, manpower, time, and danger. Here, a dead soldier blends into the woods with a face that is sodden green and "Dribbling black blood" (line 12).

9. Seeger was an American serving in the French Foreign Legion in the First World War who enlisted after graduating from Harvard University, where he shared an apartment with T. S. Eliot (M. Hill 23).

10. Robert Graves accurately predicted that Sassoon's poetry would darken in sentiment once he saw more war action, cause him to eschew patriotism, and expose the terror of war (Egremont 75). Written while recuperating from "shell shock" at Craiglockhart Military Hospital in 1917, Sassoon's "Survivors" categorizes traumatized soldiers as "broken and mad" (line 10) children whose "shock and strain / Have caused their stammering, disconnected talk" (lines 1–2).

11. Louis Simpson's war poetry shares Sassoon's sentiment that wars persist in the minds of their participants long after any armistice. Sassoon also invoked temporal shifts in "Two Hundred Years After," in which hallucinatory visions of English soldiers are seen or imagined heading up a hill in the French countryside centuries after the First World War: "Poor silent things, they were the English dead / Who came to fight in France and got their fill" (lines 13–14). For both Simpson and Sassoon, ghostly reminders of the war dead will continue to haunt the land, as if the trenches are a lasting wound on the earth.

12. The poppy's popularization in First World War poetry and the start of using the poppy as a sign of remembrance began in November 1918 ("Moina Belle Michael").

13. "The Runner" is a long, twelve-section, free verse poem, structurally similar to David Jones's *In Parenthesis,* though more direct in its presentation of dialogue and narrative than Jones's retelling of the First World War through Welsh mythological allusions.

14. Ciardi's critique of "The Runner" is similar to feedback Robert Graves wrote to Wilfred Owen about "Disabled." Amid critiquing the number of syllables Owen is using in his lines, Graves writes, "I wouldn't worry to mention all this if it wasn't to my violent pleasure" ("Letter: To Wilfred Owen" 2). He continues, encouragingly, "Do you know, Owen, that's a damn fine poem of yours, that 'Disabled.' Really damn fine!" (1).

15. T. S. Eliot also alludes to this line in *The Waste Land:* "Musing upon the king my brother's wreck" (line 191).

16. Fitting, too, that this passage may have taken inspiration from Dostoevsky's own life, when in 1849 he was arrested for antigovernment activities and brought before a firing squad, only to be reprieved at the last minute (Teuber). Dostoevsky thought his life was about to end, though it is believed Tsar Nicolas I orchestrated the event as a psychological torment and threat.

17. Echoes of this cross-generational response to war can be heard in the title of Tobias Wolff's 1994 memoir about his service as a U.S. Army officer in the Vietnam War, *In Pharoah's Army: Memories of the Lost War.*

18. The Soviet Union endured the highest combined civilian and military death toll num-

bers during World War II, approximately 24 million, an immense loss of life ("Research Start-ers"). Such severe losses were compounded by the repressive dictatorship of Joseph Stalin, and the Great Purge that preceded the war in 1936–38.

2. KEITH DOUGLAS

1. Such syntactical choices were a departure from poetic trends in the 1940s such as William Carlos Williams's "American Idiom," which encouraged using ordinary speech, a shift that would further evolve with the Beat Generation and Confessional poetry that arose in the 1950s and 1960s.

2. Douglas was among a cohort of desert war poets, such as John Jarmain, Hamish Henderson, Sorley MacLean, Sidney Keyes, and others. The Salamander Oasis Trust has published five World War II poetry anthologies, including *Return to Oasis* (Selwyn) and *The Voice of War* (Selwyn), which highlight World War II poems from the Middle East campaigns.

3. In "Goliath and David," with the enemy presented as an overwhelming Goliath, Graves positions a "calm and brave" (line 37) fellow soldier as a pure-of-heart underdog whose "Scorn blazes in the Giant's eye" (line 27).

4. In "Strange Meeting," Owen's speaker escapes battle through a tunnel (by dying, though tunnel systems were used to support the trenches through troop and supply movement) where he encounters a dead enemy soldier and realizes "we stood in hell" (10). Just as the warning Dante passes upon his entry to hell in *The Inferno*, "abandon all hope, ye who enter here," the dead soldier challenges the speaker by arguing what has been lost as a consequence of war ("Canto III" line 7). For it is "the undone years . . . Whatever hope is yours" and the hunt for "the wildest beauty in the world" which has been lost in the eyes of the enemy soldier ("Strange Meeting," lines 15–16, 18).

5. A draft of the poem suggests as much, where the line, "I am the enemy you killed, my friend," originally read, "I was a German conscript, and your friend" (Silkin 209). More notable to Owen than their differences in nationality is the fact that they share and embody a history of warfare that leaves mankind either "content with what we spoiled" or "discontent, boil bloody, and be spilled" ("Strange Meeting" lines 26, 27). These options suggest that soldiers either are complicit with the human and emotional costs of war or are at risk of being killed by a complicit opposition.

6. American poet Brian Turner is a veteran of the Iraq War and has been a leading voice for the current generation of war poetry. His poetry collection *Here, Bullet* is embedded in the Iraqi landscape, where poems are set in Baghdad, deserts, and among dunes and oilfields. The final poem in *Here, Bullet*, titled "To Sand," speaks to the permanence of such a brutal landscape, and the confluence of memory, object, and sacrifice. "To Sand" begins, "To sand go tracers and ball ammunition. / To sand the green smoke goes . . . To sand go the skeletons of war, year by year" (lines 1–2, 5), and concludes, "To sand / each head of cabbage unravels its leaves / the way dreams burn in the oilfires of night" (lines 10–12).

7. The resonance of these lines is seen in its continued use at military funerals and services, and in its echoes in historical documents, such as the speech U.S. president Richard Nixon would have delivered if the Apollo 11 moon landing mission had failed. This alternative

address concluded, "For every human being who looks up at the moon in the nights to come will know that there is some corner of another world that is forever mankind" (Safire 2).

8. Similarly, John Jarmain's June 1939 poem "Thinking of War" begins, "If I must die, forget these hands of mine" (line 1). Rather than asking to be remembered, or simplified, Jarmain's poem asks one's loved ones to forget them in order to not be constrained by memory.

9. The war narrative continues to be a compelling story, as proving oneself through the test of war is paralleled by storytelling craft techniques such as Joseph Campbell's "hero's journey" in which one traverses a series of stages, beginning with an "Ordinary World" disrupted by a "Call to Adventure" during which they will be tested before being able to return home victorious (Campbell, *The Hero with a Thousand Faces*).

10. Expressing a similar sentiment five years later, Polish poet Czesław Miłosz would write his 1945 poem "Dedication" from a Warsaw in ruins, asking, "What is poetry which does not save / Nations or people?" (lines 14–15).

3. RICHARD HUGO

1. "Testimony," as defined by *The Oxford English Dictionary*, is a written or spoken statement provided by a witness to demonstrate evidence or proof, so whether one is reading for enjoyment or analysis, poetry of testimony affirms the truth due to bearing witness or giving voice to the voiceless.

2. Sorley MacLean revisits this notion in "Death Valley," a poem that describes the death of a German "boy" (6) soldier in World War II: "he showed no pleasure in his death / below the Ruweisat Ridge" (30–31).

3. The release of Meier and Bradtke's "Der Sommerwind" and publication of "Mission to Linz" both occurred in 1965, while the song's popularity grew from Frank Sinatra's 1966 version, "Summer Wind."

4. Roy Scranton identifies "singular/multiple, man/machine, victim/destroyer" dualisms in bomber lyrics (29).

5. Similar to the Romantic poet Percy Bysshe Shelley's "Ode to the West Wind," in which the "unseen presence" (line 2) of the wind is *felt* like "breath" (line 1), and in which "the leaves dead / Are driven" (lines 2–3).

6. While early studies were conducted by figures like Charcot and Freud, the succession of First World War "shell shock," World War II and the Holocaust, and subsequent wars and traumatic events led to the inclusion of PTSD in the 1980 *Diagnostic and Statistical Manual of Mental Disorders*, a symbolic recognition of trauma in medical studies (Ringel and Brandell 5).

7. Ruth Leys reinforces that "there was in Britain considerably more continuity between the psychiatric experiences" of the world wars than typically acknowledged (192).

8. Sassoon also returned to Europe between the world wars to non-battle-related destinations, such as spending time with other artists at Haus Hirth, near Garmisch, Germany (J. Boyd 378).

9. Sorley MacLean's poems demonstrate a similar attachment to specific World War II place-names, which serve as trigger words in his poems. For example, his poems "Going Westward," "The Broken Bottle," and "The Lost Mountain" all contain direct references to

concentration camps, such as Auschwitz, Dachau, and Belsen. Additionally, MacLean's "Festubert 16/17.v.1915" uses a location and date of a First World War battle to provide context. John Jarmain believed place-names of battles in World War II's North Africa campaign, such as El Alamein and Tobruk, would become synonymous with ancient battle locations like Troy. In the poem "El Alamein," Jarmain writes, "It will become a staid historic name, / That crazy sea of sand! / Like Troy or Agincourt its single fame" (lines 13–15).

10. This limbo between royalty and criminality echoes Lord Byron's poem "Childe Harold's Pilgrimage," which begins "I stood in Venice, on the Bridge of Sighs, / A palace and a prison on each hand" (Canto IV, lines 1–2).

11. Galileo was deemed a heretic for defending the theory of heliocentrism, which argues that the Earth revolves around the Sun, against religious teachings that suggested that the Earth was the center of the universe (Shea 68).

12. The ploughman's indifference to suffering "is Auden's sign of the intellectual who can neither affect nor meaningfully comment on events," as explained by art historian Alexander Nemerov, son of Howard Nemerov (797).

13. For example, post–World War II Germans seeking to regain some semblance of normalcy in their social and working lives sought out "denazification courts" where citizens filed for an "affidavit, called *Persilschein* after a laundry detergent, that would prove their innocence" and give them a clean record, innocent of Nazi sympathies (Jarausch 266).

4. HOWARD NEMEROV

1. Despite military age requirements, many examples have surfaced of younger soldiers lying about their age in order to serve, such as twelve-year-old Calvin Graham, who lied in order to join the U.S. Navy (King).

2. According to the *Oxford English Dictionary*, a "Junker" is a term that historically refers to "A German nobleman or aristocrat, especially a member of the Prussian aristocracy."

3. U.S. Air Force radio operator Paul Montgomery said of firebombing Japan, "You kill them from a distance and it doesn't have that demoralizing effect upon you that it did if I went up and stuck a bayonet in somebody's stomach in the course of combat. It's just different. It's kind of like conducting war through a video game." Laurence Rees believed that this "distancing" is "one of the keys to understanding why such a seemingly 'normal' man can participate in the killing of woman [*sic*] and children in large numbers" (*Their Darkest Hour* 8).

4. Suspended like Jarrell's fly caught in the "amber of the histories" ("A Lullaby" line 12).

5. Twenty-seven years later, Richard Hugo would echo this sentiment in the poem "In Your War Dream," writing, "You must fly your 35 missions again" (line 1).

6. Moral injury is a concept "distinct from the idea of trauma, that relates to the ways in which ex-soldiers make sense of the socially transgressive things they have done during wartime" (Keefe 286–87).

7. This ending is an allusion to the refrain from Kurt Vonnegut's *Slaughterhouse-Five*, a novel inspired by Vonnegut's World War II experience as a prisoner of war during the firebombing of Dresden. Both uses of "so it goes" are responses to transcending time and meaning in death.

5. RANDALL JARRELL

1. Tate also critiqued the perceived absence of poets in World War II while satirizing American enthusiasm for war, writing in "Ode to Our Young Pro-consuls of the Air": "In this bad time no part / The poet took, nor chance: He studied Swift and Donne, / Ignored the Hun" (lines 55–58).

2. In *News of War*, Rachel Galvin poses the question, "Could a noncombatant ever have sufficient authority to write of war?" (2). Though Galvin is thinking of civilians and not a soldier in a noncombat role, this question of authority, and by extension, authenticity, persists in war literature analysis.

3. Jarrell takes a similar position to Joseph Heller, who described his famed novel *Catch-22* as "more anti-traditional establishment than anti-war" (Burns 111).

4. Jarrell believed Auden's poetry evolved toward a "more accessible" style, compromising its poetic qualities in the process, as he remarked in his 1941 essay "Changes in Attitude and Rhetoric in Auden's Poetry" (*No Other Book* 206).

5. "The Death of the Ball Turret Gunner" also contains echoes of Owen's "Asleep," both of which use imagery of opposites, such as life and death, sleep and waking, and "aborted life" ("Asleep" line 6).

6. Jarrell felt Freud's death "was like having a continent disappear" (*Randall Jarrell's Letters* 24) and would define literature the way Freud defined dreams, as "a wish modified by a truth" (Burt 31).

7. A spate of military losses and setbacks in 1943—Stalingrad, North Africa, and "U-boat action in the North Atlantic"—pushed the Nazis to intensify operations at concentration camps (Rees, *The Holocaust* 333).

CONCLUSION

1. The recent resurgence of right-wing extremism, fascist movements, and increasingly isolationist global policy have raised concerns over additional acts of state-sanctioned persecution and murder.

2. Questions have also been raised about the nature of Allied area bombings and the dropping of the atomic bombs, and whether these were acts of war or mass murder that could be defined as genocide (Primoratz 11).

WORKS CITED

Adams, Michael C. C. *The Best War Ever: America and World War II.* Johns Hopkins University Press, 2015.

Adorno, Theodor W. "Cultural Criticism and Society." *Prisms,* translated by Samuel and Shierry Weber, MIT Press, 2007.

"Air Force History." Military.com, www.military.com/air-force-birthday/air-force -history.html.

Alberge, Dalya. "Draft Siegfried Sassoon Poem Reveals Controversial Lines Cut from Atrocities." *Guardian News and Media,* 2 Feb. 2013, www.theguardian.com /books/2013/feb/03/siegfried-sassoon-poem-atrocities.

Alexander, Caroline. "The Shock of War." Smithsonian.com, 1 Sept. 2010, http:// www.smithsonianmag.com/history/the-shock-of-war-55376701.

Alighieri, Dante. *The Inferno of Dante: A New Verse Translation.* Translated by Robert Pinsky, Noonday, 1999.

Ambrose, Stephen E. Citizen Soldiers: From the Beaches of Normandy to the Sur- render of Germany. Simon & Schuster, 2016.

"'Angry Days' Shows an America Torn over Entering World War II." NPR, 26 Mar. 2013, www.npr.org/2013/03/26/175288241/angry-days-shows-an-america-torn -over-entering-world-war-ii.

Arendt, Hannah. *Eichmann in Jerusalem: A Report on the Banality of Evil.* Penguin, 2006.

Armstrong, Tim. "Two Types of Shock in Modernity." *Critical Quarterly,* vol. 42, no. 1, 2000, pp. 60–73, doi:10.1111/1467–8705.00272.

Arrowsmith, William. "Nine New Poets." *The Hudson Review,* vol. 9, no. 2, 1956, pp. 289–97, www.jstor.org/stable/3847371.

Assman, Jan. "Communicative and Cultural Memory." *Cultural Memory Studies: An International and Interdisciplinary Handbook,* edited by Astrid Erll and Nünning Ansgar, Walter de Gruyter, 2008, pp. 109–18.

Auden, W. H. *Collected Poems.* Edited by Edward Mendelson, Faber & Faber, 2007.

Axelrod, Steven Gould. "The Middle Generation and WWII: Jarrell, Shapiro, Brooks,

Bishop, Lowell." *War, Literature, and the Arts: An International Journal of the Humanities,* vol. 11, no. 1, 1999. pp. 1–41.

Baker, Kenneth, editor. *The Faber Book of War Poetry.* Faber and Faber, 1996.

Barksdale, Sarah Ayako. "Prelude to a Revolution: African-American World War II Veterans, Double Consciousness, and Civil Rights 1940–1955." 2014. University of North Carolina at Chapel Hill, PhD dissertation.

Barthes, Roland. *Image-Music-Text.* translated by Stephen Heath, Hill and Wang, 1978.

Bauman, Zygmunt. *Modernity and the Holocaust.* Polity, 1989.

Berry-Caban, Cristobal S. "DDT and Silent Spring: Fifty Years After." *Journal of Military and Veterans' Health,* vol. 19, no. 4, October 2011, pp. 19–24.

The Bible. Authorized King James Version, Oxford University Press, 1998.

Bloom, Harold. *The Anxiety of Influence: A Theory of Poetry.* Oxford University Press, 1973.

Blunden, Edmund. *Edmund Blunden: Selected Poems.* Edited by Robyn Marsack, Carcanet, 1982.

———. Letter to Keith Douglas. 19 Sept. 1939. MS. 56356, Vol. VI, Keith Douglas Papers, Western Manuscripts, The British Library, London.

Bodnar, John. *The "Good War" in American Memory.* Johns Hopkins University Press, 2012.

Bolin, Alice. "At the Grave of Richard Hugo." *Paris Review,* 22 Apr. 2013, www.theparisreview.org/blog/2012/05/14/at-the-grave-of-richard-hugo/.

Boyd, David. "British Sighting Telescopes," WWII Equipment.com. wwiiequipment .com/index.php?option=com_content&view=article&id=119:british-sighting -telescopes&catid=49:other-data&Itemid=61.

Boyd, Julia. *Travellers in the Third Reich: The Rise of Fascism through the Eyes of Everyday People.* Elliott & Thompson, 2017.

Brady, John C. "What Is Dasein?" *Epoché Magazine,* 20 Dec. 2017, epochemagazine. org/what-is-dasein-e11c4232771.

"British Pacifism in World War 2." Peace Pledge Union, www.ppu.org.uk/pacifism /pacwww2.html.

Brokaw, Tom. *The Greatest Generation.* Random House, 2005.

Brooke, Rupert. *1914 & Other Poems.* Sidgwick & Jackson, 1915.

Brooks, Gwendolyn. *The Essential Gwendolyn Brooks.* Edited by Elizabeth Alexander, Library of America, 2014.

Brosman, Catharine Savage. "The Functions of War Literature." *South Central Review,* vol. 9, no. 1, 1992, pp. 85–98. JSTOR, www.jstor.org/stable/3189388.

Buck, Pearl S. "Democracy and the Negro." *The Crisis,* December 1941, pp. 376–77.

Burns, Tom. "The American Narrative of the Second World War." *War and Literature: Looking Back on 20th Century Armed Conflicts,* edited by Tom Burns et al., Columbia University Press, 2016.

Burt, Stephen. *Randall Jarrell and His Age*. Columbia University Press, 2002.

Bynner, Witter. "Defeat." *New Republic*, 8 May 1944, p. 627.

Byron, George Gordon. *Lord Byron: Selected Poems*. Edited by Susan J. Wolfson and Peter J. Manning, Penguin, 2005.

Campbell, James ("J.C"). "On the Beaches." *Times Literary Supplement*, 8 May 2019.

Campbell, James Scott. "Combat Gnosticism: The Ideology of First World War Poetry Criticism." *New Literary History*, vol. 30, no. 1, 1999, pp. 203–15.

Campbell, Joseph. *The Hero with a Thousand Faces*. New World Library, 2008.

Caruth, Cathy. *Trauma: Explorations in Memory*. Johns Hopkins University Press, 1995.

———. *Unclaimed Experience: Trauma, Narrative, and History*. Johns Hopkins University Press, 1996.

Cassidy, John. "Remembering 1914: Dulce Et Decorum Est." *The New Yorker*, 6 Aug. 2014, www.newyorker.com/news/john-cassidy/war-always-hell.

"Celestial Navigation: How Did Aviators 'Shoot' the Sun and Stars?" Time and Navigation—The Untold Story of Getting from Here to There, www.timeand navigation.si.edu/navigating-air/challenges/overcoming-challenges/celestial -navigation.

Chattarji, Subarno. "Stateside Poetry: Protest and Prophecy." *Memories of a Lost War: American Poetic Responses to the Vietnam War*, Oxford University Press, 2001.

Childs, Peter. *Modernism*. Routledge, 2010.

———. *The Twentieth Century in Poetry: A Critical Survey*. Routledge, 1999.

Churchill, Winston. *Never Give In!: The Best of Winston Churchill's Speeches*. Hachette, 2003.

Ciardi, John. Letter to Louis Simpson. 1955. Louis Simpson Papers, 1943–1969, Library of Congress Manuscript Division, Library of Congress, Washington, DC.

Commonwealth War Graves Commission. 2021. *Report of the Special Committee to Review Historical Inequalities in Commemoration*, www.cwgc.org/media/noan tj4i/report-of-the-special-committee-to-review-historical-inequalities-in-com memoration.pdf.

Cooke, William. "Wilfred Owen's 'Miners' and the Minnie Pit Disaster." *English: Journal of the English Association*, vol. 26, no. 126, 1 Oct. 1977, pp. 213–18, https: //doi.org/10.1093/english/26.126.213.

Corcoran, Neil. *Poets of Modern Ireland: Text, Context, Intertext*. Southern Illinois University Press, 1999.

Cox, C. B. "The Poetry of Louis Simpson." *Critical Quarterly*, vol. 8, Spring 1966, pp. 72–83.

The Crisis. www.thecrisismagazine.com.

Currey, R. N. "Poets of the 1939–1945 War." The British Council and The National Book League, Longmans, Green, 1960.

Cuthbertson, Guy. *Wilfred Owen*. Yale University Press, 2014.

Dao, James. "Drone Pilots Are Found to Get Stress Disorders Much as Those in Combat Do." *The New York Times*, 22 Feb. 2013, www.nytimes.com/2013/02/23 /us/drone-pilots-found-to-get-stress-disorders-much-as-those-in-combat-do .html.

Das, Santanu, editor. *The Cambridge Companion to the Poetry of the First World War.* Cambridge University Press, 2013.

———. *Touch and Intimacy in First World War Literature*. Cambridge University Press, 2005.

Davidovska, Lidija. "The Poetics of Immanence and Experience: Robert Lowell, James Wright, Richard Hugo, Jorie Graham." 2013. University of East Anglia, PhD dissertation. https://ueaeprints.uea.ac.uk/47989/1/2013DavidovskaLD Phd.pdf.

Davis, William V. "*Good Luck in Cracked Italian:* Richard Hugo in Italy." *War, Literature and the Arts: An International Journal of the Humanities,* vol. 20, nos. 1 and 2, 2008, pp. 57–73.

De Havilland Mosquito: The Wooden Fighter-Bomber That Could Do It All. Imperial War Museums, 8 Sept. 2021, www.youtube.com/watch?v=JTsnMKzmdWs.

Delmont, Matthew. "Why African-American Soldiers Saw World War II as a Two-Front Battle." *Smithsonian Magazine*, 24 Aug. 2017, www.smithsonianmag.com /history/why-african-american-soldiers-saw-world-war-ii-two-front-battle -180964616/.

"Deep Image." *Poetry Foundation*, www.poetryfoundation.org/learn/glossary-terms /deep-image.

Deer, Patrick. *Culture in Camouflage: War, Empire, and Modern British Literature.* Oxford University Press, 2015.

Dickey, James. *The Complete Poems of James Dickey.* Edited by Ward Briggs, University of South Carolina Press, 2013.

Dillon, David, and Richard Hugo. "Gains Made in Isolation: An Interview with Richard Hugo." *Southwest Review*, vol. 62, no. 2, 1977, pp. 101–15. JSTOR, www.jstor .org/stable/43468937.

Dobberstein, Michael. "Rediscovering Richard Hugo: Reading the Poems." *Midwest Quarterly*, vol. 49, no. 4, 2008, pp. 416–30.

Dodson, Owen. "Black Mother Praying in the Summer 1943." *Common Ground*, Winter 1944, pp. 79–81.

Domańska, Maria. "The Myth of the Great Patriotic War as a Tool of the Kremlin's Great Power Policy." OSW Centre for Eastern Studies, 22 Jan. 2020, www.osw.waw .pl/en/publikacje/osw-commentary/2019–12–31/myth-great-patriotic-war -a-tool-kremlins-great-power-policy.

Dostoyevsky, Fyodor. *Crime and Punishment.* Translated by David McDuff, Penguin, 2003.

Douglas, Keith. *Alamein to Zem Zem*. Faber & Faber, 2014.

———. "Book Diary." Undated. From the British Library Collection/copyright © Professor Desmond Graham. MS. 56360, Vol. X, Keith Douglas Papers, Western Manuscripts.

———. *The Complete Poems*. Faber and Faber, 2011.

———. *The Letters*. Edited by Desmond Graham, Carcanet, 2000.

Douglas, Keith, and Desmond Graham. *A Prose Miscellany*. Carcanet, 1985.

Drury, John, and Mark Irwin. "An Interview with Louis Simpson." *Iowa Journal of Literary Studies*, vol. 3, no. 1, 1981, pp. 96–107, doi:10.17077/0743–2747.1038.

Du Bois, W. E. B. "The Souls of Black Folk." *Dubois: the Suppression of the African Slave-Trade, The Souls of Black Folk, Dusk of Dawn Essays,* Library of America, 1987.

Duncan, Bowie, editor. *The Critical Reception of Howard Nemerov: A Selection of Essays and a Bibliography*. Scarecrow, 1971.

Edgecombe, Rodney Stenning. *A Reader's Guide to the Poetry of Howard Nemerov*. Poetry Salzburg, 1999.

"Edmund Blunden." Poetry Archive, www.poetryarchive.org/poet/edmund-blunden.

Egremont, Max. *Some Desperate Glory: The First World War the Poets Knew*. Farrar, Straus Giroux, 2014.

Ehlers, Anke, and David M. Clark. "A Cognitive Model of Posttraumatic Stress Disorder." *Behaviour Research and Therapy*, vol. 38, no. 4, 2000, pp. 319–45.

Eisenstaedt, Alfred. *V-J Day in Times Square*. Life Magazine, 27 Aug. 1945.

Eliot, T. S. *The Complete Poems and Plays*. Faber and Faber, 2004.

———. *Four Quartets*. Faber and Faber, 2001.

———. "A Note of Introduction." *In Parenthesis,* by David Jones, Faber and Faber, 1961.

———. "Tradition and the Individual Talent." *The Sacred Wood: Essays on Poetry and Criticism, by Eliot,* Faber and Faber, 1997.

"Executive Order 9981: Ending Segregation in the Armed Forces." National Archives Foundation, www.archivesfoundation.org/documents/executive-order-9981-ending-segregation-armed-forces/.

Favret, Mary A. *War at a Distance: Romanticism and the Making of Modern Wartime*. Princeton University Press, 2010.

Featherstone, Simon. *War Poetry: An Introductory Reader*. Routledge, 1995.

Felman, Shoshana, and Dori Laub. *Testimony Crises of Witnessing in Literature, Psychoanalysis and History*. Taylor and Francis, 2013.

Ferguson, Suzanne. *Jarrell, Bishop, Lowell, & Co: Middle-Generation Poets in Context*. University of Tennessee Press, 2003.

———. *The Poetry of Randall Jarrell*. Louisiana State University Press, 1971.

"Fighting for Democracy. Japanese Americans." PBS. www.pbs.org/thewar/at_war_democracy_japanese_american.htm.

Flajšar, Jiri. "Trauma, Self and Memory in the World War II Poems by Richard Hugo." *Ostrava Journal of English Philology*, vol. 5, no. 1, 2013, pp. 45–55.

Flanzbaum, Hilene. "The Imaginary Jew and the American Poet." *ELH*, vol. 65, no. 2, 1998, pp. 259–75.

Forché, Carolyn, editor. *Against Forgetting: Twentieth-Century Poetry of Witness.* W. W. Norton, 1993.

Forché, Carolyn, and Duncan Wu, editors. *Poetry of Witness: The Tradition in English, 1500–2001.* W. W. Norton, 2014.

Frail, T. A. "The Injustice of Japanese-American Internment Camps Resonates Strongly to This Day." *Smithsonian*, 1 Jan. 2017, www.smithsonianmag.com /history/injustice-japanese-americans-internment-camps-resonates-strongly -180961422/.

Fraser, G. S. "The Part of the Natural Man." *Times Literary Supplement*, 6 Oct. 1978, p. 1124. The Times Literary Supplement Historical Archive, http://tinyurl.gale group.com/tinyurl/8n8Cdo.

———. "The Poet at War." *Times Literary Supplement*, 29 Nov. 1957, p. 718.

Friedman, Matthew J. "History of PTSD in Veterans: Civil War to DSM-5." Negative Coping and PTSD—PTSD: National Center for PTSD, US Department of Veterans Affairs, 5 July 2007, www.ptsd.va.gov/public/ptsd-overview/basics /history-of-ptsd-vets.asp.

Frost, Robert. *The Poetry of Robert Frost: The Collected Poems, Complete and Unabridged.* Edited by Edward Connery Lathem, Henry Holt, 1969.

Fussell, Paul. *The Great War and Modern Memory.* Oxford University Press, 1975.

———. *Wartime: The Experience of War, 1939–1945.* Oxford University Press, 1989.

Fynsk, Christopher. "The Self and Its Witness; On Heidegger's Being and Time." *Boundary 2*, vol. 10, no. 3, 1982, pp. 185–207. JSTOR, www.jstor.org/stable/302786.

Gaines-Lewis, Jordan. "Smells Ring Bells: How Smell Triggers Memories and Emotions." *Psychology Today*, 12 Jan. 2015, www.psychologytoday.com/gb/blog/brain -babble/201501/smells-ring-bells-how-smell-triggers-memories-and-emotions.

Galvin, Rachel. *News of War: Civilian Poetry 1936–1945.* Oxford University Press, 2017.

Garber, Frederick. "Fat Man at the Margin: The Poetry of Richard Hugo." *The Iowa Review*, vol. 3, no. 4. 1972, http://ir.uiowa.edu/iowareview/vol3/iss4/31.

Gardner, Thomas, and Richard Hugo. "An Interview with Richard Hugo." *Contemporary Literature*, vol. 22, no. 2, 1981, pp. 139–52. JSTOR, www.jstor.org/stable/120 8184.

Garrett, Stephen A. "The Bombing Campaign: The RAF." *Terror from the Sky: The Bombing of German Cities in World War II*, edited by Igor Primoratz, Berghahn Books, 2010.

Gastil, Raymond D., and Barnett Singer. *The Pacific Northwest: Growth of a Regional Identity.* McFarland, 2010.

Gates, Henry Louis. "Segregation in the Armed Forces during World War II." PBS, 19 Sept. 2013, www.pbs.org/wnet/african-americans-many-rivers-to-cross/history /what- was-black-americas-double-war/.

Gibson, James. *Let the Poet Choose.* Harrap, 1973.

Gilbert, Sandra M. "'Rats Alley': The Great War, Modernism, and the (Anti)Pastoral Elegy." *New Literary History,* vol. 30, no. 1, 1999, pp. 179–201, doi:10.1353/nlh.1999.0007.

Giles, Paul. *Antipodean America: Australasia and the Constitution of U.S. Literature.* Oxford University Press, 2013.

Glancy, Mark. "Going to the Pictures: British Cinema and the Second World War." *Past and Future: The Magazine of the Institute of Historical Research,* no. 8, Autumn/Winter, 2010, pp. 7–9.

Glick, Nathan. "About American Poetry: An Interview with Randall Jarrell." *Analects,* vol. 1, no. 2, 1961, pp. 5–10.

Goldensohn, Lorrie, editor. *American War Poetry: An Anthology.* Columbia University Press, 2006.

———. *Dismantling Glory: Twentieth-Century Soldier Poetry.* Columbia University Press, 2003.

Graham, Desmond. *Keith Douglas, 1920–1944: A Biography.* Faber and Faber, 2009.

———, editor. *Poetry of the Second World War: An International Anthology.* Chatto & Windus, 1995.

Graves, Robert. *Fairies and Fusiliers.* A. A. Knopf, 1918.

———. *Goodbye to All That.* Penguin, 2000.

———. "Letter: To Wilfred Owen." First World War Poetry Digital Archive, 25 July 2018, http://ww11it.nsms.ox.ac.uk/ww11it/items/show/8082.

———. *Robert Graves: War Poems.* Edited by Charles Mundye, Seren, 2016.

Gray, Yohma. "The Poetry of Louis Simpson." *On Louis Simpson: Depths Beyond Happiness,* edited by Hank Lazer, University of Michigan Press, 1988.

Gubar, Susan. *Poetry after Auschwitz: Remembering What One Never Knew.* Indiana University Press, 2006.

Guerin, Wilfred L., et al. *A Handbook of Critical Approaches to Literature.* 5th ed., Oxford University Press, 2005.

Hamilton, Ian, editor. *The Poetry of War: 1939–1945.* New English Library, 1972.

Harper, Glyn. *Johnny Enzed: The New Zealand Soldier in the First World War 1914–1918.* Exisle, 2015.

Harrison, Michael, and Christopher Stuart-Clark, editors. *Peace and War: A Collection of Poems.* Oxford University Press, 1998.

Hartman, Geoffrey H. *The Longest Shadow: In the Aftermath of the Holocaust.* Indiana University Press, 1996.

Haughton, Hugh, editor. *Second World War Poems.* Faber and Faber, 2004.

Haygood, Wil. "Let Slip the Poets of War." *The Washington Post,* 14 Apr. 2003, www.washingtonpost.com/archive/lifestyle/2003/04/14/let-slip-the-poets-of-war/f1d0ca6a-de32-409a-92d9-18e01442f8df/.

Hedges, Chris. "War Is a Force That Gives Us Meaning." University of California TV, 2004. www.uctv.tv/search-details.aspx?showID=9109.

Heffernan, James A. W. "Ekphrasis and Representation." *New Literary History*, vol. 22, no. 2, 1991, pp. 297–316. JSTOR, www.jstor.org/stable/469040.

Heidegger, Martin. *Being and Time*. Translated by John Macquarrie and Edward Robinson, Blackwell, 2013.

Henderson, Hamish. *Collected Poems*. Edited by Corey Gibson, Polygon, 2019.

Herman, Judith. *Trauma and Recovery: The Aftermath of Violence—From Domestic Abuse to Political Terror*. Basic Books, 2015.

Heyen, William. *American Poets in 1976*. Bobbs-Merrill, 1976.

Hill, Geoffrey. "Sidney Keyes in Historical Perspective." *The Oxford Handbook of British and Irish War Poetry*, edited by Tim Kendall, Oxford University Press. 2009.

Hill, Michael. *War Poet: The Life of Alan Seeger and His Rendezvous with Death*. CreateSpace Independent Publishing Platform, 2017.

"History." The American Legion, www.legion.org/history.

Hobsbawm, Eric. *The Age of Extremes: A History of the World, 1914–1991*. Pantheon, 1994.

Hoffman, Eva. *After Such Knowledge: Memory, History, and the Legacy of the Holocaust*. Vintage, 2005.

Hoffman, Martin L. "Empathy and Vicarious Traumatization." Unpublished manuscript, 2003.

Hoffmann, Heinrich. *Adolf Hitler in Paris 6/23/1940*. National Archives Catalog, catalog.archives.gov/id/540179.

Hogan, Patrick Colm. "Affect Studies and Literary Criticism." *Oxford Research Encyclopedia of Literature*, 2016, doi:10.1093/acrefore/9780190201098.013.105.

Höhn, Maria. "African-American GIs of WWII: Fighting for Democracy Abroad and at Home." *Military Times*, 30 Jan. 2018, www.militarytimes.com/military-honor/black-military-history/2018/01/30/african-american-gis-of-wwii-fighting-for-democracy-abroad-and-at-home/.

Horton, Alex. "Reading 'Slaughterhouse-Five' in Baghdad: What Vonnegut Taught Me about War." *Washington Post*, 13 Apr. 2019, www.washingtonpost.com/arts-entertainment/2019/04/13/reading-slaughterhouse-five-baghdad-what-vonnegut-taught-me-about-war/.

"How Is PTSD Measured?" PTSD: National Center for PTSD, 18 Sept. 2018, www.ptsd.va.gov/understand/isitptsd/measured_how.asp.

"Howard Nemerov." Poetry Foundation, www.poetryfoundation.org/poets/howard-nemerov.

Hughes, Langston. *"The Collected Poems of Langston Hughes*. Edited by Arnold Rampersad and David E. Roessel, Vintage Classics, 1994.

Hugo, Richard. *Making Certain It Goes On: The Collected Poems of Richard Hugo*. W. W. Norton, 2007.

———. "Problems with Landscapes in Early Stafford Poems." *Kansas Quarterly*, vol. 2, no. 2, 1970. pp. 33–38.

———. *The Real West Marginal Way: A Poet's Autobiography*. Edited by Ripley S. Hugo et al., W. W. Norton, 1992.

———. *The Triggering Town: Lectures and Essays on Poetry and Writing*. W. W. Norton, 1979.

"Human Fat Was Used to Produce Soap in Gdansk during the War." Auschwitz-Birkenau, 13 Oct. 2006, http://auschwitz.org/en/museum/news/human-fat-was-used-to-produce- soap-in-gdansk-during-the-war,55.html.

Hummer, T. R. "Revising the Poetry Wars: Louis Simpson's Assault on the Poetic." *Kenyon Review*, vol. 6, no. 3, Summer 1984, pp. 114–23.

Hutchinson, George. *Facing the Abyss: American Literature and Culture in the 1940s*. Columbia University Press, 2018.

"In Eliot's Own Words: Four Quartets." T. S. Eliot, www.tseliot.com/editorials/in -eliots-own-words-four-quartets.

Isherwood, Christopher. *Lions and Shadows*. Vintage, 2013.

Ivinskaya, Olga. *A Captive of Time: My Years with Pasternak: The Memoirs of Olga Ivinskaya*. Translated by Max Hayward, Collins, 1978.

Jarausch, Konrad H. *Broken Lives: How Ordinary Germans Experienced the Twentieth Century*. Princeton University Press, 2018.

Jarmain, John. *Flowers in the Minefields: El Alamein to St. Honorine: John Jarmain— War Poet: 1911–1944: A Short Appraisal of His Life and Work*. Edited by James Crowden, Flagon, 2012.

Jarrell, Randall. *The Complete Poems*. Farrar, Straus & Giroux, 1969.

———. "Item 001a Front." Series 1.1: Randall Jarrell Manuscripts—Original Poems, Box 1, Folder 7: "Death of the Ball Turret Gunner," "The Wide Prospect," and "The Snow Leopard," December 1955.

———. *No Other Book: Selected Essays*. Edited by Brad Leithauser, Perennial, 2000.

———. "Page 043." Series 1.3: Randall Jarrell Manuscripts—Criticism, Box 4, Folder 5: Recent Poetry—Rough Draft, 1955.

———. "Poetry, Unlimited: Review of *The Arrivistes*." *Partisan Review*, vol. 17, Feb. 1950, p. 189.

———. *Randall Jarrell's Letters: An Autobiographical and Literary Selection*, edited by Mary Jarrell, Houghton Mifflin, 1985.

Jarvis, Christina S. *The Male Body at War: American Masculinity during World War II*. Northern Illinois University Press, 2004.

Jay, Martin. *Songs of Experience: Modern American and European Variations on a Universal Theme*. University of California Press, 2006.

joe_538. "40's WWII Movies." IMDb, 22 Jan. 2014, www.imdb.com/list/ls059115939/.

Jones, David. *In Parenthesis*. Faber, 1963.

Kalstone, David. "Conjuring with Nature: Some Twentieth-Century Readings of

Pastoral." *Twentieth-Century Literature in Retrospect*, edited by Rubén Brower, Harvard University Press, 1971.

Kaplan, E. Ann. *Trauma Culture: The Politics of Terror and Loss in Media and Literature*. Rutgers University Press, 2005.

Kardiner, Abram. *The Traumatic Neuroses of War*. Martino, 2012.

Karlin, Mara, and Alice Hunt Friend. "Military Worship Hurts US Democracy." Brookings Institution, 24 Sept. 2018, www.brookings.edu/blog/order-from-chaos/2018/09/24/ military-worship-hurts-us-democracy/.

Kasprisin, Lorraine. "The Concept of Distance: A Conceptual Problem in the Study of Literature." *Journal of Aesthetic Education*, vol. 18, no. 3, 1984, pp. 55–68. JSTOR, www.jstor.org/stable/3332675.

Keats, John. "Ode on a Grecian Urn." Bartleby, www.bartleby.com/101/625.html.

Keefe, Patrick Radden. *Say Nothing: A True Story of Murder and Memory in Northern Ireland*. William Collins, 2019.

Keegan, John. *The Face of Battle: A Study of Agincourt, Waterloo and the Somme*. Pimlico, 2004.

"Keith Douglas." Discover War Poets, warpoets.org.uk/worldwar2/poets-and-poetry /keith douglas-1920–1944-2/.

"Keith Douglas Marginalia." *A Book of Modern Verse*. Zodiac Books, Chatto & Windus, 1939.

Kendall, Tim. *Modern English War Poetry*. Oxford University Press, 2006.

———, editor. *Poetry of the First World War: An Anthology*. Oxford University Press, 2014.

Khaldei, Yevgeny. *Raising a Flag over the Reichstag. Ogoniok*, 13 May 1945.

Kiehl, James M. "The Poems of Howard Nemerov: Where Loveliness Adorns Intelligible Things." *Salmagundi*, no. 22/23, 1973, pp. 234–57. JSTOR, www.jstor.org /stable/40546782.

Kihlstrom, John F., and Katharine Krause Shobe. "Is Traumatic Memory Special?" *Current Directions in Psychological Science*, vol. 6, no. 3, 1997, doi:10.1111/1467- 8 https://doi.org/10.1111/1467-8721.ep11512658721.ep10836842.

Kimberley, Emma. *Ekphrasis and the Role of Visual Art in Contemporary American Poetry*. 2007. University of Leicester, PhD dissertation. https://lra.le.ac.uk/bit stream/2381/9042/1/2007kimberleyephd.pdf.

King, Gilbert. "The Boy Who Became a World War II Veteran at 13 Years Old." *Smithsonian Magazine*, 19 Dec. 2012, www.smithsonianmag.com/history/the-boy-who -became-a-world-war-ii-veteran-at-13-years-old-168104583/.

Kirsch, Adam, and Kevin Young. "One Big Thing: An Exchange." *Poetry*, vol. 183, no. 3, 2003, pp. 163–68. JSTOR, www.jstor.org/stable/20606388.

Krimmer, Elisabeth. *The Representation of War in German Literature: From 1800 to the Present*. Cambridge University Press, 2014.

Kumin, Maxine. "Howard Nemerov." *Poetry,* vol. 200, no. 1, 2012, pp. 62–63. JSTOR, www.jstor.org/stable/23249373.

Kunka, Andrew J. "The Evolution of Mourning in Siegfried Sassoon's War Writing." *Modernism and Mourning,* edited by Patricia Rae, Bucknell University Press, 2007.

Kuntz, Robert. "Dreams, Machines, and the State- The War Poetry of Randall Jarrell." *Hokusei Review,* vol. 12, 1974, pp. 145–52.

Labrie, Ross. *Howard Nemerov.* Twayne, 1980.

LaCapra, Dominick. *Writing History, Writing Trauma.* Johns Hopkins University Press, 2000.

Lane, Anthony. "Diane Arbus's America." *The New Yorker,* 18 June 2017, www.new yorker.com/magazine/2016/06/06/diane-arbus-portrait-of-a-photographer.

Langbaum, Robert. "This Literary Generation." *The American Scholar,* vol. 25, no. 1, Winter, 1955–56, pp. 87–88, 90, 92, 94.

Lazer, Hank. *On Louis Simpson: Depths beyond Happiness.* University of Michigan Press, 1988.

Ledbetter, James. "Guest Post: James Ledbetter on 50 Years of the 'Military-Industrial Complex.'" *The New York Times,* 25 Jan. 2011, https://schott.blogs.nytimes.com /2011/01/25/guest-postr-james-ledbetter-on-50-years-of-the-military-indus trial-complex/.

Lee, Loyd E. *World War II in Asia and the Pacific and the Wars Aftermath, with General Themes: a Handbook of Literature and Research.* Greenwood, 1998.

Leonard, Matthew. "Muddy Hell: The Realities of the Western Front Conflict Landscape during the Great War." *Conflict Anthropology,* https://modernconflictarchae ology.com/muddy-hell-the-realities-of-the-western-front-conflict-landscape -during-the-great-war/.

Levy, Lieutenant Charles. *Atomic Cloud Rises over Nagasaki, Japan.* National Archives, catalog.archives.gov/id/535795.

Lewis, Alun. *Collected Poems.* Edited by Cary Archard, Seren, 2007.

Leys, Ruth. *Trauma: A Genealogy.* University of Chicago Press, 2000.

Locke, Duane. "New Directions in Poetry: The Work of Louis Simpson." *On Louis Simpson: Depths Beyond Happiness,* edited by Hank Lazer, University of Michigan Press, 1988.

Logan, William. *Guilty Knowledge, Guilty Pleasure: The Dirty Art of Poetry.* Columbia University Press, 2014.

Lowe, Peter. "Stripped Bodies and Looted Goods: Keith Douglas's *Iliad.*" *Cambridge Quarterly,* vol. 43, no. 4, 2014, pp. 301–24.

Lowell, Robert. *Collected Poems.* Edited by Frank Bidart and David Gewanter, Faber and Faber, 2003.

Lowery, Owen William. "A Critical and Creative Examination of the 'Extrospective' Poetry of Keith Douglas." 2016. University of Bolton, Bolton, UK, PhD dissertation.

Lukasik, Sebastian Hubert. "Military Service, Combat, and American Identity in the Progressive Era." 2008. Duke University, PhD dissertation. ProQuest.

Lyon, Philippa. *Twentieth-Century War Poetry.* Palgrave Macmillan, 2005.

MacKay, Marina. *Modernism and World War II.* Cambridge University Press, 2010.

MacLean, Sorley. *Hallaig and Other Poems: Selected Poems of Sorley MacLean.* Polygon, 2014.

Makepeace, Clare. "Male Heterosexuality and Prostitution during the Great War." *Cultural and Social History,* vol. 9, no. 1, 2012, pp. 65–83.

Matthen, Mohan, editor. *The Oxford Handbook of Philosophy of Perception.* Oxford University Press, 2015.

McCrae, John. "In Flanders Fields." *The Penguin Book of First World War Poetry,* edited by Matthew George Walter, Penguin, 2007.

McCue, Frances. *The Car That Brought You Here Still Runs: Revisiting the Northwest Towns of Richard Hugo.* University of Washington Press, 2010.

McLean, A. Torrey. "WWI: Technology and the Weapons of War." *WWI: Technology and the Weapons of War.* NCPedia, n.d., www.ncpedia.org/wwi-technology-and -weapons-war.

McLoughlin, Kate. "Beyond the Trenches." Bbk, 2013, pp. 30–31, http://www.bbk.ac .uk/downloads/bbk/bbk32.pdf.

———. *Veteran Poetics: British Literature in the Age of Mass Warfare, 1790–2015.* Cambridge University Press, 2018.

"The Military Service Act, 1916." Imperial War Museum. www.iwm.org.uk/collections /item/object/28449.

"Miller, Doris." Naval History and Heritage Command. www.history.navy.mil/re search/histories/biographies-list/bios-m/miller-doris.html.

Mills, William Ward, "A Critical Introduction to the Poetry of Howard Nemerov." 1972. PhD dissertation, Louisiana State University and Agricultural and Mechanical College. https://digitalcommons.lsu.edu/gradschool_disstheses/2352.

Milosz, Czeslaw. *New and Collected Poems (1931–2001).* Ecco. 2001.

"Moina Belle Michael: The Idea for the Flanders Fields Memorial Poppy." The Great War: 1914–1918, www.greatwar.co.uk/people/moina-belle-michael.htm.

Moramarco, F. "Reviewed Work: *The Collected Poems of Howard Nemerov* by Howard Nemerov." *World Literature Today,* vol. 53, no. 1, 1979, p. 121. *JSTOR,* www.jstor.org /stable/40132573.

Mottram, Eric N. W. "New World Poetry." *Times Literary Supplement,* 1 Nov. 1963, p. 886. The Times Literary Supplement Historical Archive, http://tinyurl.gale group.com/ tinyurl/8n85W6.

Murray, Hannah, et al. "Clients' Experiences of Returning to the Trauma Site during

PTSD Treatment: An Exploratory Study." *Behavioural and Cognitive Psychotherapy*, vol. 44, no. 4, 2015, pp. 420–30, doi:10.1017/s1352465815000338.

Murray, Martin G. "Traveling with the Wounded: Walt Whitman and Washington's Civil War Hospitals." Whitman Archive, whitmanarchive.org/criticism/current/anc.00156.html.

National Archives. "DocumentsOnline: Royal Naval Division." 25 Jan. 2006, www.nationalarchives.gov.uk/dol/popups/rndofficer1.htm.

———. "Why Did Britain Go to War? Background." 27 Jan. 2004, www.nationalarchives.gov.uk/education/greatwar/g2/backgroundcs1.htm.

National Library of New Zealand. "HEARING THE SOMME BATTLE IN ENGLAND. *The Colonist* Volume LVIII, Issue 14272, 29 November 1916." *Papers Past*, paperspast.natlib.govt.nz/newspapers/TC19161129.2.11.

Nelson, Cary, editor. *Anthology of Contemporary American Poetry*. 2nd ed., vol. 2, Oxford University Press, 2014.

Nemerov, Alexander. "The Flight of Form: Auden, Bruegel, and the Turn to Abstraction in the 1940s." *Critical Inquiry*, vol. 31, no. 4, 2005, pp. 780–810, doi:10.2307/3651436.

Nemerov, Howard. *The Collected Poems of Howard Nemerov*. University of Chicago Press, 1981.

———. *Figures of Thought: Speculations on the Meaning of Poetry and Other Essays*. D. R. Godine, 1978.

———. Letter to Parents. 28 Nov. 1941. WUSTL Digital Gateway Image Collections & Exhibitions, MSS089, Box 256, Folder 4955, Item 3, http://omeka.wustl.edu/omeka/items/show/9209.

———. Letter to Parents. Undated. WUSTL Digital Gateway Image Collections & Exhibitions, MSS089, Box 256, Folder 4955, Item 4, http://omeka.wustl.edu/omeka/items/show/9209.

———. Letter to Reed Whittemore. 22 June 1961. Reed Whittemore Papers, 84–47, Series 1, Box 8, Folder 8, University of Maryland Library, College Park.

———. "On Metaphor." *The Virginia Quarterly Review*, vol. 45, no. 4, 1969, pp. 621–36. JSTOR, www.jstor.org/stable/26443610.

———. *War Stories: Poems about Long Ago and Now*. University of Chicago Press, 1987.

"No. 236 Squadron (RAF): Second World War," www.historyofwar.org/air/units/RAF/236_wwII.html.

Norris, Margot. "War Poetry in the USA." *The Cambridge Companion to the Literature of World War II*, edited by Marina MacKay, Cambridge University Press, 2009.

———. *Writing War in the Twentieth Century*. University of Virginia, 2000.

Oostdijk, Diederik. *Among the Nightmare Fighters: American Poets of World War II*. University of South Carolina Press, 2011.

———. "Debunking 'The Good War' Myth: Howard Nemerov's War Poetry." *Bombs Away! Representing the Air War over Europe and Japan,* edited by Wilfried Wilms and William Rasch, Rodopi, 2006.

Owen, Sebastian. "'When There Are So Many We Shall Have to Mourn': Poetry and Memory in the Second World War." 2015. University of York, PhD dissertation. http://etheses.whiterose.ac.uk/11196/1/Sebastian%20Owen%20PhD%20Thesis%202015.pdf.

Owen, Wilfred. *The Poems of Wilfred Owen,* edited by Jon Stallworthy, W. W. Norton, 1986.

Palatella, John. "The War of Words." *The Nation,* 24 Dec 2003, https://www.thenation.com/article/war-words-0/

Photograph of Douglas in uniform: carboard photo frame bears inscription "Dulce et decorum est pro patria mori." 1940.

Phylon. https://radar.auctr.edu/Phylon.

Piette, Adam. "War Poetry in Britain." *The Cambridge Companion to the Literature of World War II,* edited by Marina MacKay, Cambridge University Press, 2009.

Plain, Gill. *Literature of the 1940s: War, Postwar and 'Peace.'* Edinburgh University Press, 2013.

Pope, Jessie. "The Call." *The Norton Anthology of English Literature: The 20th Century: Topic 1: Overview,* W. W. Norton, n.d., Web, 31 Jan. 2017.

Porter, Stephen, and Kristine A. Peace. "The Scars of Memory: A Prospective, Longitudinal Investigation of the Consistency of Traumatic and Positive Emotional Memories in Adulthood." *Psychological Science,* vol. 18, no. 5, 2007, pp. 435–41. JSTOR, www.jstor.org/stable/40064635.

Power, Samantha. *"A Problem from Hell": America and the Age of Genocide.* Basic Books, 2013.

Press, Eyal. "The Wounds of the Drone Warrior." *The New York Times,* 13 June 2018.

Primoratz, Igor. *Terror from the Sky: The Bombing of German Cities in World War II.* Berghahn, 2014.

Pritchard, William. "About Randall Jarrell." *Modern American Poetry,* www.english.illinois.edu/MAPS/poets/g_l/jarrell/about.htm.

———. *Randall Jarrell: A Literary Life.* Farrar, Straus and Giroux. 1992.

Randall, Dudley. "Dudley Randall." *Negro History Bulletin,* vol. 26, no. 1, 1962, pp. 76–80. JSTOR, www.jstor.org/stable/44176132.

———. *More to Remember: Poems of Four Decades.* Third World, 1971.

Rawlinson, Mark. *British Writing of the Second World War.* Oxford University Press, 2000.

Rees, Laurence. *The Holocaust: A New History.* Viking, 2017.

———. *Their Darkest Hour: People Tested to the Extreme in WWII.* Ebury, 2008.

Reilly, Catherine W., editor. *English Poetry of the Second World War: A Biobibliography.* G. K. Hall, 1986.

Remarque, Erich Maria. *All Quiet on the Western Front*. Translated by Brian Murdoch, Vintage, 2005.

"Research Starters: Worldwide Deaths in World War II." The National WWII Museum, www.nationalww2museum.org/students-teachers/student-resources/research-starters/research-starters-worldwide-deaths-world-war.

"Richard Hugo, 1923–1982." Center for the Study of the Pacific Northwest, www.washington.edu/uwired/outreach/cspn/Website/Classroom Materials/Reading the Region/Northwest Schools of Literature/Commentary/4.html.

Richardson, Anna. "The Ethical Limitations of Holocaust Literary Representation." *ESharp*, no. 5, University of Glasgow, 2005, Summer, www.gla.ac.uk/media/media_41171_en.pdf.

Ricks, Christopher. *T. S. Eliot and Prejudice*. University of California, 1988.

Ricks, Thomas E. "The Widening Gap Between Military and Society." *The Atlantic*, 1 July 1997.

Ringel, Shoshana, and Jerrold R. Brandell. *Trauma: Contemporary Directions in Theory, Practice, and Research*. SAGE, 2012.

Rivers, W. H. R. "The Repression of War Experience." *Proceedings of the Royal Society of Medicine*, vol. 11, no. Sect_Psych, Apr. 1918, pp. 1–20, doi:10.1177/003591571801101501.

Roberts, Kim. "Walt Whitman, Civil War Nurse." *American Journal of Medicine*, vol. 118, no. 7, 2005, p. 787, doi:10.1016/j.amjmed.2005.04.015.

Roeder, George H. *The Censored War: American Visual Experience during World War Two*. Yale University Press, 1993.

Rose, Kenneth D. *Myth and the Greatest Generation: A Social History of Americans in World War II*. Routledge, 2012.

Rosen, David M. *Child Soldiers in the Western Imagination: From Patriots to Victims*. Rutgers University Press, 2015.

Rosenthal, Joe. *Photograph of Marines Raising the American Flag on Mount Suribachi, Iwo Jima, 2/23/1945*. National Archives, https://catalog.archives.gov/id/32607251.

Rosenthal, M. L. "'Innocence Betrayed': Review of *People Live Here*. *Times Literary Supplement*, 4 July 1986.

Rowland, Antony. *Poetry as Testimony: Witnessing and Memory in Twentieth-Century Poems*. Routledge, 2014.

Royal Air Force Museum. FAQs, "What does the RAF motto 'Per Ardua Ad Astra' mean?," www.rafmuseum.org.uk/research/research-enquiries/faqs/what-does-the-raf-motto-per-ardua-ad-astra-mean/.

Royal Canadian Air Force. "Howard Nemerov's Royal Canadian Air Force Pilot's Flying Log Book." WUSTL Digital Gateway Image Collections & Exhibitions, MLC50, http://omeka.wustl.edu/omeka/items/show/9485.

Sadowski, Yahya. *The Myth of Global Chaos*. Brookings Institution Press, 1998.

Safire, Bill. "In Event of Moon Disaster." Received by H. R. Haldeman, 18 July 1969. National Archives, www.archives.gov/files/presidential-libraries/events/cen tennials/nixon/images/exhibit/rn100–6-1–2.pdf.

Samet, Elizabeth D. *Looking for the Good War: American Amnesia and the Violent Pursuit of Happiness*. Picador, 2022.

Santayana, George. *The Life of Reason or The Phases of Human Progress*. C. Scribner's Sons, 1905.

Sargent, Robert F. *Taxis to Hell—and Back—Into the Jaws of Death*. Photograph of U.S. Coast Guard-manned landing craft at Normandy, https://coastguard.dod live.mil/2013/06/into-the-jaws-of-death-u-s-coast-guard-manned-landing -craft-at-normandy.

Sassoon, Siegfried. *Collected Poems, 1908–1956*. Faber and Faber, 1984.

———. "Finished with the War: A Soldier's Declaration." *The Norton Anthology of English Literature: The 20th Century: Topic 1: Overview*, www.wwnorton.com/col lege/ english/nael/20century/topic_1_05/ssassoon.htm.

———. Letter: to Edmund Blunden. 18 April 1943. Papers of Siegfried Sassoon, Manuscripts Department, Cambridge University Library.

Sawicki, Donald S. "Police 10 Codes." Police Radar Information Center, copradar. com/tencodes/.

Sayer, Nina A., et al. "Randomized Controlled Trial of Online Expressive Writing to Address Readjustment Difficulties among U.S. Afghanistan and Iraq War Veterans." *Journal of Traumatic Stress*, vol. 28, no. 5, 2015, pp. 381–90, doi:10.1002/ jts.22047.

Scammell, William. *Keith Douglas: A Study*. Faber, 1988.

Scannell, Vernon. *Drums of Morning: Growing up in the Early Thirties*. Robson, 1992.

———. *Not Without Glory: The Poets of the Second World War*. Routledge, 1976.

Scott, Christopher J., and Patrick Major. "The Ionospheric Response over the UK to Major Bombing Raids during World War II." *Annales Geophysicae Discussions*, 26 Sept. 2018, pp. 1–21, doi:10.5194/angeo-2018–44.

Scranton, Roy. *Total Mobilization: World War II and American Literature*. University of Chicago Press, 2019.

Scutts, Joanna. "The True Story of Rupert Brooke." *The New Yorker*, 19 June 2017, www.newyorker.com/books/page-turner/the-true-story-of-rupert-brooke.

Sebald, W. G. *On the Natural History of Destruction*. Translated by Anthea Bell, Modern Library, 2004.

Seeger, Alan. "Sonnet 9: On Returning to the Front after Leave." Poetry Foundation, www.poetryfoundation.org/poems-and-poets/poems/detail/57350.

Selwyn, Victor, editor. *Return to Oasis: War Poems and Recollections from the Middle East, 1940–1946*. Shepheard-Walwyn, 1980.

———, editor. *The Voice of War: Poems of the Second World War: The Oasis Collection*. Michael Joseph, 1995.

Shakespeare, William. *The Tempest. The Complete Works of William Shakespeare*, Wordsworth Editions, 2007.

Shapiro, Edward S. "World War II and American Jewish Identity." *Modern Judaism*, vol. 10, no. 1, 1990, pp. 65–84. JSTOR, www.jstor.org/stable/1396050.

Shapiro, Harvey, editor. *Poets of World War II*. Library of America, 2003.

Shea, William R., and Mariano Artigas. *Galileo in Rome: the Rise and Fall of a Troublesome Genius*. Oxford University Press, 2005.

Shelley, Percy Bysshe. *Percy Bysshe Shelley: The Major Works*. Edited by Zachary Leader and Michael O'Neill, Oxford University Press, 2009.

Shires, Linda M. *British Poetry of the Second World War*. Macmillan, 1985.

Silkin, Jon. *Out of Battle: The Poetry of the Great War*. Oxford University Press. 1972.

Simpson, Louis. *Air with Armed Men*. London Magazine Editions, 1972.

———. *The Arrivistes: Poems, 1940–1949*. Fine Edition Press, 1949.

———. "Chicken Soup." Draft. Louis Simpson Papers, 1943–1969, Library of Congress Manuscript Division, Library of Congress, Washington, DC.

———. *Collected Poems*. Paragon House, 1990.

———. "In Transit." *The Hudson Review*, vol. 46, no. 4, 1994, pp. 619–37. JSTOR, www.jstor.org/stable/3852118.

———. *The King My Father's Wreck*. Story Line Press, 1995.

———. Letter to Dots and Ruth. 24 July 1944. Louis Simpson Papers, 1943–1969, Library of Congress Manuscript Division, Library of Congress, Washington, DC.

———. Letter to Lee. 13 May 1945. Louis Simpson Papers, 1943–1969. Library of Congress Manuscript Division, Library of Congress, Washington, DC.

———. "Life and Poetry." Louis Simpson Papers, 1943–1969, Library of Congress Manuscript Division, Library of Congress, Washington, DC.

———. "Love in the West and Other Memoirs." *The Hudson Review*, vol. 44, no. 1, 1991, pp. 31–54. JSTOR, www.jstor.org/stable/3851768.

———. "On the Lawn at the Villa." Draft. Louis Simpson Papers, 1943–1969. Library of Congress Manuscript Division, Library of Congress, Washington, DC.

———. "Poets of the Silent Generation." *New World Writing*. No 11. Mentor, 1957, pp. 111–112.

———. "The Poet's Theme." *The Hudson Review*, vol. 41, no. 1, 1988, pp. 93–141. JSTOR, www.jstor.org/stable/3850841.

———. "Soldier's Heart." *The Hudson Review*, vol. 49, no. 4, 1997, p. 541–52, doi:10.2307/3851887.

Simpson, Louis, and Micheal O'Siadhail. "An Interview with Louis Simpson." *The Poetry Ireland Review*, no. 29, 1990, pp. 15–28, www.jstor.org/stable/25576926.

Singer, P. W. *Children at War*. University of California Press, 2009.

Smith, A. D. *The Problem of Perception*. Harvard University Press, 2002.

Smith, Adam. *The Theory of Moral Sentiments*. Gutenberg Publishers, 2011.

Smith, Ronald. "Nick Adams and Post-Traumatic Stress Disorder." *War, Literature and the Arts: An International Journal of the Humanities*, vol. 9, no. 1, 1997. pp. 39–48.

Snyder, Timothy. *Black Earth: The Holocaust as History and Warning*. Bodley Head, 2015.

"Soldiers in World War II." World War 2, https://worldwar2.org.uk/soldiers-world -war-2.

Spender, Stephen. "Lessons of Poetry—1943." *Horizon*, edited by Cyril Connolly, vol. 9, no. 51, Mar. 1944, pp. 207–16.

———. "Ultima Ratio Regum." Poetry Archive, www.poetryarchive.org/poem/ultima -ratio-regum.

Stallworthy, Jon. *Anthem for Doomed Youth: Twelve Soldier Poets of the First World War*. Constable, 2013.

———. "Douglas, Keith Castellain (1920–1944), Poet." *Oxford Dictionary of National Biography*, 9 Nov. 2017, https://doi.org/10.1093/ref:odnb/37368.

———. *The New Oxford Book of War Poetry*. Oxford University Press, 2015.

———. *Survivors' Songs: From Maldon to the Somme*. Cambridge University Press, 2008.

Stan, Corina. *The Art of Distances: Ethical Thinking in Twentieth-Century Literature*. Northwestern University Press, 2018.

Steiner, George. *George Steiner: A Reader*. Oxford University Press, 2009.

Stitt, Peter. "Louis Simpson: In Search of the American Self." *On Louis Simpson: Depths Beyond Happiness*, edited by Hank Lazer, University of Michigan Press, 1988.

———. "West of Your City." *Poetry*, vol. 138, no. 1, 1981, pp. 46–50. JSTOR, www .jstor.org/stable/20594194.

———. *The World's Hieroglyphic Beauty*. University of Georgia Press, 1985.

Stokesbury, Leon, editor. *Articles of War: A Collection of Poetry about World War II*. University of Arkansas Press, 1990.

Stout, Janis P. *Coming out of War: Poetry, Grieving, and the Culture of the World Wars*. University of Alabama Press, 2005.

Strauss, William, and Neil Howe. *Generations: The History of Americas Future, 1584 to 2069*. Morrow, 1991.

Swift, Daniel. *Bomber County: The Lost Airmen of World War II*. Penguin, 2011.

Tambimuttu, M. J. T. Letter to Mary Douglas. 4 Jan. 1946. MS. 56356, Vol. VI, Keith Douglas Papers, Western Manuscripts, The British Library, London.

Tate, Allen. *Collected Poems: 1919–1976*. Farrar, Straus & Giroux, 1977.

Taylor, A. J. P. *English History: 1914–1945*. Clarendon Press, 1975.

Templeton, Alice. "What's the Use? Writing Poetry in Wartime." *College Literature*, vol. 34, no. 4, 2007, pp. 43–62. JSTOR, www.jstor.org/stable/25115458.

Tennyson, Alfred. *Selected Poems*. Edited by Christopher Ricks, Penguin Books, 2007.

Terkel, Studs. *"The Good War": An Oral History of World War Two.* Penguin Books, 1986, https://en.oxforddictionaries.com/definition/testimony.

Teuber, Andreas. "Fyodor Dostoevsky Biography." Brandeis University, http://people.brandeis.edu/~teuber/dostoevskybio.html.

Thomas, Edward. *The Annotated Collected Poems.* Edited by Edna Longley, Bloodaxe, 2008.

Trezise, Thomas. "Unspeakable." *The Yale Journal of Criticism,* vol. 14, no. 1, 2001, pp. 39– 66, doi:10.1353/yale.2001.0016.

Troksa, Lauren M., "The Study of Generations: A Timeless Notion within a Contemporary Context." 2016. University of Colorado, Boulder, undergraduate honors thesis. https://scholar.colorado.edu/honr_theses/1169.

Trott, Vincent. *Publishers, Readers and the Great War: Literature and Memory since 1918.* Bloomsbury Academic, 2017.

Turner, Brian. *Here, Bullet.* Alice James Books, 2005.

"Ultima Ratio Regum." Poetry Archive, www.poetryarchive.org/poem/ultima-ratio-regum.

United States Army. "Howard Nemerov's Army Separation Qualification Record." WUSTL Digital Gateway Image Collections & Exhibitions, MLC50, http://omeka.wustl.edu/omeka/items/show/9167.

van der Kolk, Bessel. *The Body Keeps the Score: Mind, Brain and Body in the Transformation of Trauma.* Penguin Books, 2015.

van Hout, Monique. *The Good, the Bad, and the Memory: World War II and the Vietnam War in Individual and Cultural Memory.* 2010. Utrecht University, master's thesis.

Vaughan, David K. *Words to Measure a War: Nine American Poets of World War II.* McFarland, 2009.

Vendler, Helen. *The Given and the Made: Strategies of Poetic Redefinition.* Harvard University Press, 1995.

"The Walls Do Not Fall by H.D." The British Library, www.bl.uk/collection-items/the-walls-do-not-fall-by-hd.

Wamsley, Laurel. "U.S. Navy to Name Aircraft Carrier after WWII Hero Doris Miller." NPR, 19 Jan. 2020, www.npr.org/2020/01/19/797756016/u-s-navy-to-name-aircraft-carrier-after-wwii-hero-doris-miller.

Waterman, Rory. *Poets of the Second World War: Douglas, Lewis, Jarrell, Causley, Simpson & Others.* Northcote, British Council, 2015.

Watson, Roderick. "Death's Proletariat: Scottish Poets of the Second World War." *The Oxford Handbook of British and Irish War Poetry,* edited by Tim Kendall, Oxford University Press, 2009, pp. 315–39.

Watson, Rodney Earl. "Memories from the Edge of the Abyss: Evaluating the Oral Accounts of World War II Veterans." *Oral History Review,* vol. 37, no. 1, 2010, pp. 18–34, doi:10.1093/ohr/ohq040.

White, Gillian. *Lyric Shame: The "Lyric" Subject of Contemporary American Poetry.* Harvard University Press, 2014.

Whitman, Walt. *Leaves of Grass.* Gibbs M. Smith, 2017.

Whitmore, Mark. "Transport and Supply during the First World War." Imperial War Museums, 28 May 2018, www.iwm.org.uk/history/transport-and-supply-during -the-first-world-war.

Whittier-Ferguson, John. "Always a War Poet: Randall Jarrell and the Returns of 20th Century War." *War, Literature and the Arts: An International Journal of the Humanities,* vol. 21, 2009, pp. 109–23.

Wilkin, Bernard. "Aerial Warfare during World War One." The British Library, 17 Jan. 2014, www.bl.uk/world-war-one/articles/aerial-warfare-during-world-war-one.

William, Charles, and C. W. Brodribb. "Poets in War." *Times Literary Supplement,* 8 Aug. 1942. The Times Literary Supplement Historical Archive, http://tinyurl.gale group.com/tinyurl/9yfix7.

Winn, James Anderson. *The Poetry of War.* Cambridge University Press, 2008.

Winter, Jay. *Sites of Memory, Sites of Mourning: The Great War in European Cultural History (Canto).* Cambridge University Press, 1998.

Winter, Jay, and Emmanuel Sivan, editors. *War and Remembrance in the Twentieth Century.* Cambridge University Press, 2005.

Wojahn, David. "The State You Are Entering: Depression and Contemporary Po- etry." *New England Review (1990–),* vol. 17, no. 1, 1995, pp. 110–23. JSTOR, www. jstor.org/stable/40242986.

Wool, Zoë H. *After War: The Weight of Life at Walter Reed.* Duke University Press, 2015.

INDEX

Air Force (Canadian, Royal, U.S.), 9, 16, 17, 22, 23, 90, 122, 123, 154, 157, 172, 174, 175, 182, 183, 186, 190, 194, 202–3, 233; Luft-waffe, 1, 192

Alfred, Lord Tennyson, 165–66, 227

Alighieri, Dante, 85, 139, 231

Arendt, Hannah, 222

Auden, W. H., 194, 234; "Memorial for the City," 201; "Musée des Beaux Arts," 148, 233; "September 1, 1939," 26, 110, 192; "Spain," 205–6

Barthes, Roland, 227

Bauman, Zygmunt, 182, 208–9

Bible: Apostle Thomas, 95; Pontius Pilate, 214–15

binaries, 9, 87, 105, 125, 132, 150–51, 184–85, 210–11, 215, 221, 232, 234

Black poets

—civilians writing about war, 17–19; Gwen-dolyn Brooks, 18–19; Langston Hughes, 18

—soldiers writing about war: Dudley Ran-dall, 17; Owen Dodson, 17, 228

Blunden, Edmund, 22, 38, 40, 41, 43–47, 76–77, 78, 80, 81–82, 92, 111, 143–44, 152, 220, 229

—poems: "Ancre Sunshine," 143; "Can You Remember?," 92; "Concert Party: Busse-boom," 43–44, 45, 46, 172; "Vlamertinghe: Passing the Chateau, July 1917," 38, 43, 229

Bodnar, John, 141, 169, 175

bombing, 129, 148, 169, 171, 234; area and precision, 171; detachment from destruc-tion of, 88, 148, 171, 180–81, 182; fire-bombing, 233; targets, 1, 126, 129, 141–42, 171, 206

Brooke, Rupert, 5, 9, 79, 98–100, 221

Brosman, Catharine Savage, 10, 11, 118, 124, 136

Campbell, James Scott, 11

Churchill, Winston, 40, 94, 116

Ciardi, John, 15, 57, 230

civilian poets: Anna Akhmatova, 19; Cze-sław Miłosz, 19, 192, 232; Dylan Thomas, 8, 111; H.D., 19, 111, 192; Miklós Radnóti, 19; Zbigniew Herbert, 19, 192

colonialism, 219

Commonwealth War Graves Commission, 228

Craiglockhart Military Hospital, 39, 49, 230

"critical neglect," 3–8, 25–26, 162, 217–18, 219–20, 223–25; and Howard Nemerov, 154–55, 161; and Keith Douglas, 76–77, 79–80; and Louis Simpson, 28–30, 73–74; and Randall Jarrell, 191–92, 215–16; and Richard Hugo, 119–22

Cuthbertson, Guy, 69, 77

Das, Santanu, 2, 37, 41, 59, 78

Dickey, James, 15, 192, 228

distance: Bauman's social production of, 208–209; Favret's distance between historical events, 184, 209; Heidegger's "distantiality," 14, 36, 87, 89; Kasprisin's extrospection as, 83; Stan's "distantiality," 14, 36

Dostoevsky, Fyodor, 65–67, 230

Douglas, Keith, 6, 7–8, 9, 11, 14, 15, 16, 20, 21–22, 23, 27, 29, 41, 75–118, 123, 127, 129, 178, 187, 189, 200–201, 210, 217, 218, 219, 223–24, 227, 229, 231; *Alamein to Zem Zem,* 77, 83, 89, 101, 102; correspondence of, 41, 76, 77, 80, 81–82, 83, 92, 102, 103, 105; and extrospective poetry, 7, 14, 16, 75–76, 77–78, 81, 83, 92, 96, 108, 116, 118, 127, 200, 224, 227; marginalia of, 78, 80–81, 97; photographs of, 76; "Poets in this War" essay, 77, 82, 117

—poems: ".303," 84, 93–94; "Cairo Jag," 95, 112, 114; "Canoe," 75, 110, 112; "Dead Men," 81, 109, 113–14, 116–17; "Desert Flowers," 21, 76, 98, 178, 218; "Devils," 104, 105, 108; "Farewell Poem," 109–12, 117; "How to Kill," 22, 78, 81, 84, 88–91, 104, 105–6, 108, 112, 114, 200, 201; "I Listen to the Desert Wind," 109, 115; "Landscape with Figures," 81, 95–97, 112; "Mersa," 98; "The Poets," 102–3; "The Prisoner," 109, 111–12, 117; "Simplify me when I'm dead," 22, 75, 84, 91–92, 100–102, 112; "To Kristin Yingcheng Olga Milena," 112; "*Vergissmeinnicht,*" 22, 84, 85–87, 88, 89, 104, 106–8, 112, 114, 116

dreams, 1, 7, 21, 25, 31, 36, 37, 44, 51–58, 59–60, 64–73, 93, 113–14, 124–27, 133, 149–50, 151–52, 162, 163, 177, 181–85, 187–88, 189, 193, 196, 200, 203, 206–7, 209–13, 216, 224, 231, 233, 234

Dubois, W. E. B., 17, 228

ekphrasis, 144–50, 233

Eliot, T. S., 4; correspondence, 81; *Four Quartets,* 111, 116, 117, 192; "Tradition and the Individual Talent," 14, 58, 77–78, 100; *The Waste Land,* 139, 230

film, 17, 25, 170, 181, 215, 223, 227

Forché, Carolyn, 13–14, 47, 216

Frost, Robert, 34, 136

Fussell, Paul, 32, 40–41, 84, 128, 153, 192, 205

Goldensohn, Lorrie, 73, 90, 120, 195, 199

"good war, the," 104, 141, 158–59, 166, 174, 175, 177, 185, 224

Graham, Desmond, 5, 15, 80, 82, 88, 90

Graves, Robert, 4, 5, 30, 40, 46–47, 67, 84, 150, 152, 220, 230, 231; *Goodbye to All That,* 46

—poems: "A Dead Boche," 46; "Goliath and David," 84, 231

"Greatest Generation," 3, 48, 158, 166

"Great War, the," 4, 5, 32, 40, 57, 60, 65, 74, 76, 77, 80, 82, 84, 87, 88, 119, 158, 163

grief/grieving, 50, 86–87, 107–108, 114, 141, 184, 211

guilt, 22–25, 54–56, 70–72, 79, 83, 88–91, 96, 103–9, 123–25, 127, 137–40, 142–46, 149–52, 162, 167, 175, 180–81, 182–83, 192–93, 200–201, 205–9, 210, 213–15, 224

Hemingway, Ernest, 48, 165, 220

Henderson, Hamish, 15, 38, 229, 231

Hitler, Adolf, 1, 18, 24, 42, 48, 63, 70, 164, 168, 229

Holocaust, 1, 2, 3, 12, 14, 25, 27, 70, 160, 193, 194, 196–99, 201, 209, 212–16, 220, 221–22, 228, 234; Adorno on, 25, 221; Auschwitz, 25, 135, 197–98, 214, 221–22, 233; film representations of, 215; history of (Rees), 27, 214, 233, 234; legacy of (Hartman), 213–14, 222; literary representations of (Richardson), 222; "second generation" perspective on (Hoffman), 25, 199, 209, 228

Hughes, Ted, 8, 77, 80, 100, 224

Hugo, Richard, 7, 9, 11, 14, 15, 16, 20, 22–23, 27, 119–53, 162, 186, 189, 210, 217, 219, 224, 233; as regionalist, 7, 22, 121–22, 129, 153, 219
—poems: "A View from Cortana," 129; "The Bridge of Sighs," 145–47, 149, 233; "Brueghel in the Doria," 145, 147–49; "Centuries near Spinnazola," 129, 140; "Galileo's Chair," 145, 146–47, 149, 217; "Galleria Umberto I," 137–40, 224; "G.I. Graves in Tuscany," 129, 140; "Here, but Unable to Answer," 151; "The Hilltop," 150; "In Your War Dream," 149, 233; "Letter to Simic from Boulder," 22, 125–27, 186; "Mission to Linz," 120, 129–32, 152, 232; "Napoli Again," 129, 136–37, 139; "Note from Capri to Richard Ryan on the Adriatic Floor," 120, 140–41; "Spinazzola: Quella Cantina La," 120, 134, 140; "Tretitoli, Where the Bomb Group Was," 130, 133, 140; "Viva La Resistenza," 140; "Where We Crashed," 120, 130, 133–34, 152; "The Yards of Sarajevo," 22, 128–29, 141–42

Iraq War, 87, 97, 182, 221, 231
Isherwood, Christopher, 101, 102, 163

Jarmain, John, 15, 231, 232, 233
Jarrell, Randall, 7, 9–10, 11, 14–16, 20, 24–25, 27, 29, 73, 117, 129, 155, 162, 180, 186–87, 189–216, 217–19, 222, 223–24, 228, 233, 234; archival material of, 191, 206–7; correspondence of, 81, 206, 211, 214, 223, 234; correspondence with Robert Lowell, 190, 208
—poems: "1914," 189, 210, 216; "A Camp in the Prussian Forest," 25, 203, 212–14; "Come to the Stone. . . .," 203; "The Dead Wingman," 203–5, 210; "The Death of the Ball Turret Gunner," 24, 191, 195, 203, 206–8, 215, 218, 224, 234; "Eighth Air Force," 191, 208, 214–15; "Jews at Haifa,"
215; "The Learners," 211–12; "Losses," 24, 191, 195, 203, 205; "A Lullaby," 195–96, 197, 199, 203, 233; "Mail Call," 24, 195, 203; "Protocols," 25, 195–99, 203, 212, 222; "The Sick Nought," 24, 194–95; "Siegfried," 200–201
Jones, David: In Parenthesis, 4, 169, 230

Kendall, Tim, 9, 76, 77, 91, 106, 112–13, 116

landscape, 2–3, 7, 8, 13, 14, 16, 21, 22–23, 24, 31, 40–47, 50–51, 83, 93, 94–97, 98, 107, 113, 118, 120–23, 127, 128–34, 135–44, 148–49, 150, 172, 204–5, 210, 219, 229, 230, 231
Lewis, Alun, 15, 117, 227, 228, 229
Lowell, Robert, 11, 190, 206, 210

masculinity, 29, 79, 101, 102, 158, 163, 165
McCrae, John, 38, 82, 183
McLoughlin, Kate, 10, 128
memory (theory), 20–26; cultural (Assman), 168; Jay Winter on, 10, 136; Monique van Hout on, 4, 168; Rodney Earl Watson on, 158
military identity and mythmaking, 18, 23, 47, 67, 85, 157, 158, 159, 160, 162, 163, 166, 168–70, 175, 180, 220

Nemerov, Howard, 7, 9, 11, 14, 15, 16, 20, 23–24, 27, 129, 154–88, 210, 217, 219, 222, 224, 228; correspondence of, 157, 172, 181; personal belongings of, 157
—poems: "30th Anniversary Report of the Class of '41," 172, 177–78, 180; "The Afterlife," 186–87; "Armistice," 181, 183–84; "Authorities," 166–68; "For W___, Who Commanded Well," 161–63 165; "Grand Central, With Soldiers, Early Morning," 155–56; "A Memory of the War," 186; "The Old Soldiers' Home," 163–68; "An Old Warplane," 172–73; "Redeployment," 24, 154, 172, 177–80, 181, 184–85, 222;

Nemerov, Howard (*continued*)
"Returning to Europe," 181–83; "Sarajevo," 186–87; "Ultima Ratio Reagan," 24,
172, 176–77, 180; "The War in the Air," 24,
172, 173–75, 177, 180, 187
New Critics, 189–90
Norris, Margot, 5, 119–20, 153, 218

Oostdijk, Diederik, 10–11, 23, 45, 66, 84,
166, 184, 190, 194, 201, 215
Owen, Wilfred, 5, 21, 22, 31–39, 42, 43, 45,
48, 51, 67, 69–70, 71, 76, 77, 79, 80–81, 83,
84–86, 93, 100, 112, 113–15, 124–25, 127,
128, 152, 157, 159, 169, 190, 192, 204–5,
206, 207, 220, 224, 230, 231, 234; referenced by Louis Simpson, 69–70, 113–14
—poems: "Anthem for Doomed Youth," 43;
"Apologia pro Poemate Meo," 128, "Disabled," 32, 39, 230; "Dulce et Decorum
Est," 76, 93, 124–25, 127; "Exposure," 21,
32–37, 45, 81, 115; "Insensibility," 81; "The
Last Laugh," 128; "Miners," 113–14, 204–5;
"Preface," 36, 69–70, 157, 206; "Strange
Meeting," 71, 85–86, 169, 192, 231; "A
Terre," 81

photographs, 1, 223
Plain, Gill, 19, 106
Pope, Jessie, 124–25
poppy, 38, 39, 46, 56, 183, 229, 230
propaganda, 124–25, 129, 163–64, 166, 168,
215, 223

race, 16–20, 228–229; desegregating the U.S.
military, 19; "double-consciousness," 17;
Japanese American internment, 19; segregation, 17–19, 228
resentment, 14, 21, 31, 40, 47–51, 63–64,
114, 136, 141, 144, 160–62, 166–68
retribution, 105–6, 11 145, 151–52, 169
Rosenberg, Isaac, 21–22, 38, 76, 80–81, 100–
101, 178, 218

Sassoon, Siegfried, 4–5, 22, 39, 40–42, 48,
49–50, 51, 58, 69, 80, 82, 90, 93, 96, 103,
112, 124, 125, 127, 128, 143–44, 152, 157,
159, 160–61, 162–67, 169, 202, 207, 215,
220–21, 229, 230, 232; "A Soldier's Declaration," 161
—poems: "At the Cenotaph," 96; "Fight to
the Finish," 166–67; "Glory of Women,"
125, 229; "The Hero," 127, 207; "Memorial
Tablet," 128; "On Passing the New Menin
Gate," 143; "Song-Books of the War," 162–
63; "Suicide in the Trenches," 49–50; "Survivors," 230; "To My Brother," 128; "Two
Hundred Years After," 230; "The Ultimate
Atrocity," 202
Scannell, Vernon, 6, 77, 79, 98, 100, 101,
112, 213
Seeger, Alan, 48, 50, 230
Selwyn, Victor, 155, 231
"Silent Generation," 3–8, 29, 220, 224
Simpson, Louis, 1, 6, 7, 9, 14–16, 20–21, 23,
27, 28–74, 79, 115, 117, 123, 129, 150, 172,
187, 189, 210, 217, 219, 224, 226, 227–28,
229, 230; correspondence and V-Letters
of, 28, 30, 51, 57; as "deep image" poet, 7,
28, 219; drafts and manuscripts of, 29, 55,
71; and PTSD, 44, 51, 64–67, 72–74
—poems: "The Ash and the Oak," 40, 42–43;
"The Battle," 31–37, 40, 73; "A Bower of
Roses," 21, 31, 58, 59–64, 74, 224, 226;
"Carentan O Carentan," 29–30, 36, 40, 42,
44–46, 57, 73, 172, 229–30; "The Heroes,"
32, 37–40, 56; "I Dreamed That in a City
Dark as Paris," 1, 36, 52–54, 55–56, 59–60,
73; "In the Suburbs," 63; "Memories of
a Lost War," 30, 64, 67–69, 72, 73; "The
Men with Flame-Throwers," 62–63; "On
the Lawn at the Villa," 52, 54–56, 60; "On
the Ledge," 56, 64, 65–67; "The Runner,"
56–58, 230; "The Silent Generation," 40,
48–49, 63; "A Story About Chicken Soup,"
42, 64, 70–72; "To the Western World," 63

Spender, Stephen, 176, 191, 193, 219
Stallworthy, Jon, 6, 39, 112, 181

Tambimuttu, M. J. T., 77
"telescopic sight," 78, 83, 84, 88–89, 91–92, 195, 200–201
Thomas, Edward, 100–101, 152, 159, 168–169
trauma and PTSD, 2–3, 7, 8, 12–16, 20–27, 30–31, 44, 46–47, 51, 53, 55–56, 64–73, 76, 78–79, 83, 96, 103, 118, 121, 123, 124–25, 134, 135–44, 145, 148–52, 154, 158, 160, 162, 172, 174, 177–82, 184–86, 187, 193, 195, 199, 200, 206, 208, 209–11, 213, 216, 217–19, 222–25, 224–28, 230, 232, 233; among drone operators, 88, 182; Cathy Caruth on, 14, 55–56, 177, 180, 206; Sigmund Freud on, 14, 26, 55, 209–10, 232, 234; Hoffman's "second generation" and, 25, 199, 209, 228; Kaplan's "vicarious trauma," 14, 20, 24–25, 66–67, 78–79, 193,

199, 209–10, 213–14, 216, 224; LaCapra on, 127, 208–9; Leys' trauma of world wars, 232; Murray et. al on returning to sites of, 15, 23, 135–44; and "then-now discrimination," 23, 135–36, 142–44; "traumatic superiority argument" vs. "traumatic memory argument," 68–69, 72, 227–28; van der Kolk on, 30
Turner, Brian, 97, 231

Vaughan, David K., 5, 133, 157, 181, 184

"war books" boom, 98, 160, 220, 221, 223
Waterman, Rory, 4, 10–11, 99, 227
Whitman, Walt, 36, 45–46, 54, 229–30
witness, 2, 9–10, 13–14, 25–27, 28, 69, 83, 85, 93, 96, 124–27, 150–51, 161, 179, 192, 198, 199, 206, 208–9, 213–14, 216, 218, 222, 224, 225–26, 228, 229, 232; Forché's poetry of, 13–14, 47, 216; "proxy-witnessing," 206

www.ingramcontent.com/pod-product-compliance
Lightning Source LLC
Chambersburg PA
CBHW030300100426
42812CB00002B/515